Holy Hustlers, Schism, and Prophecy

THE ANTHROPOLOGY OF CHRISTIANITY

Edited by Joel Robbins

1. Webb Keane, *Christian Moderns: Freedom and Fetish in the Mission Encounter*
2. Matthew Engelke, *A Problem of Presence: Beyond Scripture in an African Church*
3. David Smilde, *Reason to Believe: Cultural Agency in Latin American Evangelicalism*
4. Francio Guadeloupe, *Chanting Down the New Jerusalem: Calypso, Christianity, and Capitalism in the Caribbean*
5. Matt Tomlinson, *In God's Image: The Metaculture of Fijian Christianity*
6. William F. Hanks, *Converting Words: Maya in the Age of the Cross*
7. Kevin O'Neill, *City of God: Christian Citizenship in Postwar Guatemala*
8. Frederick Klaits, *Death in a Church of Life: Moral Passion during Botswana's Time of AIDS*
9. Chris Hann and Hermann Goltz, editors, *Eastern Christians in Anthropological Perspective*
10. Allan Anderson, Michael Bergunder, Andre Droogers, and Cornelis van der Laan, *Studying Global Pentecostalism: Theories and Methods*
11. Richard Werbner, *Holy Hustlers, Schism, and Prophecy: Apostolic Reformation in Botswana*
12. Omri Elisha, *Moral Ambition: Mobilization and Social Outreach in Evangelical Megachurches*

Holy Hustlers, Schism, and Prophecy

Apostolic Reformation in Botswana

RICHARD WERBNER

University of California Press
BERKELEY LOS ANGELES LONDON

University of California Press, one of the most distinguished university presses in the United States, enriches lives around the world by advancing scholarship in the humanities, social sciences, and natural sciences. Its activities are supported by the UC Press Foundation and by philanthropic contributions from individuals and institutions. For more information, visit www.ucpress.edu.

University of California Press
Berkeley and Los Angeles, California

University of California Press, Ltd.
London, England

Library of Congress Cataloging-in-Publication Data

Werbner, Richard P.
Holy hustlers, schism, and prophecy : Apostolic reformation in Botswana / Richard Werbner.
p. cm.
Includes bibliographical references and index.
ISBN 978-0-520-26853-1 (hardcover : alk. paper) — ISBN 978-0-520-26854-8 (pbk. : alk. paper)
1. Pentecostal churches—Botswana—Gaborone. 2. Gaborone (Botswana)—Church history. I. Title.
BX8762.A45B58 2011
276.883'083—dc22 2010047448

Manufactured in the United States of America
20 19 18 17 16 15 14 13 12 11
10 9 8 7 6 5 4 3 2 1

This book is printed on Cascades Enviro 100, a 100% post consumer waste, recycled, de-inked fiber. FSC recycled certified and processed chlorine free. It is acid free, Ecologo certified, and manufactured by BioGas energy.

For Muriel Sutherland Snowden and Otto Snowden

Contents

Illustrations

MAPS

FIGURES

Acknowledgments

Around the Pond of the Buddha in the Japanese city of Suita, spring brought a fleeting, magical moment. Lace-like blossoms covered the cherry trees, swayed gently with the fresh winds, then gradually faded away. It was in that vibrant season, in 2009, that I wrote the first draft of this book, while I was Overseas Professor at the Graduate University for Advanced Research and the National Museum of Ethnology (Minpaku) in Osaka. My hope is that my colleagues and friends in Japan, who received me so graciously, will recognize the charm and freshness of their spring inspiring the book itself. I thank them all, collectively.

In particular, and first of all, I want to thank Kenji Yoshida, my caring host at Minpaku, with whom I have long shared interests in the study of ritual and performance, of self and other (Yoshida and Durrans 2008), and now of new Christian movements. I am grateful also to other colleagues in Japan who gave me the opportunity to screen my films and exchange ideas for this work in progress: Hirochika Nakamaki, Yasuhiro Omori (Minpaku, Osaka); Akira Takada (Kyoto University); Eisei Kurimoto (Osaka University); Akira Okazaki (Hitotsubashi University, Tokyo); Kozo Watanabe (Ritsumeikan University, Kyoto); Jeremy Eades (Asia Pacific University, Beppo). Itsushi Kawase (Kyoto University) made me a part of his world of filmmakers, in Japan and elsewhere, and with his wife, Fujimi, and their family generously received my own family and lifted our spirits: may we again hear your temple bell resounding for us. For two members of Minpaku's staff, the administrator, Setsuko Ikuta, and IT engineer, Akimase Kanatani, I became virtually a full-time project, which they brilliantly finessed past one hurdle after another: Arigatou gozaimasu.

Reading the first draft chapter by chapter, three friends, Fred Klaits, David Maxwell, and Mattia Fumanti, spurred me on with their immediate and very helpful comments in numerous emails. I want to thank them and also Paul Henley and Matthew Engelke for giving me the benefit of their advice on chapters linked to their own studies. Given the first draft as a whole, my wife, Pnina Werbner, and then, for the University of California Press, Joel Robbins, the Anthropology of Christianity Series editor, and Reed Malcolm, the senior commissioning editor, made me work a great deal harder to realize the book's potential in the light of their insightful criticism. Hopefully, also, Johannes Fabian, who read the book for the Press, will find that his suggestions have helped to raise the theoretical interest in the book to a higher level.

Peter Blore, David Henderson, John Lancaster and Jon Tipler of the Media Centre at Manchester University generously freed time to meet my many needs for media assistance during my long-term research project on well-being in Botswana, of which this book forms a part. For inspired editing and many discussions about our work in progress, I wish to thank Andy Lawrence, currently resident filmmaker at the Granada Centre for Visual Anthropology, and James Uren, Ravensbourne College of Design and Communication. I am grateful also to the Nuffield Foundation, the Economic and Research Council, and the International Centre for Contemporary Cultural Research for providing funds for the project.

For my research in Botswana, I owe a lasting debt to my research assistant, Njebe Molefhe Gabanakgosi, and his wife, Martha Masika. I carried out my research as a Professorial Research Fellow of the University of Botswana and with the kind permission of the Botswana Government, Ministry of Labour and Home Affairs. When I met Archbishop Jakoba Keiphile at his headquarters in Tsetsebjwe and in Gaborone, he made me and my research welcome in his church, Eloyi; he consented to my filming him and the church, and watched and commented on raw footage of church events (see also Werbner 2008) when I returned to visit him. We shared meals together, and he even gave me the satirical moment, during preaching, to perform as Esau (evoking much laughter) with himself as Jacob in his own playful version of the Bible story. I mention this at some length for an important reason. It is not only to express my thanks to the archbishop, but also to convey the lasting warmth with which he received me, despite the turmoil of the schism that I discuss in the book and which eventually, toward the end of my research, kept me from filming the Eloyi city branch at the request of local committee members. Throughout my research Boitshepelo Jakoba, the city bishop of Eloyi, later archbishop of Conollius, generously welcomed me with his unwavering support, as did pastors-general Mogotse and Solomon, and Prophets Joshua, Andrew, Matthew, Ruben, Obed, Lesego, and Johannes. To them and many other members of the Eloyi and Conollius churches, I offer my greatest thanks.

Introduction

Around the world, the quest for well-being and personal security brings new Christian churches vast numbers of followers. Many come to the inspired—the charismatics[1] felt to have extraordinary spiritual gifts. A relative few become charismatics themselves. The most successful enjoy popular reputations for faith healing, for providing spiritual protection, for visions or the interpretation of dreams, or for especially insightful counseling or moral guidance in everyday life.

It is widely recognized in the literature on charismatic Christianity, and indeed on charismatic Islam also, that to be a charismatic and to fulfill one's inspired mission creatively within an institution, such as a church with a hierarchy or a bureaucratic organization, is highly problematic. The broad issues are familiar—they have been much rehearsed in the social sciences in a long line stretching from Max Weber's seminal distinctions between charisma and routinization, the innovative and creative versus the bureaucratic, and along with that the instability of spiritual recognition in the eyes of others (Weber 1948; Eisenstadt 1968; Lindholm 1990; P. Werbner 2003:22–29, 285–287).[2] The tensions between charisma and institutionalized structure have been much discussed and well theorized, following Weber.

In going beyond that familiar sociology of charisma, I want to open out an alternative field of analysis around what I call "holy hustling," specifically holy hustling by Apostolic charismatics known as prophets in Botswana's capital city, Gaborone. My main interests focus on the subjectivities of the charismatics in contexts of religious change, their understandings of self and other, and their intersubjective engagements with their patients in prophecy and in faith healing.

Perhaps most strikingly different in the present moment for African churches is the identity of some of the new urban charismatics themselves.

Thrust into the very front line of what is perceived to be an intensifying war of good and evil, the unlikely charismatics are urban youths. "Street kids" their enemies call them. It is cleverness in the ways of the city, street smarts, that sets them apart from earlier charismatics. With that comes for the new urban charismatics a remarkable bringing together of apparently contrary aspects of holiness and hustling that calls for explanation: How can willful individualism and caring empathy exist together? This is an issue that the literature on churches in Africa has so far failed to address. It is all the more remarkable because such empathy, the present study shows, is vicarious beyond the divide between self and other—the urban youth as charismatic endures and suffers momentarily in place of another.

In certain moments of spiritually moving intersubjectivity, the self-experience of the urban youth at the center of this study is like that of earlier charismatics. Their very selves, unlike the selves of wholly autonomous individuals, are *permeable,* for they feel others' pain penetrating them as if it were their very own, when they are overcome by the Holy Spirit. At other moments, however, they are domineering; and dominant in being autonomous, self-seeking, and self-interested, they hustle others for personal gain. They are not surprisingly held by many to be manipulative and greedy individuals.

These young men, intense in their faith and in their bonding with the faithful, are felt to be interdependent with the people they serve in moving ways. In submitting themselves totally to religious passion, they become deeply *pitiable* for the suffering they endure on behalf of others. Even more, they are *publicly* seen to be vulnerable, to have put themselves in danger in their efforts to give protection against witchcraft or occult attack. They are, paradoxically, selfless and yet also self-willed; they are highly individualistic and yet engaged with deliberately confronting the risks and dangers as subjects who are not merely individuals but also permeable dividuals.[3] Here the study of holy hustling leads to questions of intersubjectivity and the making of self and other in ritual practice, questions that I open out further, in Chapter 9, by comparison with the making of what Thomas Csordas' calls the "sacred self" among New Englanders in the context of twentieth-century American individualism (Csordas 1994).

For the latest generation of young Christian charismatics, now responding to the quest for well-being and personal security in African cities, the present is a time of escalating moral crises. Many African churches have already turned into arenas not only of spiritual protection and faith healing but also of endless testing and dissent over faith. The struggles from generation to generation move forward in surprising ways as churches founded in the countryside grow in the city and gain more urban-oriented branches.

A key issue repeatedly agonized over is: What is Christian and what is not? Is there "back-sliding," a lapse from the orthodox into the heretical, even into the perceived sins of the ancestors' ways or those of latter-day witchfinders and "traditional" doctors? Rarely is the charismatic response straightforward. With creative innovation often comes restoration, and the mix of the old and the new arouses controversy.

Charismatics often come to the fore in religious reform from generation to generation. Religious reform, once begun against original belief and practice, has the prospect of becoming not a single moment or phase in history—the Reformation—but the keeping of a reactive spiral of changes ongoing from generation to generation. Each generation's initiative, once an accomplishment in reformation, becomes, in turn, grist for succeeding generations. Spiraling over several generations, the turn taking returns on itself—reprise reoccurs, for example when a third-generation brings back certain original beliefs or practices, refreshing them as another reformation.

FILM FIRST, BOOK SECOND

Accompanying this book is my film *Holy Hustlers* (2009). It foregrounds much that is left in the background of the book's textual analysis. The reader is asked, therefore, to turn now and first to the film: before reading the rest of the text, watch the film and know and feel more of the aesthetic appeal, the sensuous and the sensual realities, the desire and even the disgust, in holy hustling as Apostolic prophetic practice.

Holy Hustlers is evocative and cinematic, of course. From the very start, some of that aesthetically sensuous appeal has to be kept in mind. One reason is the need to appreciate that holy hustling gains its moving urgency through actual aesthetic force. Another and perhaps even more important reason is the high religious value that aesthetic force has for the Apostolics themselves. Beauty and splendor beckon God; they have a powerful and transformative significance for Apostolics, and explicitly so.

I want to introduce their moving practice with a subjective impression of my own, which the film reflects and, of course, qualifies. On first seeing Apostolic services, I felt an overwhelming impression of dazzling brilliance. The great vibrance in song and dance moved me, and I enjoyed the laughter and richly spontaneous entertainment Apostolics share even in the long, rambling sermons with their stories and parables, their indispensable readings of the Bible.

What I see, and *Holy Hustlers* registers, is a brilliant whirl of color. It is the rich vestments of men flying off, billowing in swaths of red, orange, green, white, and yellow (but, and it is a deliberate and highly significant absence, no black, no color of the dead). The men whirl together in a round dance, as if soaring in spirit beyond the earth itself. Around a once brilliant red sun, worn down on the floor, they make an inner ring; women dance, more gently, on the outer ring. A few of the young men wear fezzes, but most adorn themselves in high miters, towering above the women's modest head coverings, copes, and sashes, mainly white with red crosses. Some Apostolics have moments when they look lost in reveries, but for much of the time, the congregation is together in intense concentration. Prophets lead the music—the singing and dancing, the playing of the tambourines, the ringing of the bells, and the clapping—and they try to tune their own and others' bodies to be in harmony with the Holy Spirit.

The major subjects of care and spiritual comforting, with prayer, in some of the most dramatic moments, during trance, are the young prophets themselves. The prophets' bodies fall out of their own control and need support from other Apostolics. Rallying around the swooning prophets, the congregation comes together; the most prominent women who are the Mothers of the Church draw nearest to the men around the prophets; and the congregation as a whole is strikingly overwhelmed in Apostolic fellowship.

The moment is emotionally moving. It also arouses moral passion. The prophets are, at once, heroic and pitiable, before God and the Apostolics. Heroic, because they have rushed back to the church from a wild, dangerous hunt for hidden things—the obnoxious and evil work of church enemies. Pitiable, because driven in disgust by their prophetic impulse and in humiliating contact with the obnoxious, they bear, beyond doubt, the heaviest burden of pain and suffering, on behalf of everyone in the church. It is this bringing together of the heroic and the pitiable, I come to understand later, that exalts prophets as devotional subjects—that is, subjects around whom a community of suffering[4] emerges and shares moral passion, above all compassion, in devotion to the Holy Spirit. In being transfigured, becoming devotional subjects through a humiliating act, young men as prophets serve for the sake not of their individual salvation, but the salvation of each and everyone in the congregation as a whole.

Prophets are also exalted during services, in the eyes of Apostolics, as I came to see also, through their whirling youthful energy in the round dance. In the lead, and joined by some church servants, become as one, prophets let their feet fly off the ground and their bodies swing high in abandon; they offer other Apostolics the example of rising together in spirit closer to God. Their whirling follows a practice that is widespread among other Apostolic churches in southern Africa—the shared intent is to bring the divine presence nearer and into the interior of a holy circle (West 1975:93; Niehaus 2001:35).

Prophets tell me they deliberately intend to be exemplary. Their dance is meant to give hope to the suffering and lift up their "morale." Prophets, in their youthful energy, activate what they call *matlakase*, spiritual electricity, empowering Apostolics.[5] Soaring in ecstasy, and so, by example, animating the feelings of other Apostolics, the young prophets movingly incarnate a higher state of being. They are transfigured by the Holy Spirit.

My own sense is that Apostolics share aesthetic experiences of very great pleasure in the dancing and singing. The shared pleasure leaves many people, and here I include myself after filming a vigorous all-night vigil, not exhausted at the end of a long vigil, but refreshed and intensely revitalized.

Around prophets, the Apostolics themselves are, I realize, moved toward a highly sensuous, powerfully intimate sense of spiritual transfiguration. The Apostolics' waves of powerful emotion surge in moral passion. The Apostolics are much animated by prophets as devotional subjects, and they are energized by these youthful holy hustlers as transfigured incarnations, drawing everyone nearer to the Holy Spirit. For Apostolics, to sing and to dance fervently, as they are led in the most dramatic moments by transfigured street-wise youth—not elders or figures of ancestral authority—is to undergo a religious experience that is profoundly new and passionately Christian.

It takes some time, I found, to recognize sacred illumination—the display of light and the celestial economy of charisma in the church. Initially, church members appear to be dressed as if in heavenly bodies; their vestments bear stars, moons, and crosses (for the risen Christ), and their dancing and swaying seem to reconfigure celestial constellations. Later, I learned that each member has a spiritual gift ranked according to the receiving of celestial light from a heavenly body, the highest ranking being that of the gift of the sun for the archbishop and certain others, but not the city bishop. The economy of charisma, activated in dance, is constantly present to the eyes of church members who see it in its sacred illumination.

My early impressions, too, grew stronger as I heard more of the Apostolics singing. I heard the pastors say in greeting the Apostolics, "This assembly is loved and glorious in the Lord." Above all, I realized that the shared yearning for the body at peace with Jesus, and cooled by Jesus, runs deeply among Apostolics. So, too, does the desire to experience Jesus, to know Him directly; "I want to see Jesus, I want to see my Lord," runs the Apostolics' favorite English hymn. Again and again, throughout their services, they sing of their devotion to Jesus:

Ga le mpotse tshepo.	Ask me of trust.
Ga a ka ke tlaare, ke Jeso.	I will say, "Jesus."
Ke tapeetse go Morena.	I am raised in the Lord.
Gae, ke ga etsho.	Home, that is ours.

Expressed even further, this is their appeal in a song, with the first three lines in Zulu then the rest in Tswana:

Khulula, Messiah.	Liberate, Messiah.
Tina sibochiwe. Amen, Amen.	We are bound Amen, Amen,
Amen, Amen, Moyana, Moyana.	Amen, Amen, Holy Spirit, Holy Spirit.
Tsela e eya, eya legodimong	This path is going, going to Heaven.
Tsela e e thata, e e yang legodimong.	This path is hard, going to Heaven.

Apostolics, singing of their suffering, appeal to God their Judge to be compassionate:

Suna maru a sa thaga.	Kiss the clouds, bursting forth.
Moathodi, moathodi ke wa batho.	The Judge, the Judge is for the people.
Yo nana yo, yo nana yo.	Woe is me, woe is me.
Ke le *tstatsi, ke letsatsi le bothoko.*	The day, the day is painful.

Charismatics are the men with faith in the Word of God, faith in their own voices calling out the Word, men who are not put off by any bitter experience of past failure as seers and healers. But rather than triumphalism, what dominates their felt ethos is the sense of vulnerability, in a Tswana term, *matemeka,* the precarious and unreliable.[6]

This term, *matemeka,* is one of a good number, including *moitseanape*—the "seer" as tricky occult expert—that make up a distinct semantic field in the prophets' diagnosis. It is a semantic field of slippery entrapment

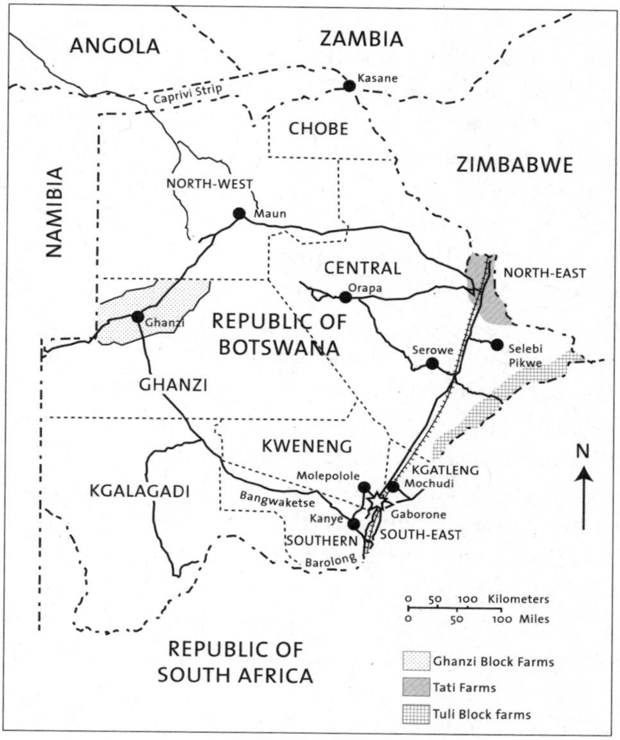

Map 1. Botswana

terms, and it is used by prophets in exposing that the familiar world is a dangerously deceptive appearance. I regard this semantic field and its significance more fully in Chapter 7.

APOSTOLIC CHURCH HISTORY, ORIGINS AND SCHISMS: ELOYI AND CONOLLIUS

Throughout this book, I concentrate mainly on young urban charismatics in the Eloyi Christian Church and its offshoot, the Conollius Apostolic Church. Each church has its city branch based in a poor neighborhood of Gaborone. Eloyi itself is one of many small churches known as Apostolic, after the Apostles of Christ. At the time of my research in 2005 and 2007, it was without doubt the largest and most famous in sensational media coverage, with its very dramatic, explosive exorcisms. Its total congregation is estimated at between four and six thousand members. It is transnational and has dozens of branches across Botswana and in South Africa.

I made no census of church membership. My impression is that the members are not overwhelmingly the poorest of the poor, but that many, if not most, are low-paid but steadily employed workers who are, relatively speaking, among the better off, though a very few are university graduates, with only one being a university lecturer. To trace recruitment and personal histories in the church, I give an account in Chapter 3 of the lives of the city bishop (now archbishop), the village archbishop, and five of the young charismatics.

Eloyi and Conollius belong to the great stream of Apostolic and Zionist churches in southern Africa. Its main source, coming from America, was in late-nineteenth-century Christian revivalism, as Bengt Sundkler suggests in the foundational text on the churches, *Bantu Prophets in South Africa* (1948, second edition 1961). This text, like so much of the later literature, has much to say about syncretism; it foregrounds what has become a major debate about continuities and discontinuities, about the Christian and the non-Christian, in new African Churches.[7] In Chapter 9, I review Sundkler's text along with the later literature in order to situate their contributions comparatively within broader theoretical debates about religious change.

The legacies of American revivalism keep being re-created in southern Africa's history of Christian reformation. Perhaps most influential for the Apostolic and Zionist stream, originally, were the Christian Catholic Apostolic Church in Zion and the teachings of its founder, John Alexander Dowie, the self-styled First Apostle and Prophet of the Restoration (Sundkler 1976:54). These teachings came to Africa in 1897 from Zion City in the American Midwest, and they were spread among Zulu by the preaching of an ex-Dutch Reformed Church missionary at the turn of the century.[8]

To these origins, Sundkler traces the name Zionists and similarly that of Apostolics, also. Among Apostolics, the appeal is to apostolic succession from John the Baptist (Sundkler and Steed 2000:427, cited in Ashforth 2005:186.). Their name reflects the high value Apostolics put on baptism and full immersion in Jordan, so that every river is Jordan, during baptism. For some Apostolics, the name also registers their yearning to be in another time, the time of presence with Jesus, as were the first Apostles (Amanze 1998; Engelke 2007).

I witnessed no baptism in the city branch of Eloyi, which practices full immersion according to its village-based archbishop. "How do you baptize in your country?" he asked me at the very beginning of our first meeting—it was clearly the most important thing he wanted to know, and he explained that Eloyi practices full immersion. The Limpopo River, which flows year-round unlike most streams and rivers in Botswana, is near the archbishop's headquarters in the countryside.[9]

Eloyi's founder, Jakobo Keiphile, comes from the country's Central District, to the east near the border with Zimbabwe. Archbishop Jakobo belongs to an ethnic minority, Birwa, whose language is now virtually a dialect of Tswana, the main national language in Botswana. Eloyi itself, while having core members from the Central District, is ethnically diverse. The origins of the church among Birwa are reflected in little more than certain words in church songs, perhaps composed by the archbishop himself.

Originally, when Archbishop Jakobo founded his church in 1955, he called it the Conollius Apostolic Church after a New Testament figure who urged people to return to their home places. The name was poignant, because Archbishop Jakobo suffered religious persecution in his home village, Tsetsebjwe.[10] He told me his church members were flogged at the headman's court, because the tribe had one official church, that of the Congregationalist London Missionary Society—no other was then allowed. He was forced to flee, finding a safe haven as a young charismatic in exile within a village in the big railway town Mahalapye, at the center of Botswana. There he built up his church, which remained relatively small, until Independence in 1966 brought freedom of religion and his return to Tsetsebjwe. The church still keeps a major center and, for some purposes, its official headquarters, in the railway town.

The first part of this book illuminates the prophets' impact during the escalation of a moral crisis and the latest major church schism. I give a brief sketch of that, at this point, by way of introduction. In recent years, Apostolics, and above all their church leaders, have become increasingly embittered by their many moral and religious differences. Their struggles have escalated within the church hierarchy, which I discuss in Chapter 3, between the elderly village-based archbishop and the middle-aged bishop based in the city—father and first-born son—and, within their family and across the generations, until reaching a schism. It is one of a number of schisms, since the founding of the church, which continue the abundance of schisms Sundkler originally found to be a feature of such churches (Sundkler 1961:161–180).

Late in 2007, the church split in two. The established church has remained under its founding and only archbishop, Jakobo Keiphile. It has

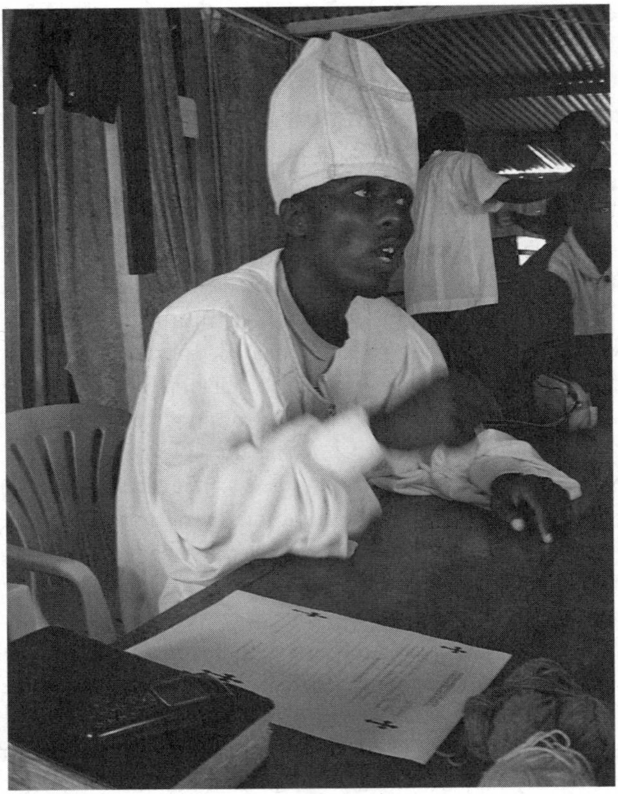

Figure 1. Diagnostic consultation with prophet.

kept its name, Eloyi, and a favorite hymn is this, after the last words of Jesus on the cross:

> *Eloyi, Eloyi, Lama Sabaktani,*
> Lord, Lord, why hast Thou forsaken me?

Named the Conollius Apostolic Church (again after the biblical Cornelius), the new church was founded by Boitshepelo, the old archbishop's son.

Archbishop Boitshepelo, whose own name means Place of Holiness, has revived Eloyi's original name. He casts his move as a return to the primal authenticity of their original church. It is not secession or a complete break from his family's heritage, he claims with good reason, although his innovations within Eloyi have been highly controversial. They were passionately opposed by his father and others in the church hierarchy but much

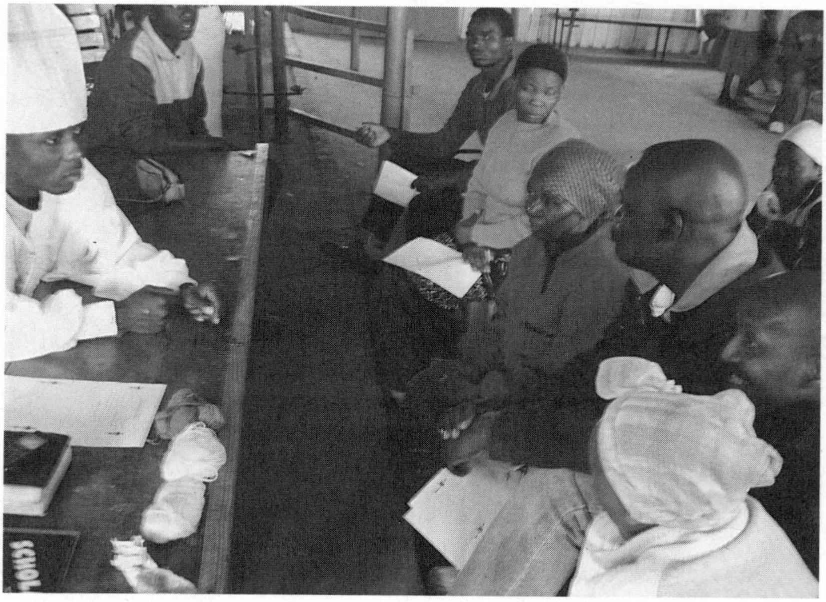

Figure 2. Hospital-style consultation, forms, and rows.

supported by the young men who are the faith healers and charismatics in the church's city branch.

In the city much is made of command by these charismatics and their archbishop of documentation and modern technology as it applies to people. This includes, among other things, formal techniques of people processing, queuing procedures, official documentation of identity, dictated prescriptions on clinical forms, and even what a charismatic calls a "report," in English, of diagnosis. Such charismatic practice appeals to popular expectations and experiences of everyday life in dealing with officialdom, bureaucracy, and other organization in the city. It is a church practice that goes beyond mere mimicry of the bureaucratic to proof of inclusion in the mastery of the people technology in the modern city. After all, as the city archbishop sees it, his church is part of the public health service, which the government gets for free.

A gale, at the very height of the crisis, destroyed the old church building of Eloyi, completely, during my fieldwork. Some saw the fulfillment of prophetic vision in the devastation. For others, it was a judgment of God upon the pillars of the church, the family of bishops themselves fallen in disarray. Still others suspected the work of malice in witchcraft by the

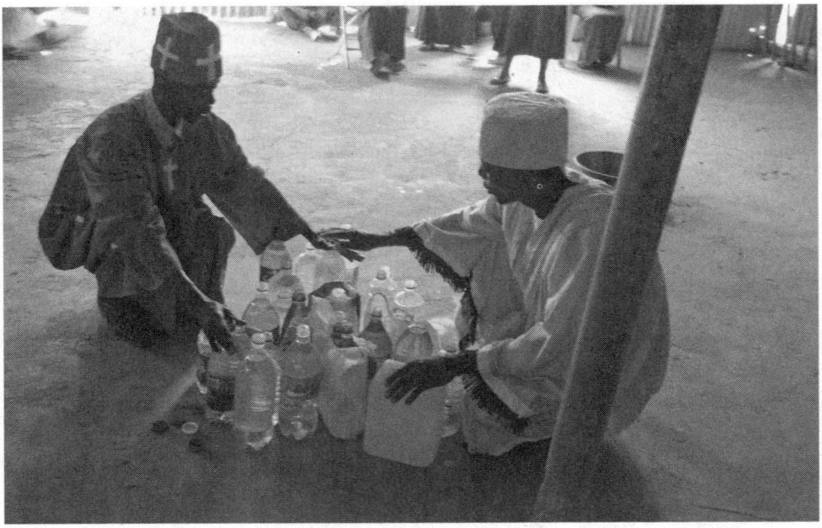

Figure 3. Church servants preparing holy water and prescriptions.

otherwise spiritually powerful turning to evil. Chapters 4 and 5 show how the dissonance, like the destruction, is an ordeal for the church, because it drives forward the anxious moral questioning, the felt uncertainties and the counterassertions in the schism. The Apostolics transcended the ordeal in moments of renewal and fresh appeals to the power of the Word of God. The new archbishop has taken with him into Conollius roughly half of the young charismatics from Eloyi's city branch.

DIVIDUAL, INDIVIDUAL, AND THE OCCULT

The notion of "a complete break with the past," so widespread in recent literature on charismatic Christianity, foregrounds the individual as the new person reborn in Christian churches. Against that, in Eloyi and, indeed, in many other Apostolic churches across southern Africa, Christians face problems of the person being individual and, alternatively, dividual, partible, and permeated by others' emotions and shared substances, including body dirt or sexual and other fluids, and also words.[11] The moral and metaphysical problems of alternating personhood[12] are often experienced as dangerously unsettling—in need of intersubjective management, of careful spiritual regard, protective guidance, and inspired remedy, lest the person suffer ill-being and disease (*bolwetsi*), turmoil (*dikgoborego*), loss of *mahumo* (wealth and prosperity), occult darkness or "bad luck"—*sefifi* (in Tswana) or *senyama* (in Zulu)—perhaps even occult harm (*boloi*). Dividuality opens the vulnerable person both to attack by demons and witchcraft (enemies work upon and fabricate organic bits for occult purposes, with malicious intent) and to pollution, especially in contact with birth and death.

That said about pollution, the demonic, and witchcraft, I need to spell out and better conceptualize what, among the Apostolics, is their distinctively Christian turn in their approach toward the occult. One reason why such conceptualization is needed, at this point, follows from the current critical rethinking among Africanists.

We are now reaching beyond a mainstream of Africanist studies from the nineteen nineties onward. In that mainstream, many phenomena were lumped under the rubric of "the occult"; it was for the sake of a fresh interest, and to address questions of political and moral economy in studies of 'the occult economy' (see Comaroff and Comaroff 1993, 2000, 2001) and 'the modernity of witchcraft' (Geschiere 1997). Given the surfeit of such studies, and the now evident limits of their insights, the tide is now turning toward analysis that splits, rather than lumps phenomena (Kiernan 2006, West 2005, Ranger 2006).

In support of that emerging turn as a useful way forward, I want to advance my own analysis by disaggregating certain phenomena in accord with Apostolic practice. Elsewhere, in my studies of the occult among Tswapong, I write of sorcery, because Tswapong belief and practice fit sorcery and not witchcraft, according to the classic distinction we owe to Azande and Evans-Pritchard (Werbner 1989, 2001). Here, writing of witchcraft, I follow common usage among English speakers, including Apostolics, in present-day Botswana, and I suspend that distinction.

Apostolics speak of witchcraft and witches in English or even in Tswana, as it were in shorthand terms; that is, somewhat broadly and, one might say, loosely. In such shorthand, Apostolics' usage covers *tokoloshi*, demons, and almost any evil attack by invisible means. But in practice, and especially in the practice of diagnosis and healing prescription, Apostolics do observe certain distinctions. Apostolics are themselves more splitters than lumpers, when it comes to the occult; they have an occult repertoire of their own.

What is important, for Christian reformation, is how concern for the dead figures in the way Apostolics disaggregate the occult. If demons loom large in the Apostolics regard for the occult, completely disregarded are, for example, zombies. In response to my asking, Apostolics could tell me a well-known notion among Tswana—*matholwane*, zombies, are the living dead forced to serve their masters by evil, hidden means. Zombies are also part of occult stories in the media in the city and in other gossip and rumor in the countryside. But in no Apostolic diagnosis that I recorded is there any mention of zombies; nor are they the subjects of casual talk or healing treatment: they are simply outside the Apostolic repertoire of the occult. Demons dominate that repertoire to the exclusion of zombies.

The occult burden of the dead still weighs heavily, at times, among Apostolics. But Apostolics have changed that occult burden in Christianizing it, in various ways. One of these has to do with *kgaba,* which traditionally means wrath or the just anger of the dead (Schapera 1934; Werbner 1989:28; Lambek and Solway 2001). Prophets speak of *kgaba* in diagnosis, they tell me, though I myself heard no case of it; and they have a treatment for *kgaba,* by spraying ash and holy water from a green whisk and by green wool that they tie around certain body parts. But while using the word *kgaba,* they obviate its old meaning with a new one, which is in no sense the anger or wrath that is just.[13]

In prophetic usage, *kgaba* overlaps with *senyama* or *sefifi* in the sense of "bad luck," and it is about the dead being uneasy and restless for bad or evil causes. Prophets mention various causes, such as neglect of a tombstone, the disturbance of the grave by a witch, or even the fact that not having been baptized as a Christian the dead is restless, not at one with God. Something of the old moral idea of *kgaba* remains in the linked notion of *tlhola,* the ominous. According to *tlhola,* the unhappiness of parents affects their children; it is, in my view, an aspect of their dividuality, as is *kgaba.* Prophets tell me that when something ominous occurs, they sometimes warn patients to attend to their parents at home in their villages, to see them, to make them happy, to buy them something to please them. Prophets say they send the patients home, but they also treat them with a bath, which is considered essential for healing in that it cleanses them of darkness as bad luck, *sefifi.*

This concern with the ominous and bad luck relates also to the Apostolic version of the old Tswana notion of *seriti,* the essential shade or aura of a person.[14] Currently, dignity is the English word commonly used by many people in Gaborone to translate *seriti,* and for many, *seriti* no longer has any metaphysical or substantial meaning. I was even told by some staff and students at the University of Botswana that I was wrong to translate *seriti* as shade; they insisted, also, that *seriti,* dignity, has nothing to do with *moriti,* shadow—this, despite the view of the University's leading linguists that these nouns share the root *riti,* and by its noun class *seriti,* shade, is the essence of *moriti,* shadow. More in accord with the older

Tswana usage, in the condition of bad luck, the archbishop tells me, your body is not in harmony (*utlwana*, in mutual understanding) with other people's bodies. *Seriti*, as the shade of the dead, burdens you down in *sefifi*, occult darkness. It is the same condition as the one you have when you are fearful of the shade of a dead person, because it has not left and gone away. Nowadays, the archbishop himself fears, people are "carrying the shades of many dead," having been to too many funerals, without proper cleansing; they are overcome, "overburdened by the weight of the darkness."

What the archbishop demands is much more spraying and careful cleansing. Such treatment is another example, in my view, of the transformative practice, from dividuality to individuality, by which Apostolics manage their alternating personhood and overcome having bits of significant others in themselves. The substance they seek to share is the one by which they go beyond their past burdensome dividuality; in holy water, they partake together in Jesus.

CHRISTIAN REFORMATION: DIALOGICS AND DIALECTICS

My argument about religious change among Apostolics and other charismatic Christians in Botswana advances the concept of reformation in Christian history. The present book proposes that the study of the consequences of the reformation in present-day Africa now calls for better understanding of shifts in rhetoric; of how problematic the power of the Word becomes, and what are the new words of Power. It calls for close, theoretically informed analysis of change or continuity in religious language, both in content, in what is being said, and in dialogics, in how the saying is accomplished. This is importantly in something of a spiritual monologue or in dialogue, for example, the direct talk between charismatic healer and patient. That is why, in much of this book, I document in depth the distinctive religious language that is deployed among African Christian charismatics in prayer, diagnosis, and prescription.

It has been argued that spiritual egalitarianism often prevails, at least ideally, in numerous African charismatic churches. This refers to one extreme where almost any of the faithful can be graced with charisma, perhaps with the gift from the spirit of inspired speech. But often there is a division of spiritual labor, so that, at another extreme, as among the urban youth, charismatics are specialists. They are set apart even from the church hierarchy, which includes the routinized officials in regular posts, such as the priests, evangelists, and pastors.

From this division of labor, however, as I show in the present study, it does not necessarily follow that young charismatics and old patriarchs or surviving founders of a church hierarchy oppose each other consistently. Nor does it mean that opposition between them is the usual source of the many schisms in African charismatic churches. My evidence is that the hierarchy is often divided against itself; patriarchal authority, if exercised in well-defined offices, is not monolithic. Moreover, I show that along with the ordinary church members, the young charismatics, too, take sides. They form more or less permanent coalitions with some church elders against others; they contest command of the moral high ground, and they insist that at stake is privileged access to divine Power not earthly power or influence alone.

The comparative and theoretical interest in the dialectics of Christian reformation in Africa is all the greater, because that often takes place, at least among African charismatics, through repeated schisms, each distinguished in turn by what Gregory Bateson calls schismogenesis (Bateson 1958:175–197). Bateson argues that ideological difference in value or practice is exaggerated and opposition increased in distinct processes of complementary and symmetrical schismogenesis. My account shows the process of schismogenesis that occurs among charismatics in a single church and its offshoot. It highlights the fact that reformation is not, at least among southern African charismatics, merely new, nothing but "a break with the past."[15] Some of the past is so very present that it continues unquestioned, underlying or informing predicaments from generation to generation. My argument is that such axiomatic continuity holds fundamentally for personhood in new Christian churches, especially the Apostolics and Zionists, in southern Africa.

Drawing on Gregory Bateson's theory of schismogenesis, my arguments in the first part of the book move beyond the familiar institutional sociology of charisma and provide the basis for my focus on semantic and dialogical analysis, primarily following Mikhail Bakhtin (1984), in the second part of this book. Urban charismatics are creative in the very language of religion that they use, including city slang and trendy imagery. Hence one challenge, also met in the book's second part, is to show how and why young streetwise charismatics rework or Christianize old forms of speech, from prayer to the dialogue of diviners and mediums. Here I draw also on Alfred Schutz's (1944) phenomenological approach to the stranger and his insights into the contingency of the natural attitude in common sense. I show how charismatics subvert the natural attitude of their patients; how they shock them by exposing that what is familiar actually hides disturbing things of the occult. Pursuing the phenomenological approach further, I take up the somatic treatment given in charismatic practices and consider it in the light of Marcel Merleau-Ponty's understanding of intercorporeality (2002).

My discussion pursues issues raised some thirty years ago by Johannes Fabian in his seminal approach to charismatic movements; Fabian addresses "prophetic discourse" and attends to the discursive and to critical narratives (Fabian 1979). The challenge for the present study is even greater than the one put by Fabian, however. In part this is because of the importance of charismatic practice for the growing interest in the anthropology of the senses. In part, also, it is because the Apostolic prophets intend to reach beyond "story" telling and interpersonal communication in words. The need is to document and analyze how charismatics themselves, as Apostolic prophets, go beyond text making or even commentary on commentaries (cf. Fabian 2008). Accordingly, I show how they not only intensify the visualizing of imagery but also somatize passionately by cultivating the refined substances and cosmetic means (see Chapter 8) to redress the bodies, the personal conditions and the life situations of the afflicted. The issues take us to questions of aesthetics and even psychotherapy, as I suggest in Chapter 9 in my comments on Catholic charismatics in New England.

In Chapter 9, I foreground more of the comparison that informs my ethnography. This further illuminates the bearing that holy hustling has for a substantial body of research on African charismatics. This research has a great deal to say on faithful experience, moral agency, persuasive language, and intersubjectivity. In response, I make most explicit in Chapter 9 what are the theoretical implications of my argument and where it leads in current debate, primarily among anthropologists but also among social historians, theologians, and other scholars interested in comparative religion. The main issues I address are about syncretism and antisyncretism in prophecy and divination, about the importance of sin, conscience, and moral policing among charismatics, about the re-creation of the self and person in healing ritual, and, very generally, about religious innovation and cultural change.

My Conclusion integrates this book's text reflexively with my film *Holy Hustlers* (2009), taking its lead from Richard Rorty's perception, according to Clyde Lee Miller, of the enduring importance of Aristotle's ideas of *dianoia* and *noesis* (Miller 2003). I build my argument on a fact of urban charismatics' experience of the moving image, which these young men speak about explicitly and very articulately. They are seers of the cinematic, of the moving image. In their diagnostic experience, the prophetic *is* the cinematic.

Prophecy goes beyond diagnosis, of course, just as ethnography goes beyond mere narrative. But what is remarkable, I argue, is that seen in terms of the creative process, prophecy and ethnography have much in common, and all the more so when a film is the father of the written text, as in the present case. Hence I draw on the ideas of *dianoia* and *noesis* to shed light on the creative bond between my ethnography and charismatics' prophecy, and to open out the question of how we similarly engage with fragments and fabrication, with the presence of absence, and with discovery that goes beyond the surface of things.

More broadly, by deepening the analysis of holy hustling, my account illuminates the tensions and dilemmas emerging in African Christianity among charismatics, but widely prevalent also in the comparative study of religious change elsewhere.

PART I

To and from Crisis and Beyond

1. Holy Hustling

CHRISTIAN PASSION IN HOLY HUSTLING: MIMESIS, EMPATHY, AND DEVOTION

The urban young men who are the charismatics in the city branch of their Apostolic church, Eloyi or Conollius, undergo moments of religious passion. As faith healers, they are seen to have vicarious experiences of the Holy Spirit burning fiercely within them. What they endure is not their own but their patient's suffering. It is overpowering and involuntary; it is visceral. The suffering is mirrored on their own bodies and dramatized by their gestures of pain. They turn their own gaze inward, while becoming a living and moving image in the gaze of others. In sacred mimesis, they feel a compulsion inspired by the Holy Spirit to be and behave like someone else, their patient.[1] Such sacred mimesis serves their patient for reflection, for knowing an interior condition that the patient cannot otherwise grasp clearly.[2] To be a patient is to suffer from not understanding oneself or one's situation and to be in need of someone whose extraordinary insight comes from a spiritual gift: charisma.[3]

With prophetic charisma comes both the compulsion to embody sacred mimesis and also the recognized capacity for sacred empathy. Prophets themselves are self-conscious about empathy in their practice. They say that they have to feel others' pain for them, put themselves in the others' position, identify with them as intimate others, as if they were one's mother's own children or even parents. The prophets' expressed intent is to make others' pain more bearable by being shared. But the sacred empathy of prophets surpasses mere identification or feeling for the situation of the other because, being understood in terms of divine inspiration, it is empathy that is revelatory, free of the other's misrecognition of self and situation. Or, at least, it is presented as if it is the truer, higher insight. The Apostolic faith-healers as charismatics diagnose in the words of the Holy Spirit about the source of the patient's suffering; they reveal its causes and its remedies.

In dialogue with the patient, young Apostolic faith healers become assertive, even aggressive. The turn has come for the patient to become the object of subjection. It is subjection to the power of the young charismatics. They dominate forcefully, because they are sure they know the truth better than the patient, who may be an elder or perhaps some other person ordinarily owed respect and deference apart from such diagnosis.

In Chapter 2, I give in full the response by one of the most prominent prophets, Prophet Joshua, to my question about what happens in diagnosis. More briefly here, by way of introduction, Prophet Joshua's answer explains that he brings together both his bodily experience in empathy with his patient and, also, his intellectual activity in reasoning *akanya,* like a chess player. He reasons very quickly and intuitively to get a configuration as an arrangement of the bits; the bits flash by, as if it were on a "film" (he uses the English word). His "film" shows him who is the witch and the witch's techniques of occult attack.

What Prophet Joshua tells me is that as a prophet he has the sight of a "camera" (in English) with a "film" which reveals the occult. He is drawing a contrast to my camera. Mine merely shows what anyone can see, whereas his eyes, looking through his "camera," see what people do not know about themselves, their unwitting collusion in witchcraft. His reasoning, however, is human reasoning, and thus limited.

Even beyond the comparison to my camera, prophets alert their patients, in modern terms, to the prophets' use of an extraordinary means of visualizing the otherwise hidden and unseen. For example, in diagnosis with a patient who is a sophisticated civil servant, Prophet Andrew speaks of doing a scan, after a hospital model for internal investigation; he carries out her needed scan under the guidance of the Holy Spirit, as I show in Chapter 3.

Patients have to realize that they do not know even themselves truly. *Ga o itlhaloganye,* "You do not understand yourself," is a favorite truth that prophets insist on telling their patients. To see what is truly inside someone is the gift only prophets have, and it comes ultimately from the *mowa,* Holy Spirit.

Knowledge is elusive, especially self-knowledge, according to prophets' warnings. For prophets, knowledge is not absolute or total. It is not the knowledge of and for the four corners of the earth, which only God has. Prophets see and know fragmentary pieces, which have to be put together, bit by bit, with the help elicited from the prophets' patients. It might be thought that prophets are simply bricoleurs, another instance of Levi-Strauss's famous insight; but if so, they are the bricoleurs who never claim authorship and who innovate in the name of a higher truth, partially glimpsed—the true author is the Word.

Having made discoveries from the Holy Spirit, Apostolic faith healers promise hope and relief. Often, the revealed need is for demonic exorcism. The occasion becomes a moment of prayer, song, and dance by a supportive church congregation and yet also a moment of wildly tearing things to bits, of attacking furniture and even walls and ceilings. The destruction is meant to be liberating. Apostolic charismatics run amok in pursuit of the harmful, hidden matter of demons and witchcraft. Contact with the obnoxious things which they expose overpowers them with disgust; they swoon and have to be restored to consciousness with prayer by a man (bishop, pastor, or other prophet) who catches them protectively in his arms.

I call these young urban charismatics holy hustlers not to dismiss them, as if they were—and they are not—cynical charlatans or mere fakes. As streetwise hustlers, these young men push with impatient energy, when they dance ecstatically, diagnose affliction, treat patients, and exorcise demons. They sometimes say they are told by the Holy Spirit, by the Word, to *gatelela*. That means to subjugate, to press hard, down to the ground as in wrestling, or even rape. In youthful enthusiasm, charismatic prophets jostle and even batter their patients emotionally with fear of evil intent, death, and disease, and they may not always be "nice" in that they exact excessive gifts or extort cash fees, contrary to their church rules for free healing services. Contrary to their church rules, also, some of the young urban prophets dare to hold consultations and healing sessions privately at home, and they are accused of stealing from the church the holy ash they need for treatment. Their enemies—and they do have seriously hostile critics both within their church and beyond it—would find the label hustlers all the more apt, given the earliest usage in eighteenth-century England: gangs of pickpockets were hustlers.

In calling charismatics prophets, I follow Apostolic usage. Apostolics speak of prophets, in English, and *baprofeti*, using the term in the Tswana translation of the Bible—and for Apostolics, their *baprofeti* are the successors to the prophets of the Bible. It is, of course, a usage that is not common or standard for the English words, prophet and prophecy, which have a strong sense of telling the future. The Apostolic prophets tell more about the past and the present than about the future, except as it is or has been fabricated maliciously to become an unwelcome expectation.

As holy hustling, the charismatic practice is distinctively youthful, masculine, and urban. The charismatics themselves are twelve young men. Mainly in their early to mid-twenties and nearly all unemployed, they have the clairvoyance of the streetwise, of seeing clearly into a world of tricksters. Urban slang in some parts of Africa takes over a traditional term for a seer or diviner, one who "sees clearly" into the invisible world, and associates that with street smarts.[4] The urban slang introduces—or perhaps sharpens from past ambivalence toward the seer—what is a double edge in its sense of duplicity: the clairvoyant is able to see through the scams of tricksters but able also to con others, who don't see clearly, or at all.

Urban slang among Eloyi's charismatics treats "the seer" to a similar remaking with a double edge, which sometimes is turned against the charismatics themselves. In nineteenth-century Tswana, dictionary compilers found, *moitseanape* was a "diviner, a soothsayer," derived from "*itse,* know, and *nape,* god of wisdom" (Matumo 1993: 253). Any expert is now termed *moitseanape* in common usage today. More specifically, in the urban slang of young charismatics, the term refers to someone with cunning that is suspect and used for harmful, occult purposes. The expertise is that of traditional doctors who fabricate organic substances, "medicines" as Tswana call them in English. What people call witchcraft—that is, malicious occult attack that causes affliction, including affliction by demons—they blame on the use of medicines by others who are jealous and malicious. "Seers," including traditional providers of medicines, are the tricksters whose fabrications in witchcraft charismatics claim to be able to see and expose.

In my argument, what "holy hustlers" signals is not a pejorative judgment, or even an obvious contradiction, but a problematic, perhaps a synergy between contraries. Put generally: How do holiness and hustling fit together? More specifically, how do prophets bring one to bear on the other in prayer, diagnosis, prescription, and exorcism? In other words, how do they sanctify hustling in purity and holiness and, at the same time, energize holiness forcefully? How do prophets swing between extremes, between moments of reckless energy, most strikingly when they whirl until "flying" in their ecstatic round dance, and careful moments in prayer, reflection, or healing meditation? How do they dominate in prophecy and yet also endure vicarious suffering, on behalf of others, and become the transfigured subjects around whom Apostolics glorify their devotion to Jesus? These are the questions to which I return throughout much of this book.

MASCULINIZING PROPHECY AND DEVOTIONAL SUBJECTS

Asserting a gendered dogma of inspiration, the young men who are prophets say that women have soft bones, too soft to bear the most intense energy of the Holy Spirit. Instead, women cry weakly; only men can endure the spiritual charge until they fall unconscious, at one in trance with the Holy Spirit, and then released, glorifying their Lord.

I call this masculinized inspiration a dogma in the sense of "an arrogant declaration of opinion." No woman was ever a prophet in the Bible, prophets told me, certain I would not contradict them. At Eloyi's city branch but not at Eloyi's headquarters in the remote rural village of Tsetsejbwe, the young male prophets, masculinizing their own domain, have effectively hustled older women away from prophecy. The change in the city toward an exclusively masculine and youth domain of prophecy is all the more distinctive, seen against the more general practice in similar churches in southern Africa. In other Apostolic and Zionist churches, women are commonly prophets; often, they are the only or main prophets.[5]

In Eloyi's city branch, men are held to be the right ones to take over from the traditional witchfinder. The archbishop prohibits that takeover at the village headquarters; he does not allow it in his presence, and he condemns it as not Christian. In the city, prophets accomplish their reprise of the traditional in Apostolic guise by becoming "sniffer dogs," in resonance with traditional practice of witchfinding. In the way of male dogs, their mission is to find the personal bits witches use to harm church members and weaken their prayers.

At a peak in a Sunday service, the bishop or, in his absence, the pastor-general sends prophets on the masculine hunt in their mission. Rushing wildly outside, here and there, sometimes to the roof of the church, sometimes to a distant crossroads or the very limits of the neighborhood, prophets sniff about, partly on all fours. When they burst into the church, dramatically, on their return, they bear one prophet, comatose and rigid in trance. He clutches the noxious bits, such as a church cape or photographs, worked on by the witches.

The electrifying feel of the moment is all the more intensely masculine because the prophet swoons and is manhandled, patted, then cradled by other men until he recovers from trance. "A woman's cape, nasty with blood, from a beast of prey or something else," announced the pastor-general at one such moment. "Maybe one of you women will be killed by something. Let us pray." It is striking, also, that the strong, tactile feel in the church is even more dominantly masculine in that only men hold hands when dancing, making a whirling unity, and men are the ones to lay hands in blessing women and each other. Such masculinizing is not a reflection of touching in everyday life practice—where there is no such male bias—but a transformation in ritual, which creates a gendered imbalance in favor of men and which further sets church life apart in sacredness.

Earlier, I argue that prophets bring together the pitiable and the heroic, in being devotional subjects effectively in faith healing. Carrying the argument forward, I suggest that prophets also serve Apostolics by being the devotional subjects who enable the spiritual realization of parental virtue in ritual. After prophets swoon, the cradling itself, along with the surrounding by concerned elders, is thus a transformative rite for youth and elders. Enduring spiritual passion, youth become submissive and elders become assertive in devotion and care, in moral passion that brings them all closer to God.

One gets the impression, also, of a sensually masculine display during youthfully vigorous dance, showing off in the presence of women, and indeed prophets have an aura attractive to women, somewhat like pop stars, and like them, generally, a perhaps well-deserved reputation for being promiscuous.

Not surprisingly, and in accord with a general pattern in similar faith-healing churches, women are the prophets' main patients (Engelke 2007; Ishii 2008). It is said, also, that a prosperous woman sometimes keeps an attractive prophet to look after her and protect her, because of his charisma and power. Women form the supporting chorus during services. It is the prophets who take charge by usually leading the singing, dancing, and clapping, and by playing the tambourines and ringing the bells; they are the ones who give each other a break in diagnosis, sometimes at potentially awkward moments, by intervening and bursting out into song.

I witnessed one exorcism when a woman went on the rampage, in a fit much like a prophet, as if she were a sniffer dog. At first Prophet Andrew held her back, then, told by a pastor-general to let her go, he freed her. She grabbed a mattress, tore and ripped to get to the bits inside, and used her mouth dog style. But what she got, according to Prophet Andrew, was nothing, and eventually the pastor-general stopped her dismantling further. Having ordinary senses, I, of course, smelled and saw nothing different from the other stuffing that prophets wrenched from nearby furniture. "It was," Prophet Andrew told me, "her imagination." In using that English word, I take it that he meant "a fantasy, not inspired by the Holy Spirit."

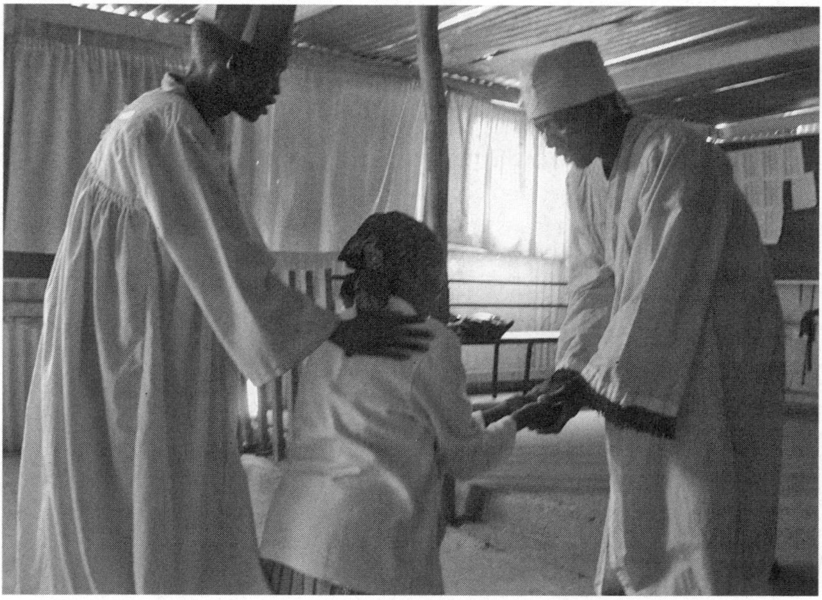

Figure 4. Church servants laying on hands.

It might be thought that the assertion of masculinity in prophets' holy hustling makes for triumphalism. Elsewhere, and notably among Catholic charismatics in the Philippines, participation in the spiritual war of good and evil is taken to be empowering, at least from an analyst's perspective, because these Christians confidently know their ritual brings victory (see Wiegele 2004). Eventually, the good will triumph.

By contrast, prophets of Eloyi, like many other Apostolic Christians in Botswana, are not so sure, especially at the height of Botswana's AIDS pandemic.[6] These Apostolic Christians are often fearful their prayers may fall short, that enemies may be too cunning in their occult expertise, that malicious witches and demons may be too strong. To stand up to these dangers and uncertainties calls for men in the lead, prophets insist, but men who are able to climb the city hills by themselves, go out in the wild, pray and get closer to God, away from people. According to Prophet Joshua:

> The Bible says old men and women cannot be caught by the spirit like the one which catches young men and young women. The old see when sleeping. On waking up in the morning, they say I dreamt like this and that. That's the spirit of the old. Their visions come when they

> sleep, as the Bible says, because their bones are tired. They don't have the marrow to withstand the force of the spirit. When the spirit enters you, it can make you fall down. But old women who fall down will be unable to stand up.

It was Prophet Joshua who, in a moment of fierce inspiration, hit the church's first and powerful crystal ball with his fist, shattering it to bits, and in so doing frightened away the women, especially the elderly women, from presuming to be prophets. With the shattering, the women felt their inspiration ebbing away; they were struck silent, I was told. More modestly and with less fear, the women continued to present nighttime dreams for the congregation's consideration.

CHRISTIANIZING THE WITCHFINDER'S EXTRASENSORY ATTITUDE

Although prophets in name and confirmed by Eloyi's bishop, the young charismatics are, nevertheless, diviners and mediums in many of their ideas and practices.[7] But as prophets, they aggressively oppose diviners and mediums. Even in the face of their archbishop's outraged condemnation, however, some deliberately go to *sangoma,* mediums of ancestral spirits, to get training in divinatory trance, in dream interpretation, and in the extraction of harmful occult substances from the body.[8]

Certain prophets want to know all of what some say are the tricks of the *sangoma* and other "traditional" doctors, the more effectively to counteract them. In this turn to an older religious tradition, anathema for Eloyi's founders, a third generation of the church led by the young prophets takes up a legacy of occult practices from grandparents or other relatives, who were diviners. There is in recent Eloyi prophecy at its city branch—for somewhat more than a decade—a Christian reappropriation of an old attitude toward the senses—the extrasensory attitude. According to the extrasensory attitude, the gifted specialists who go beyond ordinary knowledge of the world have an extraordinary and powerful capacity that is extrasensory. Power and knowledge come together in this extrasensory attitude, which is linked to the dead. More specifically, and in a version widespread across southern Africa, this extrasensory attitude is the perceived ability, like that of dogs, to "sniff out" witches and witchcraft substances (Ashforth 2005; Niehaus 2001). Just as dogs smell a trail beyond human capacity—they smell what is out of sight—so too do prophets "sniff out" the invisible: they know the unseen according to the extrasensory attitude on their occult hunts.

It is a religious act, prayer, which Christianizes the old extrasensory attitude and turns it into something new. In Eloyi, the ancestors and the dead are more a burden of darkness, *sefifi* (also, "bad luck," *senyama* in Zulu), than a means of access to power and knowledge, which come from God. If, in the past, extrasensory ability was given by or in harmony with the ancestors, once Christianized, it is for the avowed purpose of getting the prophet closer to God and, through his intercession, getting the patient closer, too. In addition, the Christian attitude is meant to be realized with the sincere, moral passion of wholehearted faith in God's mighty glory and active benevolence.

Charismatic intercession in Eloyi takes prayer out of the context of the ancestors and descent into a context of trust and faith in the church. But it does so, with some unease—one might say an existential anxiety—in the presence of the continued perception of descent as a force in everyday life, a matter of one's very substance and essence, and also, for many if not most church members, in the presence of ancestral intercession, pleading for relief with the dead, as a commonplace practice at home or in their original villages.

There is an underlying point, which Chapter 6 advances more fully. Charismatic prayer, like the faith upon which it is predicated, is intersubjective, and not the unburdening of the subject as an individual. Even more, for Eloyi members prayer is one of the most important religious means they use for the management of their intersubjectivity. Of all the linguistic modes charismatics use as prophets in intercession, prayer is the framing mode. It is the one that, for charismatics, is essential—without it the others are of no avail.

RELIGIOUS LANGUAGE AND DIALOGUE BEYOND DIVINATION

The Apostolic prophets are more like Tswana diviners than the classic non-Christian prophets in the Africanist literature, such as prophets among the Nuer. Arguably, as Thomas Beidelman has suggested, the Nuer prophet is perceived to have little or no agency (Beidelman 1971). When he undergoes a visionary experience, it imposes itself upon him, and he is merely the means through which some Power as a refraction of Spirit communicates.

By contrast, the Apostolic prophet, while undergoing the experience of the Word, wonders in amazement, according to his own report. When he tells this to his patient, he presents himself as an active agent in conversation with the Word and the angels: he tells of asking the Word and the angels so that he can reason through his amazement. In turn, he elicits from the patient participation in their direct dialogue. This reflects on the wondrous conversation that he keeps reporting and about which he asks the patient—the patient has to identify and recognize familiar bits, reported as unfamiliar by the prophet in his revealed vision. The prophet thus has the questioner's agency in the dialogue, questioning the Word and the angels and, in turn, the patient. Not that the prophet has nothing to say of his own—he does offer advice and reasoning, he counsels forcefully, but he usually does so only after understanding the patient's answers or response.

I call this linguistic form a doubled dialogue because it flows back and forth, interactively, between two registers of dialogue, the interior monologue and the direct dialogue. The interior monologue, which I conceptualize after Mikhail Bakhtin, is one speaker's talk that resonates with other speech which the speaker reports or alludes to. Commenting on "dialogized interior monologue" in Dostoevsky's *Crime and Punishment,* Bakhtin writes of a "model of the *microdialogue*: all words in it are double-voiced, and in each of them a conflict of voices takes place" (italics in the original, Bakhtin 1984: 74). The interior monologue conveys its register through idioms of citation, such as "It is said," "I wonder," and "I ask." In this register, the prophet rehearses his inner conversation for the patient, who hears only the prophet's voice speaking of, to, or with the Word. One of the most articulate of the prophets, Prophet Joshua, calls his interior monologue "the report" in English and *mafoko* (news, words) in Tswana.

By contrast, each participant in direct dialogue is an interlocutor. Each speaks and hears; the conversation is mutual. This is the register that patient and prophet use directly with each other. How and when shifts are made from one register to another is an important question, and I return to it later in my close analysis of actual cases, most fully in Chapter 7.

My immediate interest is more broadly to introduce the religious change in holy hustling by which divination and prophecy are brought together and Christianized, and yet opposed in competition and, even more, in declared hostilities.[9] Prophecy is now contemporary with divination and the practices are consulted alternatively by some people, even otherwise devout Apostolics. For Apostolics, the prophetic dialogue is borne of the divinatory, with which it shares the shifting between interior monologue and direct dialogue. The pattern is familiar in religious change that involves observable distinctions between reproduction, replication, and replacement; being "borne of" does not mean being "the same as" or necessarily "taking the place of."

One hallmark of the birth of the prophetic from the divinatory is in the call for consent from the very beginning of the consultation—the appropriate response in the séance being "Yes, I hear and understand (i.e., agree)," and for the Christian and pious answer in diagnosis, "Amen." Another such hallmark in dialogue is the common use of citation idiom, for example, "It is said." In the prophetic interior monologue as in the divinatory, the reporter of what is said is not its author; prophet and diviner alike address and question an answering agency that is authoritative—the lots being the agency for the diviner. The Christianized citation idiom refers to the otherwise inaudible, the remote speaker, as the God of Gleaming Brilliance, *Modimo wa Kgalalela,* the King, the Voice, the Doctor of Life, and the Angel of Might and Life, *Lenyeloi le Maatla le Botshelo*—with each divine remote speaker saying and answering what the prophet reports in his interior monologue.

The approach to verse and the textual is, moreover, significantly different in the interior monologues of divination and Apostolic prophecy. The diviner draws, at least in wisdom divination, on a repertoire of archaic verse, mellifluous in sound, rich in imagery, cryptic and condensed in significance. The diviner's interior monologue is highly allusive. It has a superabundance of meaning much of which is so beyond ordinary comprehension that it takes an expert, the diviner, to unpack it in plain speech. The diviner displays specialist command of a cultural archive, with more or less depth according to his expertise and personal wisdom (Werbner 1973, 1989:19–60, 2001).

By contrast, if also ambiguous, the Apostolic prophet's interior monologue is free of allusive verse. Unlike the diviner as poetic specialist, he reports in everyday language, which may shock or surprise but is not in itself mysterious or an index of knowledge open only to an initiated expert. *Ranolela,* to clarify, is the prophet's intent in speech with the Word, and simple clarity is its form of expression. Texts are not the prophet's forte; they are not the means of his assertion of the wiser, more authoritative understanding than that of his patients. He is not set above them in diagnosis by any esoteric command of texts and their truth. Nor is he the one who gives the indispensable Bible readings at services—the reader is often a woman—and his knowledge of the Bible is something he shares much in common with many other Apostolics. The prophet has Power, and thus knowledge beyond that of others, such as his patients. But what characterizes the prophet's language is sharing with others, intersubjective inclusion: as in his dialogical revelations, so too in his language.

Like the wisdom diviner, the prophet is a specialist in knowledge beyond that of ordinary people, but unlike the diviner, the prophet is a charismatic who speaks the street language of the common people. If, currently, wisdom diviners are keepers of culture, their successors and competitors, streetwise prophets, are today's trendy men of God.

In their practice, prophets introduce a religious language of their own, new in spiritual idiom and forms of divine address, yet old in dialogics. What resonates through the prophets' diagnostic monologues and dialogues is an *artful* echo of the séances of diviners and witchfinders. I stress *artful* to draw attention to the poetics of moving, persuasive language; it does not remain the same in the move from the divining séance to the prophetic diagnosis, but the continuing narrative art and the play of rhetoric, evolving from one to the other, is remarkable.

Even more, what is deeply shared, from divining séance to prophetic diagnosis, is their common, logocentric perception of the power of the word and the voice.[10] For prophets, however, the logocentric perception takes a Christian turn, embedded in prayer and religious dialogue with the Word and Voice of God: power becomes Power.[11]

HUSTLING IN DIAGNOSIS AND EXORCISM

An important part of prophets' hustling, in diagnosis and in subsequent treatment, constitutes the materiality of witchcraft. In this respect, also, prophets belong to the long tradition of hustling by witchfinders. Witchfinders discover things, which they produce as proof of witchcraft. Their hustling concretizes the unseen and the invisible, manifesting their perceived capacity for extraordinary knowledge. Prophets dominate their patients in making witchcraft something material, first as realized objects of reconnaissance—fabricated objects exposed, envisioned, and reported in diagnosis—then as actual objects, the things found and torn apart in exorcism. Good as exorcism is intended to be for patients, it is more than very good for prophets—they know it is their moment of popular recognition, of dramatic triumph in the war of good and evil.

As masters of the materiality of witchcraft, prophets greatly enjoy exorcism. It is wildly exhilarating for young men on the rampage. It shows youth at the height of their manly powers. Praised for being like hunters of old, they are held to be the heroes in the vanguard, driving out evil; safely behind and urging them forward stay the women, their bodies deliberately vibrating with the music, for the glory of God. Exorcism brings prophets generous gifts from supplicants; it makes them loved, even sexually, and makes the church famous and popular. It is not surprising, therefore, that a great deal of diagnosis is devoted to the discovery and exposure of fabricated objects in reconnaissance for exorcism.

During diagnosis, the prophet tells of a journey in which, with the aid of angels and God, the prophet does reconnaissance around and on behalf of the patient. Each prophet usually has a special angel of his own, but on the journey he may consult angels speaking the patients' language and ethnically identified with them. It is not an ordinary journey, but a spiritual one, and the reconnaissance, uncovering hidden fabrications, is in advance of the prophet making any physical visit to the scene, a visit he might make in exorcism.

It might be thought that the prophetic journey is the same as that of the shaman in many parts of the world. If perhaps a variation on well-known shamanic practice—and the prophet does get nearer the exalted world to hear the Voice—the prophetic journey is, however, distinguished by a significant difference in the regard for the familiar. Shamans are famous for going beyond, to the land of the dead or to some alternative world usually invisible or even unknowable. By contrast, when inspired, prophets report that they make their way spiritually round a familiar world—that is, familiar to their patients, not themselves usually—and they expose it as dangerous and threatening because fabricated things are hidden, or yet to be understood in that familiar world. "Smelling out," using extrasensory powers and a heightened sense of the uncanny, prophets defamiliarize the familiar, in diagnosis and exorcism. The familiar becomes mere appearance, not true reality.

Following the phenomenologist and sociologist Alfred Schutz and his insight into the stranger, I bring into my argument the concept of the natural attitude that is the attitude of common sense in everyday life (Schutz 1944). It is the natural attitude that patients take for granted. For that very reason—the patients' sense of life going on as usual despite their troubles—the prophet subverts the natural attitude; he has to shock, to expose and disturb what the familiar actually hides. This is all in the name of truth—the revelation of the patient's naivety; and renewed awareness is the aim. The prophet presents a monologue that undoes the natural attitude by introducing the stranger's approach of defamiliarization.

At first in such a monologue, what the prophet visualizes is fleeting and puzzling—"wonders" (*dikgakgamatso*). Or rather, what he says he sees and what his posture conveys is his vision, *pono,* of fleeting fragments and his hearing of puzzling bits. His is an experience of the uncanny. He continually remarks on the remarkable and the surprising, even shocking, "I am amazed, and I ask . . ." Prophets say that they themselves become light, quick, and weightless in diagnosis.

Telling a story in fragments, not as a whole all at once, the prophet exerts leverage upon patients. He presses them to go from their natural attitude toward detachment, toward more of the stranger's approach to themselves and the significant things and others around them. In turn, and from one story fragment to another, each reported object from the patient's everyday, familiar world—an object such as a tool box or a pillow—becomes something fabricated, a threatening topic of defamiliarization, in the dialogue of diagnosis. The reconnaissance and later exorcism reach into the intimate interior of the patient's everyday, familiar world. Uncovered is the occult danger in the near object. I am tempted to say that the prophet resembles the Surrealist whose art, seeking the renewal of the image, reveals the mystery in familiar objects; the revelation is shocking, and it is according to Magritte's principle of the visible thought: everything visible conceals something visible—visible to the seer. Against misrecognition comes the shock of recognition.

To say that the prophet is the father of all suspicion would be wrong. Feeling that they are victims of undue affliction, or fearing they might become such victims, patients are already suspicious when they arrive for a diagnosis. Given their suspicion, the prophet is the one who works upon their understanding of the world as it is as usual; he defamiliarizes that world, breaks it down, even to bits, and reveals malicious fabrication. The implicit promise goes beyond diagnosis to prescription: the prophet is expected to find a remedy for restoring the everyday world to what it should be, as usual, or even more desirable than usual—blessed with Christian goodness from the heavens above.

In their holy hustling, young prophets deal in suspicion and guilt, they shock yet try to arouse hope and trust, and finally, at their most promising and caring, they work to undo evil and redress or remedy occult attack. It fits their youth-generated vision, in diagnosis, of malice, cunning, and entrapment that the streetwise charismatics have a blind spot. This dark limit in their diagnostic vision of a personal situation obscures what is highly illuminated in many séances by Tswana village diviners, most of whom are from older generations. Very frequently, when village diviners disclose malice and blame for witchcraft, they also reveal, for the same clients, their responsibility for failure in meeting obligations to others, particularly in relation to the dead.

As prophets, charismatics see and say almost nothing about duty and obligation; much about evil, *bosula,* and the dirty, *maswe,* virtually nothing about sin *sebe.* They remind patients of a fault, *molato,* such as the need to come back to the church, and they themselves feel at a loss, if they fail to attend services, and thus become distant from the Holy Spirit. "Rely on the law of the Lord (*ikanyeng molao wa Modimo*)," exhorts one of the young charismatics in a rare sermon. But, apart from the avoidance of beer, tobacco, and snuff (rejected for being offerings to the ancestors, as in many Apostolic and Zionist churches), young charismatics hardly attend at all to the moral discipline of the individual as a Christian person.

Prophets journey as seers and sniffer dogs from diagnosis to exorcism, on the same trail as other witchfinders of the past and present, such as the diviner or the *sangoma.* Prophets share and carry forward a common heritage of the occult hunt on the trail of discovery in search of malicious fabrication. A patient's own home is the main end of the trail. In the yard, by the four corners where traditional witchfinders place their potions of substances to protect the bounded home space against occult attack, prophets replace that untrustworthy treatment with faithful holy water, the substance of Jesus's dew. Like the body, the inner space around it has to be brought in harmony with the Holy Spirit. As in the diagnostic dialogue, so too in the occult hunt, divination and prophecy proceed, if somewhat uneasily, in tandem with and against each other.

PRAYER, CHRISTIAN PROTECTION, AND INNERMOST SINCERITY

That said, I must take care not to leave the impression of a view of the same again and again, and difference, never. On the contrary, my argument is that there is a reactive spiral in religious change; the return takes its turn along with the new, particularly in what I call Christian reformation.

For the new, one important difference from other witchfinders is much stressed by prophets themselves. In moral and spiritual terms, prophets distinguish their practice of *sereletsho,* protection, which is good, from others' practice of *buseletsa,* retaliation, which is evil. In retaliation, occult aggression is met by counteraggression intended to harm the original aggressor. By contrast, in protection there is no such counteraggression but mere defense, for example, by exorcism that drives away the demon. Although prophets say other witchfinders try to retaliate, I found they too claim to be protective and none are willing to admit openly, and when not drunk, that they counterattack with more occult aggression, despite demands among their clients.

The point is that prophets insist—and in this they follow a strong lead by Eloyi's archbishop—that *buseletsa,* retaliation, is not Christian; that to try to retaliate, because it makes one more distant from God, weakens one's ability to pray and reach God: seek retaliation and you soon stop being a prophet; you lose your Power.

The example for a prophet is the way of Jesus. It is Jesus's way, as I mention above, about which Apostolics sing their hymn of the cooling dew, the very essence of Jesus, who opens the body to peace and quiet, free from pain. It is that cooling dew of Jesus that Apostolics seek in water become holy by blessing and which they spray to make themselves, their bodies, their vestments, their homes, and, above all, their church at one with Jesus and the Holy Spirit. With the same appeal to assuaging, prophets and the archbishop unpacked, for me, the appearance of their staff's trident of the cross, which has an arrow head. This deliberate copy of witchcraft spears and knives is meant to counteract occult aggression, lowering its fierce heat, they say, the way the cool water lowers the boiling.

After prayer, diagnosis is the move that opens the occult hunt and is intended to be the reconnaissance for it, providing the guide, as it were, "the film" in advance. For other witchfinders, there is a mere struggle between foes, the witches, and friends, allies led by the witchfinder. By contrast, it is a Christianized, spiritual and moral war, having the hopeful trust in good winning over evil, that prophets wage as they journey with the Holy Spirit. One song, urging them on, is:

Tsepha Morena oya golala.
Tshepa Morena oya kganya ga golo.
Trust the Lord in all His Glory.
Trust the Lord in His Dazzling Magnificence.

Another song, often sung during exorcism and its hunt, exposes the evil and deceit in the ways of traditional witchfinders, which are false and untrustworthy:

Ga gona nnete, ga gonna botshapegi.
There is no truth. There is no trust.

Prayer, sustained by the continual invocation of the many, mighty, and redemptive names of God, of Jesus, and of the angels, Christianizes the common heritage of the occult hunt and makes it truly Powerful for Apostolics.

COSMETICS IN COUNTERFABRICATION

There is a fundamental dividual understanding—an understanding of the person as partible and permeable by the substances of others—that motivates the Christian passion in the prophets' prescription of remedies for their patients. Bad fabrication calls for good counterfabrication—that is, in essence, the logic of the witchfinder of old. With Christian faith, that dividual logic gets reworked by regard for the substantial visible manifestation of the Holy Spirit as a holy presence.

A favorite song during exorcism is,

Shadows of the night have fallen.
Pass the night in dew and open.

Sholwane, the word for dew, is in Birwa. According to the archbishop, the cooling dew in the song is Jesus, welcomed to stay the night, and open the body of each and everyone to peace and quiet, free from pain. *Fola,* to cool, is to heal, and Apostolics sing again and again during exorcism:

Fodisa, fodisa badumedi.
Heal, heal the faithful.

In such healing, they seek to be cooled by Jesus, by his soothing substance, all together and as one.

The Apostolics do not focus their concern on the agony or torment of Christ in the crucifixion. They want the Holy Spirit to attend to their own pain, their bitterness in everyday life. They want the dew of the risen Christ, of Jesus at peace, in the cooling holy water. They do not make the holy presence evident by flagellation or by the return of Christ's stigmata on the body—and for Apostolics, of course, the cutting of the body through incision and with bloodletting is dubious or even un-Christian.[12] Incision with the injection of protective substances is the speciality of the Apostolics avowed enemies, the *sangoma* and other traditional healers.[13] Rather, the holy presence draws near in the material means of Christian cosmetics for making the body beautiful as a whole, in harmony with the bodies of others and with the Holy Spirit.

In my usage of *cosmetics* I follow Thomas Beidelman, who reminded anthropologists that in its classical derivation from *cosmos,* cosmetics conveys "the idea of making something orderly and therefore attractive and right" (Beidelman 1966:376). More specifically, as Christian, cosmetics beautify for an order of the world, a cosmos, in harmony with the Word and the way of Jesus, the Lamb of God. For the sake of such Christian cosmos, the mixing up of things through *boitseanape,* occult expertise, must be undone; the fabricated evil must be undressed, its invisible fabrication, exposed.[14] Things get *thebetsa,* blocked and frustrated, by occult fabrication, and the aim of prescription is, according to the youngest of the prophets, Prophet Matthew, "to *bula,* open your things of life so that they *ditlhamalale,* should go straight and *disiame,* be well and good." Most strikingly, blessed strings of wool provide the right fabric to redress the wrong one, the occult and evil one. The blessed strings serve in counteraction, *tsosalosa ditshika,* to loosen the veins (the strings) that witchcraft blocks.

Where the work of witchcraft maliciously fabricates the occult, Christian healing treatment must counterfabricate benevolently, the goal being the visible blessing of the Holy Spirit, of the Lamb of God in Heaven. So runs the underlying logic of Apostolic prescription as Christian healing by charismatic prophets, I argue.

SINCERITY, CARING, EMPATHY, AND VICARIOUS EXPERIENCE

For hustlers who, as prophets, are holy, sincerity matters, and it matters above all in prayer. In prayer, a prophet avows before God silently or in the hearing of his patient that he is pleading in good faith, without deceit; that his very breath is at one with the patient's so that in his own diaphragm he breathes the patient's suffering: he feels the other's troubles in the inner depths of his own being. This avowal of empathy affirms that what is hidden and invisible to the patient—namely, the prophet's intent in the very interior of his being—is known before God, who sees the invisible interior, to be truly for the patient's sake.

Expressing this, one of the most prominent among the prophets, Prophet Andrew, prayed for a suffering woman:

> Mighty Judge, God of Heaven, God of the Holy Ones, I bring closer your servant to make her holy with your Voice, Good Father, and to report the troubling situations before you, because we know you are *tshepego,* trustworthy and reliable, in the hands of the holy ones. I am not pleading with you like someone who is *tsietsang,* cheating and not in good faith. I call on you from my chest, *tsa letswalo* (from the very diaphragm, inner being), when troubles get to my very breathing.

What the prophet declares, in concluding his prayer, is that just as in heaven among the holy ones, God is trustworthy and reliable so too is the prophet, who is interceding for the patient, for God's servant on earth.

There is a caring duty between the prophet and the patient. Each has to attend—listen, *reetsa*—to the other, and "to listen to oneself," *iteetsa*, is also what the prophet asks of the patient. But Apostolic diagnosis, I want to stress from the start, does not overwhelm one sense by another, as if understanding were merely hearing *or* seeing. For Apostolics, to diagnose is to listen *and* to see.[15]

Among Apostolics, the Word is, of course, not reducible to any spoken word. Accordingly, for revelation of suffering and embodiment of the Word, Apostolics go beyond verbal monologue and dialogue to body language. There are moments during diagnosis when the prophet shuts his eyes, overcome in trance and evidently withdrawn, away from the exterior world around him. Often, while his eyes are still shut, his hands move reflexively from part to part of his body; his gestures and body language, sometimes writhing in torment, mirror the pain of the afflicted other who faces him; and he conveys his consciously great empathy with human suffering—he knows and says he knows the suffering of the other in himself.

Vicarious experience is divine passion among Christians everywhere, but exceptional in Eloyi is the passion for human empathy. Rarely in church ritual is empathy[16] for others and their mortal frailty so powerfully realized as in Eloyi during a diagnosis and, most strikingly, at its peak. Earlier, I highlight the evoking of moral passion in Apostolic services, when prophets, overcome in trance, undergo being what I would call devotional subjects. The passion of prophets in such moments, I argue, facilitates that other Apostolics have the ritual experience of a community of suffering.

THE HEALING TRADITION OF EMPATHY AND VICARIOUS EXPERIENCE

Is there any tradition of ritual healing that Apostolics could or did draw upon or were perhaps aware of, when they began to prophecy, with empathy, while undergoing vicarious suffering and the searing heat of the Holy Spirit? In other words, is the Apostolics' practice wholly exceptional in the southern African region, apart from churches? To ask is easy, but it is much harder, and possibly beyond our immediate reach, to answer.

In the regional cult of Mwali, which extends across the original areas from which Eloyi spread, adepts do undergo vicarious suffering when seized in trance by Mwali. But their suffering in highly dramatic fits is on behalf of whole communities, and it is not for the sake of individual healing or the revelation on their bodies of the interior condition of others (Werbner 1989, 1997).

Beyond that, and for the nearest strong resemblance to Apostolics healing practice with vicarious suffering, I would look to the Transkei and the Ciskei in South Africa and to Xhosa ritual of affliction, one of the many variations on *ngoma* across eastern and southern Africa, and including *sangoma* (Janzen 1992, 1994). If a nearer or more closely alike example exists, I have not found it yet, although I am tempted to look, also, to perhaps the oldest healing tradition in Botswana. Among the Kalahari !Kung in the borderlands of Botswana and Namibia, sickness is an existential condition. It calls for the healer to suffer vicariously in pain and confusion, to go beyond his ordinary self, to endure the gift of charisma, the power of spiritual energy (*num*), as fierce internal heat running up and down the healer's trembling body, to see things with an extraordinary clarity in deep understanding, to lay on hands, and to draw the sickness into his own body and then to expel it into space (Katz 1982:100–102; on *num*, Katz 1982: 93–95).

What is striking in the Xhosa ritual is the healer's display of intuition, called *umbelini* (Buhrmann and Gqomfa 1981, 1982). It is an inner feeling, basically a gut sensation, sometimes running through the body, which is perceived to be in contact with the patient's interior. It has to go up the right way to clear the healer's mind (Buhrmann and Gqomfa 1981:193). The healer—known as *igquira*, a name that reflects Khoisan linguistic influence and may also reflect some influence of Khoisan healing practice in shamanic trance—immediately senses the pain of the patient and reveals it bodily. It is evident that "the tension and agitation [of *umbelini*, gut sensation] in their [the healers'] case is used as a diagnostic and therapeutic tool" (Burhmann and Gqomfa 1981:199). The healer is also a visionary who dreams and has extrasensory perception of hidden things.

All of that closely resembles prophets' healing practice among Apostolics. In addition, the Xhosa healer, too, has the power of the voice, being a singer. But, and this is common among *ngoma* cults elsewhere, the singer has an ancestral drum and moves urgently in a round dance for communication with the ancestors, for knowing the ancestor within himself (Burhmann and Gqomfa 1982).[17] The importance of Apostolic round dance, as I suggest in the Introduction, is great for moving the faithful in a distinctively Christian religious experience. The difference with the Xhosa healing tradition is thus most striking where the Apostolic is most profoundly Christian.

As a transnational church, Eloyi now extends into South Africa, but I cannot say whether Eloyi's founder and early Apostolics knew of such Xhosa healing rituals. Given the flow of labor migrants at the time of Archbishop Jakoba's early church, and his stay in the railway town of Mahalapye, some Xhosa influence is possible. I speculate here not to claim an answer but to open the question for further research. What is beyond speculation, however, is the Christianizing that imbues healing with new Apostolic realities whatever was borrowed or old, perhaps from the millennia of the Khoisan healing traditions.

EMPATHY, TRUE KNOWLEDGE AND SUBJECTION

Diagnosis involves empathy, but it is not an egalitarian communion of minds or a sharing of fellowship in Christ. Instead, as the holy hustlers who are mediators and brokers of divine Power, prophets exact submission, artfully and persuasively but forcefully and with the deliberate intent of effecting a Christian recreation, of spiritually changing the patients' inner being, their minds, *tlhaloganyo,* as well as their bodies and their outward situations.

In all the consultations I observed, the patients, while themselves questioned, did not cross-examine the prophet, in turn, but at most grumbled in muted discontent. They preferred to respond, if they could, with polite deference. If they expressed some measure of doubt or puzzlement, they usually, at some intense moment, looked quite bowled over. My impression is that patients tolerate much fumbling on the part of the prophet, his missed targets and caricatures of their situation, because what is often uppermost for them is an eager desire to reach the later stage of prescription and treatment. It is not that patients are uncritical—they prefer some prophets over others, and they recognize some to be better at prophecy than others. A patient sometimes comes back to the same prophet for diagnosis over years, as did my assistant's wife, Martha.

Patients do sometimes tell a prophet where he is mistaken. Even more, they sometimes flatly contradict a prophet's assertion in some detail. But often enough, patients go on to say where the prophet is partially right, as it were, collaborating in his recovery from error by turning the error into a half-truth. The prophet dodges artfully, from fumble to fumble, and patients dodge along with him.[18]

Above all, Apostolics start from their understanding that man is distant from God;[19] that because the prophet, like the patient, has to be brought nearer to God, a prophet cannot get everything right all at once; that with wholehearted support, quietly devoted in patients' cries of amen and loudly in the whole congregation's rising song and clapping, the prophet gets close enough for true revelation: the Word rises in him. The artful dodger is the holy hustler.

In the next chapter, I say more about the religious controversy and the skepticism around such hustling, exorcism, and Christianized witch-finding, and I relate my discussion to concerns about purity and power that divide the prophets from the archbishop and others in the church hierarchy.

2. Between the Prophetic and the Pastoral

HIERARCHY, CHARISMATIC GOODS, AND A SPIRITUAL DIVISION OF LABOR

In the Eloyi Christian Church becoming and being a prophet, gifted with the Word of God by the Holy Spirit, positions the charismatic outside the church hierarchy. Inside it are pastors, *baruti'* ("the teachers"), who hold the ministerial offices of the church, from archbishop, bishop, assistant bishop, pastor-general, deacon, evangelist, to preacher, supported by the Executive Committee of Overseers, *baokamedi,* including an elected chairman, vice-chairman, vice-secretary, publicity secretary, and treasurer. Their official duties are detailed in a formal constitution registered at the Registry of Societies in Botswana's Ministry of Home Affairs (Registry of Societies 1994).

For example, heading the hierarchy, the archbishop has the constitutional duties "to teach the entire congregation the Word of God, to make burnt offerings (Sacrifices), to appoint ministers and delegate duties to members." *Go tlajesa selaelo,* "to feed the sacrament of the last supper," is also his responsibility. Much lower in the hierarchy, the deacon's duties are "to preach the gospel of God, to pray for the sick and water to be holy, to baptize believers, to teach subordinates how to relate the Word of God to the people and Rules of the Congregation." Not mentioned in the hierarchy are *basebetsi* (from the Sotho word, *sebetsa,* to work), the servants, who have the holy gift of healing hands.

The constitution also calls for ministers to be formally trained, in accord with standard requirements kept, at least on paper for official purposes, in the 1990s by the Registry of Societies. For example, the "Archbishop shall be a person with a Diploma and or Degree in theology from any recognised theological Institution, University or College whose teachings and training is approved by the executive committee." The founding archbishop is illiterate, but cites and expounds biblical verse constantly, having memorized a considerable number. His son, the bishop, did a theological course and does have a diploma.

Although the constitution asserts Eloyi's right "to determine by Prophecy the sickness of people and how their diseases should be cured," nowhere does it authorize prophets or define duties for them.

Each prophet holds a commission that is personal. It has to be confirmed by the archbishop or a bishop, if the prophet is to serve within the church. Only when a bishop has laid hands on the prophet, empowering him with Spirit, can the prophet have true revelation, *senolo*. What the prophet has, however, is not a definable office within the church hierarchy but a spiritual gift of charisma from God that is thus extrahierarchical.

Yet prophets and pastors have to serve together in Christian amity for the good of the church. All claim to seek *tlhaloganyo ya Modimo*, 'the understanding of God. The ideal is inclusive. In the bishop's words at the 2007 church conference, "Everybody should be equal, men and women. We need to respect the rights of everybody wholeheartedly *ka butalo*, literally, 'with greenness.'" The need among the Apostolic leadership is for a working partnership between hierarchy and extrahierarchy.

In practice, the partnership is volatile. Sometimes euphoric, trustful, and mutually supporting, other times fractious, adversarial, awkward, and even mutually subversive, it is an ambivalent partnership, constantly being tested and, within certain limits, renegotiated. None of the prophets come from the archbishop's family and his relatives who dominate the church hierarchy and the executive committee, the domination being so great that even relatives, when disgruntled with the bishops, complain to the government's Registry of Societies (Ministry of Home Affairs) about "nepotism." In Chapter 4, I return to the intervention of the Registry in church affairs, when I discuss how and why Apostolics are highly litigious. There I argue that long prevailing in Botswana is a process that I call democratization. By that I mean a bureaucratic tendency in which government officials have actively tried to re-create civil society in an ideal democratic image of their own, bound by written rules, efficient, modern, and thoroughly documented (see also van Binsbergen 1993). At this point, however, I keep the relations with the state and government bureaucracy in the background in order to focus upon church hierarchy and extrahierarchy.

At the very height of their experience of charisma, prophets must rely on pastors, above all. In submission to the Holy Spirit, on a mission of exorcism or witchfinding, prophets become devotional subjects, selfless, unconscious, no longer in control of their bodies or themselves. Swooning in trance, their limbs fail them; some get stiff, others fall limp. Pastoral care lifts them bodily and, interceding with prayer and the laying on of hands, restores them to themselves spiritually, in God's name. An example of such prayer is this appeal by a pastor-general, while the prophet lies limp in trance, having found witchcraft bits used by enemies of church women:

> We need you to be awakened unto us, Mighty Lord, you King of Kings, Great Savior of Jerusalem. Lord we beg you, protect us from our enemies, Jehovah. Here they are attacking us day and night.

Released from trance, from the convulsion of being, as it were, spaced out, prophets often raise their arms to heaven, shouting, "Glory, My Lord!"

Even beyond such essential help, prophets' dependence reaches to the most important goods they need for healing patients. These goods are the substantial remains from burnt offerings: *sowatsho,* holy ash, and *tomololo,* sacrificial blood in holy water. *Sowatsho,* like *isiwasho* in Zulu for Zionist churches, is a Tswanaised version of the English word "wash." With water made holy by prayer, it is the prime means of cleansing and purifying the body from occult dirt. *Tomololo* sets Apostolics apart from ordinary people in their daily lives, because it literally stinks to heaven—so much so that, I am told, some "combi" (minicab) drivers and their passengers won't ride with the smelly Apostolics. Even among the Apostolics, there is doubt and dissent about *tomololo,* the bloody water. One of the devoted church servants says,

> If you just use this *tomololo,* it can't work. But through human faith, *tumelo ya motho,* through your own faith, *tumelo ya gago,* you might use it thinking something will happen. Everyone sees it his own way.

Nevertheless, the fluids that are the mainstays of the church and essential for prophets include *tomololo,* above all, along with milk, paraffin, and sea water. Sea water is held to be inherently powerful, able to drive you down to depths beyond your control. But, even beyond that, sea water and salt are Christianized by Apostolics. Salt sprayed in the form of a cross is used to drive away *tokoloshi,* demons, and it is an important means of exorcism. Salt is also said to counteract evil after the precedent in the Bible for Gomorrah and the pillar of salt.

Prophets refresh themselves after a morning sessions of examination and prescription by drinking *moreto,* which they call "afternoon tea" and which is a brownish drink of holy ash, paraffin, and salt—it is very salty, indeed, to drive off the demons, and it can be an emetic. As a good primarily from the burnt offerings and as a drink for an inner circle, after the patients are gone, *moreto* is for these Apostolics the Christian version of the light beer in the early stages of fermentation that village intimates shareFor Apostolics on the inner circle, the taste of the church is *moreto*; its stink, for all Apostolics and the wider public, is *tomololo*.

I ask one of the prophets, Joshua, about communion, because he often prescribes sacrifice, for example in the case of my assistant's wife Martha which I discuss later. Prophet Joshua has a Bible to hand, as we talk in the bishop's office, and he opens the Bible, cites a verse, and tells me that the instruction from Jesus is to hold the annual *Paseka*, Passover, for a communion meal, but not any regular communion otherwise. It is at *Paseka* that Apostolics have to take the body and blood of Jesus, which is turned from wine. Otherwise, sacrifice is for an exchange, taking the life of the goat or sheep and giving it to the patient who is a pleading supplicant. Prophet Joshua explains that such sacrifice is to rid the patient of old and bad blood, and transfer that to the dead goat or sheep.[1] All of that, I come to understand, is church orthodoxy, though as I discuss later, Prophet Joshua is inspired to be unorthodox, when it comes to drinking, powerfully, the blood of sacrifice, as it were, apart from blessed wine.

In Prophet Joshua's view, putting oneself in the right state by telling the truth about oneself, in the presence of God and the church hierarchy, matters for sacrifice. To come to the altar and make a sacrifice, one first ought to make a public confession before God and the preachers. Such confession, which affirms hierarchy, while closer to that of the Catholic Church, differs from what is perhaps the most familiar Protestant model. In that, it is the congregation that hears the self-account. Prophet Joshua makes this need for confession, before the hierarchy, clear during a diagnosis in one public service, when he exhorts his patients:

> At the very start, you should *boipolelo*, confess (report on yourself) before the Hand of Life, in front of the pastors, then you can step at the altar of *tefelo*, recompense (the burnt offering).

Authority over sacrifice and its goods is held by the bishops and, with their consent, a pastor-general, who are expected to make the burnt offering while they are pure, according to the priestly code in Leviticus. The church hierarchy rests on command of the ash and the blood as the holy means of spiritual transformation, with faith, toward well-being. Reserving these at the church keeps them for use there during services or elsewhere on church occasions, with a bishop's permission. Individuals are meant to get them free as the public goods of the church, from God, because faith healing, in the way of Jesus, has to be free, as his was. Taking fees is a sin of greed, the archbishop insists.

The church has no income, officially, from payments for services. Much fundraising is mainly by members' monthly subscriptions and by frequent "concerts" open to everyone for a small fee and raising donations, given spontaneously to honor competing choirs. At Sunday services, with sometimes large congregations of over 200 people (the largest I saw was well over 300 people), no funds are raised. No one is supposed to receive earnings from church funds. While pastors, like many church members, usually have steady jobs, as mainly low-paid manual or clerical workers, traders, police, or soldiers, with a very few being teachers (including at least one at the university), almost all prophets are unemployed.

Most prophets find themselves unable to be regular enough to keep a full-time job for long. Keen to be on the road and fond of speed in fast cars, many prophets are great travelers. At every opportunity and often enough on the spur of the moment, they visit the church's distant branches across Botswana and into South Africa. A favorite boast is that to be a prophet is to be restless, ready to go here and there. A prophet is not a stay-at-home. Prophets cannot devote themselves to work at the expense of constant church service, they say, without suffering fierce headaches or nose bleeding. They feel driven erratically as the Holy Spirit moves them to serve the church, in the city, or elsewhere, in prophecy.

In need of an income, and at times for the sake of patients who demand confidential consultations unseen by the congregation, prophets, such as Andrew and Matthew, do hold private, fee-paying home séances, against church rules. Getting essential ash has driven some prophets to steal from the church's reserve and be suspended by the bishop. When the harassed bishop relented on the suspension, gossip in the church has it that he was fearful of the prophets' powers, and their threat to use them in a plot against him—"We will fix up *tlaloganyo* ('an arrangement', 'an understanding') for you." The bishop himself tells me that it was his younger brother, the assistant bishop at Pikwe town, who ended the suspension; that this subversion of his authority as bishop was one of the important reasons for his leaving Eloyi. If selfless in trance, prophets are often strikingly self-willed when it comes to obedience to hierarchy against their own and their patients' perceived interests.

There is a somewhat overlapping spiritual division of labor between prophets and pastors. The dreams pastors have at night make them also visionaries, if not in trance. Prophets, especially as they grow older, sometimes preach, drawing on biblical verse and stories; one pastor-general is still active as a prophet also. At the top of the hierarchy, the founding archbishop, Jakobo Keiphile, began as a prophet. He still undergoes trance, when filled with the Holy Spirit.

If complementary, at least ideally, the spiritual division of labor is sometimes awkward, even morally contentious, and increasingly full of problems, as a new, third generation is providing the prophets. The problems involved are such that I must say something about personhood and the occult first and then return to how the spiritual division of labor actually works.

REFORMATION, EXORCISM/WITCHFINDING, AND CHARISMATIC MEDIATION

Reformation is the Apostolics' response to the changing moral and metaphysical problems of what I call alternating personhood—the dynamic of the person being dividual and also individual—in Eloyi as in many other Apostolic churches. They abandon *bongaka ba setsho,* the "medicinal horn" or "doctoring of tradition." They reject that indigenous tradition with its charms, magic, and organic medicines as sinful, against God's commandments, Satan's work, and not Christian—but they do not deny the existence of witchcraft; nor do they start wholly afresh, even with the baptized.

Suspicious that others fabricate charms to put them in contact with dirt and dress them in *sefifi,* "darkness and bad luck," Apostolics have their hands cleansed and protected with ash. It is, also, to stop money slipping from the Apostolics' fingers. Ash is changed by the fire of sacrifice, and so too, Apostolics say, is the person changed by using it: dressed in a holy condition of purity. Or, again for protective illumination against *sefifi,* darkness, Apostolics have prophets or church servants give them prayerful flame baths. The servant appeals to God, while rotating a basin with a burning paraffin candle around the kneeling sufferer. A flick of the servant's robe envelops the sufferer in wind, spiritually, for wind is spirit. Witches are said to dress themselves in black in order to cast black and darkness on others, and so must the counteraction bring white and light to the targets and victims of witchcraft.

This is Prophet Andrew's prayer, declaring his sincerity in such service, while the wind from his golden robe and the vapor from the flaming paraffin envelops a kneeling sufferer in the Holy Spirit:

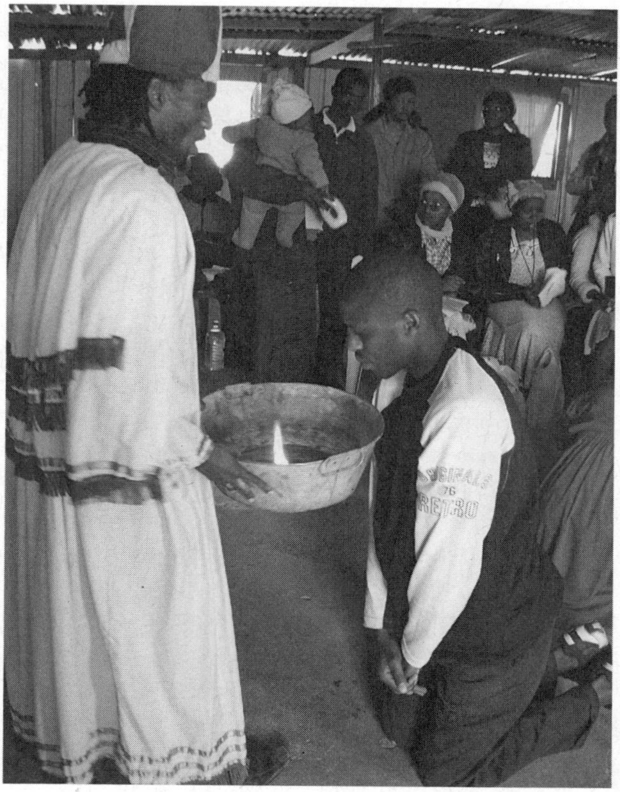

Figure 5. Paraffin vapor bath illuminating darkness from patient.

> Dress her, God Full of Peace. We do not pray to you like one without faith and trust in all the paths on which you go. Oh Lord, God the Overseer, let her be cared for, as she is asking, in the name of the Son and the Holy Spirit.

The rite is something of a reprise in that the notion of *sefifi* is, among Tswana, a long and well-established reading of occult darkness. Occult darkness is a condition against which traditional doctors and diviners, like Apostolics after them, treat by illumination, usually with a lamp or the light from burning herbs. Speaking of the vapor rite itself, Apostolics use the term *aromela,* "envelope in incense"; it is the same as is used for the traditional rite that the Apostolics' rite replaces. The shared understanding that the traditional and the Apostolic rites carry forward is that the subject has to be dressed afresh—no longer in the dark or dirt but made presentable to others by illumination or incense—for the sake of harmony with others and, thus, well-being.

Apostolics confront the predicaments of alternating personhood within an ongoing war of good and evil, *molemo le bosula*. They do so, as it were, on two fronts: on one they pray for the good, and they combat evil on the other.

On the good front, as earthly beings, they appeal to God in heaven for protection and prosperity. To get closer to God, if only vicariously, Apostolics approach charismatic prophets as mediators for hearing the Word of God, effectively and powerfully—the prophets' very bodies speak revealingly, in the gestures and postures of trance, to the needy condition and turmoil of the faithful. Inspired in trance or overcome by Spirit, the prophets feel themselves physically moved to take the part of their patients. Their own bodies "reflect" the patient's suffering, and "reflect" is their own word, in English, for that. The bodies of the prophets, at one with the innermost truth of their patients' bodies, are not at peace. Prophets writhe and sweat noticeably, when overcome by Spirit, and they say they feel their temperature doubling and their faces weighed with sorrow, when they get to understand the reality of a patient's suffering even before the patient knows it.

Apostolics turn the young men who are prophets into what I call devotional subjects. By that I mean, as I suggest in the Introduction, subjects around whom, in moments of ritual, a community of suffering emerges and shares moral passion, above all compassion, in devotion to the Holy Spirit. As devotional subjects, prophets serve their fellow Apostolics, ritually, in faith healing; they offer the living proof of bearable pain; and they become the means of Christian exaltation, beyond pain, in the Apostolics' moments of care and compassion during a service.

On the other front, and concerned about their vulnerability to occult attack as dividuals, Apostolics want to find out who might be attacking them and how. Here they turn to the prophets as having supersensory powers, being able to smell witchcraft substances, things otherwise hidden from ordinary senses. It is not a break with the past but a *controversial Christianizing* of the old tradition of witchfinders who *dupa* ("sniff out," "diagnose") witchcraft.

The prophet takes on the part of a dog, nose down or up high. He sniffs, barks loudly, and makes whistling sounds, until the trail ends and he reaches the earthly things and substances of witchcraft. Overwhelmed by disgust, he is transfixed, grabbing the occult bits and unable to let go without the help of prayer and the laying on of hands, usually by a caring pastor.

The pastor Christianizes the witchfinding from the very start of the sniffing by addressing a prayer to God or the Messiah: for example,

> We beg you loving Messiah, rock full of life, pillar full of strength, against evil spirits. You, full of pity, give us the strength to remove everything hidden, oh Lord. All will be removed easily with your hand full of life's strength, great pillar of heaven.

I emphasize *controversial Christianizing* because such witchfinding is divisive in the church, and all the more so because it is highly popular and has greatly raised public interest in the church through press and television coverage. Above all, Christianized witchfinding divides the prophets from the archbishop. Their disagreement arises from a difference in religious basics.

Purity is the over-riding concern for the archbishop. God cannot be truly approached without it. It is essential for holiness: the verb *itshekisa,* to make oneself clear or clean, is to make holy, and the undoing of that, *itshekologile,* is polluting, ritually impure and thus unholy. The archbishop fears the prophets are becoming polluted by their continual contact with earthly things, things of witchcraft, and their failure to cleanse themselves carefully before contact with other Apostolics in prayer and laying on hands. He accuses them of learning the ways of *sangoma,* traditional witchfinding mediums: they proudly register for the certificates that a now-professionalized healing association gives such *sangoma* and others.

In accord with his purity concern, the archbishop sets a holy example, having in mind his understanding of the priestly code in Leviticus. He wears a biblical beard, cleanses himself and bathes with stored rain water—water from heaven—provides the pure holy water for others, and avoids contact with certain earthly things, especially the witchcraft substances prophets sniff and grab. Never in his presence, he insists, do prophets *dupa* or *ipolola,* dig out charms or extract them by biting or incising the body. Archbishop Jakobo condemns such witchfinding as not Christian, not the original way of his church, and against *tlholego,* its nature or basic principle.

AUTHORITY AND THE ECONOMY OF CHARISMA

So far my account may give the impression that prophetic charisma, being boundless and ultimately indefinable, completely escapes hierarchy. I must now qualify this impression. It is important to recognize the problematic assertion by the Eloyi church of its authority over prophetic charisma and, indeed, the prophets themselves. Making this qualification also enables me to say more, in Chapter 5, about the involvement of prophets in contesting that authority and in the redesign of it after the major schism between Eloyi and the new Conollius church.

In Eloyi, the orthodox cosmology elaborates the heavenly imagery, according to an underlying premise of valued distance from God: the closer to God, the greater the power and blessing. Hence, in heaven above the elements of the firmament—from the lowest, the star, to the moon to the sun, the highest—are relative in value. This is the cosmic order recognized in Eloyi—though unmarked in the official constitution.

Eloyi is not unique or the first in the region to have a celestial iconography. It is found in some older Apostolic and Zionist churches in South Africa, where "the drawings of sun, moon and stars on flags and clothing have significance because they are sources of celestial light."[2] It is worth saying, also, that dressing and being transfigured according to spiritual merit and the order of charisma has its counterpart in an even older tradition of ritual healing, exemplified by, among others, Xhosa healers who dress according to spiritual qualifications and rank (Burhmann and Gqomfa 1981:189).

According to the cosmic order so, too, does the value of the spiritual gift vary among Apostolics. Apostolics are given more, or less, from the Holy Spirit relative to the origin of their gifts in the celestial firmament. The idea is, also, that healing has to fit that origin. Only a healer with the encompassing gift of the sun, the highest of all, can heal everyone else, whether spiritually of the sun, moon, or star. Others with lesser gifts are limited accordingly. In practice, applying this premise creates rank. It comes from the archbishop with the gift of the sun downward—and the archbishop's paramount gift, like the rank of his charisma, is powerfully imaged in red suns on the outside walls of his church headquarters. Cosmic order reigns supreme.

What is decisive is the vision of the archbishop himself, irrespective of any visions of a spiritual gift's origin that prophets may have. By overturning a prophetic vision, for example by revealing that the gift is not of the moon but of the sun, the archbishop can and does assert a measure of centralized and hierarchical control over the economy of charisma within his church. It is when such control is disputed, as during the schismatic crisis, that orthodoxy is subverted, and there is iconoclasm, rejecting the imagery.

In my film *Encountering Eloyi* (2008), I show a salient example of the archbishop's assertion of cosmic authority over charisma during the crisis. Bearing a second prescription from Prophet Joshua, this time for a sacrifice

Figure 6. Pastor-general in full regalia before sacrificial pyre.

among other things, Martha comes to the archbishop for the burnt offering. She seeks relief from being childless and suffering terrible menstrual pain. The intent, promised by the archbishop's own pastor-general during the actual offering, is hopeful. It is to take the life from a female kid yet to give birth, to offer it to God, and to make Martha unbound, like other people. It is a promise of fertility for Martha by an exchange through a burnt offering—that her life and her birth potential will be replaced by the kid's.

Starting with a diagnosis to review Martha's condition and the prescription, the archbishop reveals to her that her pain is not that of an illness. On the contrary, the Holy Spirit burns within her. Not mere pain, her experience is the spiritual one of being fiercely entered by the Holy Spirit. Most importantly, it comes with the highest spiritual gift, that of the sun. This is what the archbishop himself knows from his own experience, and what he shows in body language and says in words.

But, the archbishop insists, the trouble with her healing goes beyond the mere failure to recognize the true nature of her affliction. Even worse, it is a matter of capacity and charisma, far out of the young Gaborone prophets' diagnostic and healing reach—she is a sun person being treated as a moon person, by moon people with lesser spiritual gifts and thus unable to deal with her condition. Her bishop in the city is merely moon-gifted. The one she needs instead is the archbishop himself, as he makes plain to her. And, in her higher standing, she needs a new robe, bearing a red circle and thus bringing to her body the blessings of the warmth of the sun. Normally, to be conferred, a robe has to be blessed by a bishop in public in the presence of the congregation, but in Martha's case, the archbishop makes clear, the right one to invest her with her robe is, of course, the archbishop himself. In due course, he does that for her, on her return with a sun-imaged robe.

The archbishop's assertion of authority goes even further, because he is bitterly aware of sin and wrongdoing in his church, seen from his orthodox perspective. The prophet's prescription calls for Martha to drink drops of the sacrificial blood in holy water. But for the archbishop, that is worse than merely an unorthodox innovation, additional to the cleansing use of the blood. The archbishop is appalled—for him, drinking the blood is dirty, nasty, and polluting. Even worse, it is another instance of the sin in the Gaborone branch against the holy code of purity; he prohibits it.

Martha does not accept all that easily or with grace, at first. She trusts the prophet and sticks to her ritualistic faith in the prescription—it has to be carried out meticulously to work. Eventually won over, in part under her husband's influence (after a quarrel) and in part by the recognition of her highest spiritual gift and its allure, Martha submits to the archbishop. It is a win for orthodox cosmic order. The hierarchy captures her, now more confident in the archbishop than any other charismatic. She continues to side with the archbishop against the bishop and remains in Eloyi after the schism.

HUSTLING, EXORCISM, AND THE DEMONIC

There is a further prophetic practice that the archbishop condemns: the exorcism of demons, *tokoloshi*. *Tokoloshi* are new to the city, demons never known in the archbishop's home village. *Tokoloshi* are said to be alien things or spirits bought by consumers and mailed in the form of a powder imported from South Africa, the immediate source of most consumer goods in Botswana. A doll, sometimes pierced with pins, is one of the imported means of striking with a *tokoloshi*, and to my amazement, while filming, the bishop reached into his briefcase dramatically, for the camera, and held up one used against him. The occult attack was unsuccessful, he said, because he prayed, was warned by God, and found the doll's pierced arm hidden in his car. The word *tokoloshi* itself is Zulu, for alien and wild spirits, and people in Botswana associate it with Durban. The streetwise expression in Gaborone, using Zulu, for *tokoloshi* is *mfana wa mafetshwane*," lad of tricks," or after the great Zulu war, "lad of destruction."

Tokoloshi have to be activated for pay, and then like goods in a supermarket with a barcode, they have a limited life, people say. At first, they serve your desires, but then they get ravenous for desire beyond desire, until they burn up all your goods and luxuries. To get rid of them calls for exorcism, much of which is very public and costly. It draws in spectators from a whole neighborhood and usually a big congregation of Apostolics for whom a bus, a feast, and a tent have to be provided at considerable cost to the host, sometimes more than 5,000 pula, or more than two months of a manual worker's income.

Hustling by the prophets around exorcism is a topic of church gossip. One complaint, even by devout Apostolics, is that some prophets offer a deal to their own advantage. They would be willing to perform the trapping of the *tokoloshi,* their first part of the exorcism, and then the later cleansing, without any congregation. There would be no expensive bus, no costly feasting. The exorcised Apostolics would merely have to pay half of the usual cost to the exorcist prophets. I was told that such bargains became a scandal that had to be dealt with by the bishop. He excluded some, and wanted to exclude all the prophets involved. According to church gossip, after a series of his own troubles and accidents, including the death of close kin and his own near death, he changed his mind—being fearful of the prophets' power—and merely suspended some prophets, temporarily. The bishop himself told me that one of his reasons for leaving Eloyi for his own church was that his younger brother, the assistant bishop in Pikwe town, subverted his authority by readmitting the suspended prophets. Another matter for gossip about exorcists' hustling is that some prophets are said to promise, without mentioning any fee, to come for the exorcising of a yard, and then they delay until the suffering Apostolics get their unspoken message—the patients need to offer a substantial gift if the prophets are to come. Time is of the essence in hustling.

In the course of the exorcism, many goods are destroyed or taken apart, left in bits. The attack on property, from mattresses and blankets, to amplifier cabinets and other furniture, to ceilings and a yard's four corners is, at first sight, staggering. Its impact, even on people who have heard about such attacks, is overwhelming, and I myself was astonished on first actually seeing it.

At that first exorcism, I, like the yard's owners, hardly grasped the usual warning from a leading pastor, "We will borrow a Caterpillar bulldozer from the Council. But you shouldn't say, when it passes, then shoves you aside, and maybe takes your house, that I didn't call it here." His words resonated with a trauma suffered by the church itself. At an old site, Eloyi was itself razed to the ground, without warning, by a bulldozer under a city council scheme. Eloyi has never received any compensation from the Council for the church building and its contents, although a High Court decision put a morally damning stop on further Council bulldozing.

The bishop calls exorcism's destructive attack "maintenance." He compares it to the essential removal of a thorn in one's foot—in Tswana, pity is literally taking out a thorn—and in preparing a whole congregation to descend on a demon-ridden home, he exhorts his congregation to save some of their singing for when it is needed, while they *kgakgamololo*, "take things to bits."

According to Prophet Andrew:

> You have to destroy, because people are terrorised by demons and evil spirits. You have to decide what you value, things or life. If life, then you need to destroy things with *tokoloshi* in them.

The church has gained a dark side, too, in its reputation for exorcism, because with the opening of mattresses and the search through drawers and cupboards occasionally comes, to the chagrin of church elders, very substantial theft of money and valuables, which the prophets and other exorcists are accused of hiding in their robes.

The exorcism materializes occult and nasty-looking things, such as a living puff adder, a witchcraft horn full of noxious substances, a knife, and even the abused mantle of a rival church. The practice is the traditional one of witchfinders to offer, as Isaac Schapera argues in a classic analysis, proof of witchcraft beyond doubt (Schapera 1955). It is a practice that is, and perhaps always was, the object of much skepticism.

Schapera's argument goes further (see also Schapera 1969). It brings in the state. In the Bechuanaland Protectorate under the British authorities, witchcraft beyond reasonable doubt was regulated under state law. One consequence was that even greater backing was given to the practice of witchfinders, legitimizing it as a public service in the mastery of the materiality of witchcraft—witchcraft had to be seen to be fabricated and the material evidence of fabrication, discovered. Any accusation of witchcraft without such evidence was libel, by law, and libel litigation over witchcraft accusations continues in local hearings in postcolonial Botswana.

Traditional witchfinding has thus been something of a state-made practice, which Apostolics continue to rework in their Christian prophecy during the present postcolonial period. None of the prophets' material evidence of witchcraft is ever evidence in court, as was that of traditional witchfinding. Nevertheless, the exposure in exorcism is very much an open, dramatic matter for the court of public opinion, so to speak, sometimes merely that of a local congregation and neighborhood but sometimes the widest public for the media's sensational stories.

When I asked Prophet Andrew about the material proof of witchcraft in found objects, I raised the suspicion some people have, both within and outside the church, that the practice is merely what people call a trick by a magician, *masala mose*. In response, Prophet Andrew drew a comparison to Jesus and the unbelievers and to miracles. The unbelievers drowned out the believers by shouting "yes" for crucifixion, so the "no" of believers was not heard. Now, as with Jesus, less than fifty percent of the people believe in the miracles of destroying *tokoloshi*. Explaining further, he mentioned Moses and miracles. God saw Pharaoh was hard-hearted, so he gave Moses the power to turn his staff into a snake. So too with miracles against *tokoloshi*, Andrew told me; they are needed otherwise people don't believe.

Andrew carries his reasoning further in the light of Moses' example. God taught Moses. Before that Moses did not know how to perform miracles. Now Andrew himself has to be taught; he wants to learn from a "teacher," *moruti*, and plans to spend a month at Mmadinare, a village remote from the city but not far from the archbishop—there he would learn miracle making from a famous expert on demons. Andrew says he can't yet do so, because it is costly in food and other expenses, including gifts to the teacher.

THE POWER OF THE WORD, SPIRITUAL ELECTRICITY, AND ICONOGRAPHY

My own understanding is that for prophets what is paramount is attacking the demonic with the power of the Word and the Voice. Secondary to that is the substantial materialization, the miracles and wonders of destroying the *tokoloshi*, controlling and cleansing it with holy ash and holy water. It is the people who need to see the objects with their ordinary senses. For faith, the prophets have the Word, the people have the miracles.

By contrast to the archbishop and his stress on the priestly code of holiness, the overriding concern of prophets is power. Of course, they do also value purity, and highly so, as their prescriptions show. They practice ritual cleansing, holy bathing, and protective purification, even with flame vapors and candles, for themselves and their patients (the archbishop does not use or approve of flame baths). They keep their robes, *purapura* (singular, with the connotation of a garment of rank), set aside, safely, for use for church purposes. In daily life, however, by contrast to the biblically bearded archbishop, they are unmarked as prophets, though some indulge, when they can, in a taste for flashy clothes and sporting designer labels.

The prophets' concern for power dominates their sense of "spiritual electricity," which they speak of using the common Tswanaized word for electricity, *matlakase*. The church building, the prophets' robes, and other wonderfully pleasing holy objects, such as a crystal ball and bold, color-coded cloth hangings, are felt by prophets to be energized, hopefully enough to raise morale. All such holy things and holy places, prophets say, are charged, more or less, with an electricity of their own. The electricity in holy objects can boost, even jolt, the tired off their chairs into ecstatic dance and song at church. As Prophet Joshua tells me,

> Our very church building should have the power to help make things not be hard, that "morale" should be good when we enter the church, and we shouldn't feel tired or sit exhausted. The church itself should have electricity of its own, enough to give you an electric shock when we want to sit down and make us stand on our feet and dance.

Prophet Joshua tells also of being charged by too much Spirit:

> We are eager and overcome by too much spirit. High as the ceiling is, you can jump to it, then fall down, but not feel pain. You see a prophet turning over, overcome by too much spirit. While the talk with spirit goes on, they [prophets and other Apostolics] burst into song, blocking the spirit a little. It's like petrol in a sealed tank. It blasts in the air, because it's got hot.

This same force can be felt burning fiercely inside a patient or a wayward prophet, when the Holy Spirit gets blocked, perhaps by willfulness. Such a prophet writhes, involuntarily, and screams in agony, only to be released by crossing his chest with cooling, holy ash.

Prophets resort to power dressing. They change their robes in the knowledge that one robe now feels more powerful than another, more dazzling, brilliant, and glorious, or, if white, more spiritual, and thus more appealing and closer to the angels and the Mighty One. The prophets' aesthetic is that

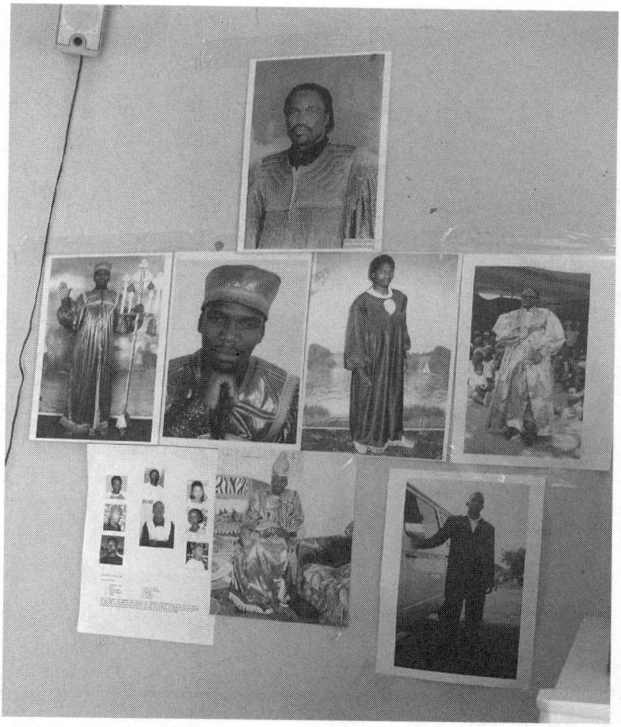

Figure 7. Iconography on prophet's wall.

of glorious revelation. Power dressing transfigures them and is a means of ascendance to a higher, more powerful state of being. It is also a means of protection against attack from enemies, such as witches and traditional doctors, envious of a prophet's power.

A prophet's own room has a characteristic iconography, self-imaging in powerful glory. On the walls and even on the refrigerator door are studio portraits of the prophet himself, elegantly poised in one gloriously rich robe after another; there too, usually, is a mentor's portrait, for example, the assistant bishop, again majestic, robed with epaulets in his splendid best. None of the prophet's kin figure in the wall pictures. Prophet Andrew's album has a few kin and school days' pictures after many of church figures, including the white-robed Catholic pope with arms raised in blessing opposite Prophet Andrew himself, virtually the pope's mirror image in robe and posture. Prophets buy their portraits in the city, Prophet Andrew proudly showed me, at a favorite digital studio, fully equipped with the

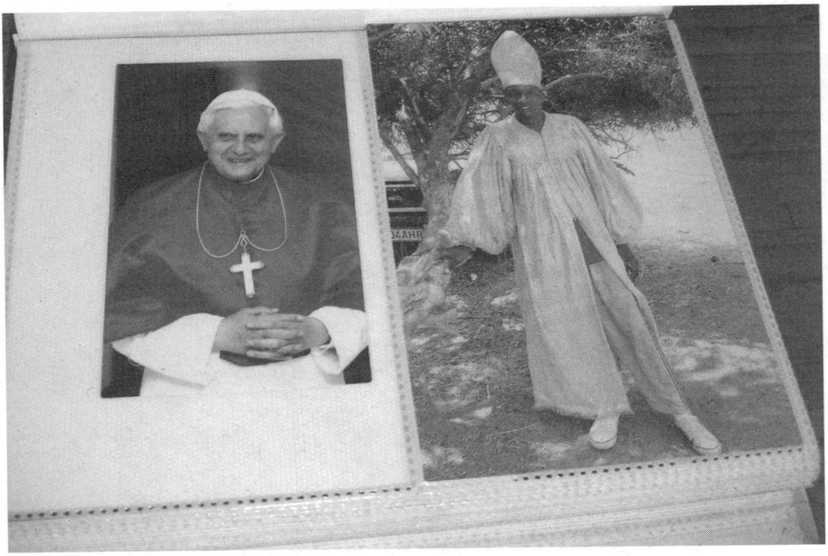

Figure 8. Iconography in prophet's album.

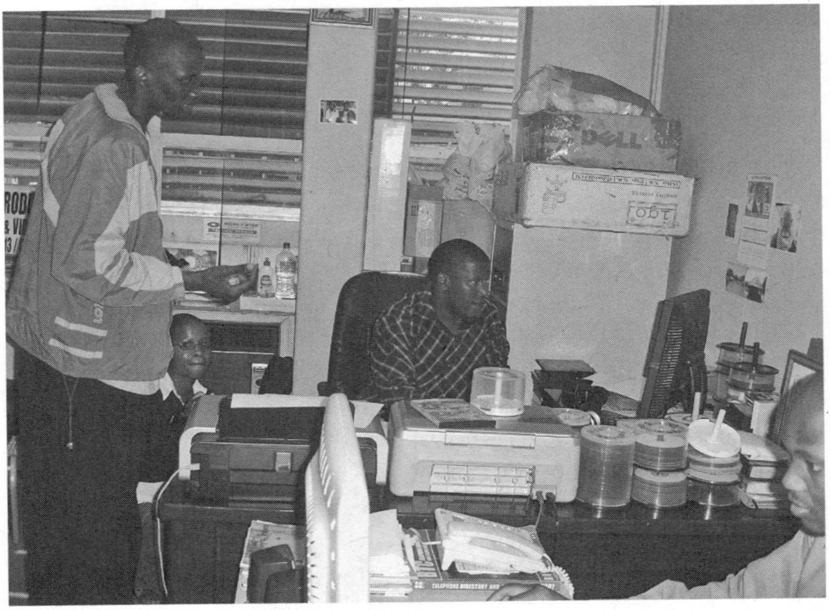

Figure 9. Introducing the prophets' digital studio.

latest computer technology. He advised me to use the studio, and I found myself already in an editing suite, even before shooting my own film.

It was a still image, the latest portrait of the archbishop, that opened the way for my research in the church. Shortly before I began my fieldwork on Eloyi in 2005, my assistant, Njebe, and his wife, Martha, spent nearly a month with the archbishop at the village headquarters of the church in Tsetsebjwe.[3] Following in Njebe and Martha's footsteps, in accord with my project, I went to Tsetsebjwe with Njebe to visit the archbishop. It was, among other things, to get the archbishop's permission for my research and filming.

I found the archbishop eager for a new portrait of himself to replace the old one widely hung as an icon in his church and on Apostolics' walls. With the portrait in mind, we went to Pikwe town to his chosen studio, had lunch together, spent the day on his errands, and finally got the new icon of him resplendent in his towering miter and red robe. Obviously very pleased, the archbishop gave me one of the copies and along with that, his permission and blessing for my research. Greatly relieved, I then presented myself, icon in hand, to the bishop, who, in turn, introduced me to the whole congregation at a Gaborone branch service. "You need not fear being invaded," he told them as I filmed, "because the film makers (Njebe and I) come for the whole church by arrangement with the Old Man, the archbishop. They carry his photograph." He held the archbishop's portrait up for all to see. Throughout my fieldwork I kept the archbishop's portrait prominently displayed on my own wall, in the room where I most often received Apostolics.

The image that matters most to prophets is, however, not the still but the moving image. Prophet Joshua, himself the owner of a very good and costly digital camera, tells me about his cinematic vision:

> We see a sort of film. Sometimes we can dig from here and take out something, a horn or bottle or whatever, something for witches. From the beginning, you see that film showing how they did it, what they put in there. Then you take it out, but first you see the film showing what technique they were using. It tells you if this person is witching, so you can chase that person away.
>
> I become alert and turn my camera on someone, asking my eyes what is happening on this person, and then I am told the witches use this person, or he is a witch or he has been sent unwittingly not knowing it. We know but the person doesn't know anything at all.

To strangers and on trips outside Gaborone, some prophets were fond of introducing me, jokingly, "He is also a prophet and our photographer." If meant for fun, it says something serious, also, about prophets' perception of themselves as seers of the moving image. They understand their spiritual trance to be cinematic, and what they imply in their joke is that we have the cinematic in common. It is something that would please the anthropologist and renowned filmmaker Jean Rouch: their spiritual trance is my cine trance.[4]

I return to the subjection and domination in the prophets' diagnostic practice and to issues of embodying empathy in the second part of this book. First, in Chapter 3, I discuss the lives of some of the prophets and bishops, their backgrounds, and church careers. Then, in the following chapters, I say more about the escalating crisis among the Apostolics, their visions, and their dilemmas when their church building is destroyed by a gale. In turn, this leads me back to Apostolic prayer and diagnosis.

3. The Lives of Prophets and Bishops

FIVE EXEMPLARY PROPHETS

For their own lives, in reflection with me, prophets tell the story of inspired vocation and faith, sometimes from childhood but more commonly from their teens. It is a story in which they come to understand the troubles of others, gain the power of the Word, and eventually learn to protect themselves against the evil and the envious.

The prophets themselves are diverse. But all come originally from villages and most from northern homes near the archbishop or in his subdistrict. Their origins are as follows:

NORTH: a) relatively near archbishop's headquarters, Lerala 1, Mmadinare 5, Pikwe 1;
b) elsewhere in the Central District, Shoshong 1, Tonota 2;
SOUTH: a) near capital city, Mochudi 1, Gaborone 1.

They represent something of a third generation, at least in the history of their church, though usually not in their own families, where they are sometimes the first generation. Somewhat more than the senior pastors, they also come from widespread places and represent the ethnic diversity in the congregations; none are close kin or members of the same family. I turn to five examples in order to document prophets' personal lives and vocational stories.

PROPHET JOSHUA

Joshua is the most dynamic, expressive, and forceful of the prophets. A spectacular dancer and ritual performer, he features the most in my film

Holy Hustlers, and I begin with his story. Along with Andrew, he is one of the most trusted prophets; they are the ones who, being closest to the bishop, advise and stand by him as he decides to leave Eloyi and become the founding archbishop of a new church, Conollius.

Joshua is short, stocky with the muscular body of a remarkably athletic dancer, and he wears his hair Rasta-style in ringlets. Very convivial, he smiles quickly and often, without embarrassment showing his teeth blackened by the bad water of his childhood village in the south. His clothes, usually smart and pressed, contrast on weekdays with the often shabby clothes of his patients. Overall, he has the look of a with-it young man of the city, and like many of his peers, he mixes his Tswana freely with many Tswana versions of English words—it is city-smart jargon and not, I must add, anglicized Tswana or Tswanaized English only for my benefit.

Joshua grew up in Eloyi, the church of his parents, and remained true to it, until he followed his bishop into the Conollius Church. He tells me he was born in 1983 in the north of the country, which he still knows well, but was raised in the south.

Joshua first started "becoming wise," *tlhalefa*—aware of a vocation as a prophet—in 1989. He was six years old when he first watched church dancers with Bishop Boitshepelo 's younger brother, Assistant Bishop Sekai, at Pikwe, the mining town not far from the archbishop's village headquarters. He remembers looking at them, wishing he could join them. Then, in 1990, he himself began to dance until, in 1996, he was able to dance within Assistant Bishop Sekai's church. He couldn't do other things outside (i.e., climb on roofs and hunt in exorcism), he says, but in church his feet were strong in ability, light and full of skill, *matlhofo*. From 1996, having entered the church, his heart would beat fast, then he would see many things he wouldn't understand. Finally, pastors said, "This child has the Gift of God, he was born with it. After a time, he is going to be a prophet."

In 1997, in class at school, he saw many "wonders," *tiro e e kgamatsang* (his ironic phrase both for miracles and for shocking things of witchcraft). It disturbed him in class, and sometimes he would shout and have to be taken home. Then he started dancing in church, and the more he danced in church, the more he saw many things in heaven above, here and there. Sometimes, he told me, he would see the troubles of 20 people, all at one go; he could also see a single person's troubles, one by one.

One of the descriptions Prophet Joshua gave me of his visionary experience as a prophet is this:

> Sometimes I hear the Voice coming, or sometimes I feel that pain reflecting in my body. Or if it's a headache, I feel it stronger than it is in you. It is very much worse, *bothoko thatha*. I sometimes see something like a board written with so many things. So I have to play chess. I have to arrange those things the way they should be, *fa di tshwanetseng*. I have to arrange them very quickly. I use intelligence, *tlhaloganyo*, to reason quickly, *akanya ka bonako*, it's something like chess. You have to go fast and use lots of intelligence, *tlhaloganyo* (understanding).

Joshua completed Form III at school and worked at the Spar supermarket in Palapye, another nearby town along the railway. But he suffered headaches, because he had to work on Sundays. At 1:00 o'clock, they would start bothering him, when his angel would be waiting, wanting to talk to him. He gave up his job, and he feels that if he found a job, he would be punished for missing church on Sundays. He is unmarried, has a child and a steady girl friend, but does not live with them, though he tries to support them; he lives off donations and sometimes feels hard-pressed for money late in the month and when he needs to pay his rent.

THE CASE OF THE SLIPPERY MONEY

Money is a concern Prophet Joshua often addresses in his consultations. It is somewhat in advance of my fuller analysis of diagnosis in prophecy, but to illustrate briefly that concern and Prophet Joshua's style in prophecy, I extract the following from a longer diagnosis. In this, he addresses a Gaborone couple he knows well from repeated consultations:

> I don't know how it is going. It is not right. First, it is said that we should pray. As for me, when I pray and ask the King what is the fault, it is said that things are not going well. It is said that your money just slips from your hands. It is that you are going to grasp money, but when you should use it, it loses its work [it is useless]. This thing is going to cause complaints between you. They worked [witchcraft] against you using money. At the end of the month, when you should have taken money home, it just finishes somehow or other, *ka tsela nngwe*, in an odd way, *go sa itsagaleng*, a way not knowable.

The prophet's words were on target for closely receptive listeners. For the couple, money is indeed a source of friction. The wife regards the husband, with good reason, as feckless with money and too ready to gamble it away; the husband finds his wife too tight with her earnings, which she regularly tries to salt away, hidden in the house or beyond his access in the bank. She is the one who takes the lead in seeking the prophet's diagnosis and prescriptions.

For one interview, Joshua and I met in the bishop's office. Sitting behind the bishop's big desk but not on his chair, which was significantly and powerfully covered with red cloth, Joshua came and went busily in response to the press of church affairs. He appeared in charge in the bishop's absence. In response to my questions, he enjoyed opening the Bible to relevant passages and took evident pride in his knowledge. He was following the example of pastors, making a show of textual command, while appealing to textual authority.

When I ask Prophet Joshua about his favorite red robe, he replies,

> It is as if I am bulletproof against those witches and doctors, who can start something, being jealous. We are all children of God, but some wish evil to happen to you. That red robe protects me powerfully, so I use it most.

He speaks of the need a prophet has to protect himself from envy, especially from witches and traditional doctors, who want to fight. He must take care not to "retaliate," *busoletsa,* or seek vengeance, lest he so dirty his hands that at the end he destroys their healing power. He has to be strong and have something that can protect him, his robe.

The red robe, being the color of blood and thus vital, is the most powerful of his robes. When he wears it, people can think he has wings and is flying, Prophet Joshua told me. His white robe re-empowers him with the gift of prayer. He relies upon his white robe to bring him even closer to God, for sometimes, Prophet Joshua said, he himself feels distant from God or overwhelmed by bearing the troubles of so many people. His robes—gold, white, red, gray, and with different miters and caps or fezzes—are many. Their glorious variety is meant to suit the rich variety in his religious experience of being a prophet who undergoes the pressures of the Holy Spirit in the faithful service of Eloyi.

PROPHET ANDREW

The second prophet, Andrew, is an unmarried southerner, about thirty years old, who was born in a village near the capital. Andrew grew up in the capital, "the best place, ahead of the rest of the country," where he still lives in his grandmother's house. After he suffered a mild illness and heard the voice of his angel, he became the first in his family to join Eloyi, while a teenager. He knows other prophets suffered more and were more disturbed than he was when he first had his visions. As befits a usually balanced person, less given to extremes, he went to school and completed his studies without any difficulty. Nevertheless, he has experienced the loss of control with the Holy Spirit, and he remarks,

> At times the Holy Spirit comes with a pressure on us, so we can't even manage to control ourselves, and end up falling. You cannot injure yourself when you get the Holy Spirit. The Holy Spirit cannot hurt you. But if you are doing something without the Holy Spirit, you definitely get hurt. With the Holy Spirit, even if you can fall from the roof of a house you can't actually be broken.

In fact, never did he fall in any of the services I attended. He leaped on roofs, ran with the "sniffer dogs," but never himself caught witchcraft bits by hand or mouth. He told one of his patients, "Smelling out witches, no, I don't like doing that. But there are things that can force you to do it to help a person." With extreme care at an exorcism, while collecting the noxious remains at Boitshepelo's request, he avoided contact by handling them fastidiously with a plastic wrapper. For Andrew, trance is now mild, no longer the fierce burning within that other prophets often still experience, when overcome by the Holy Spirit.

Compared to Joshua, Andrew—tall, thin and elegant, if perhaps somewhat self-consciously—is less ecstatic, less gifted in vigorous church dance (pop music brings out his dazzling style) and accomplished more in preaching—which he much enjoys. He has fewer robes, preferring white and gold, *diphatsinang*, glittering, with sparklers for Power dressing, but he avoids red, which he finds too dangerous; red is beyond his temperate religious disposition.

Andrew, like Joshua and all the prophets, shows much bodily empathy with others' suffering in his diagnoses. He is authoritative, never hesitant in manner. He gives intensely knowing looks, often with long pauses, when he gazes deeply into a patient's eyes. Reflecting a patient's pain as experienced on his own body, he touches his own shoulders, back, hips, and navel, pointing to his head for headaches. In diagnosis moments of inner spiritual withdrawal, being with the Holy Spirit and his angel, he shuts his eyes, then opens them, searching through his patient. His ability to convey the holy presence working within him is impressive.

Telling of his communication with the Holy Spirit, Andrew gave me this account, in his own words, in English:

> I do see the Holy Spirit is within me and is showing me things, if you are a patient, if you have got a pain somewhere or even if you have got

> a problem at your house. It is coming like a vision, like a dream but a dream that comes even when my eyes are open. It touches me, so that I get to that state of the patient, so that I can easily feel the pain the way the patient is feeling it.

Perhaps more than most prophets, Andrew willingly takes on many tasks in the church, including those of the humble servant who gives flame vapor baths and ties cords to protect the afflicted. A characteristic prayer of his, given in a very soulful manner, is this, over an old woman:

> Dress her, God Full of Peace. We do not pray to you like one without faith and trust in all the paths on which you go. Oh Lord, God the Overseer, let her be cared for, as she is asking, in the name of the Son and the Holy Spirit.

A favorite topic of his in diagnosis concerns ingratitude, dispossession, and failing to get one's due in life, as if one were not truly blessed, a topic which he expresses in this address to a weary-looking mother, accompanied by her roughly twenty-year-old daughter:

> The situation isn't right where you're living. You aren't holding well. For you don't attend church well. Inside yourself you feel nauseous, even if you haven't eaten anything. There's something affecting you. It is said that's the way it is. These are the things that dispossess you of what should be yours. It is so not only for your daughter. You yourself were once denied things rightfully yours, *distswanelo tsa lona*. When I ask Heaven, "How?" it is said you once tried to work for yourself, and failed. Now, it is as if you could tell people you were blessed with nothing at all.

In one of our many conversations, the prophet tells me of how in his own life, he has had to overcome a similar situation. He is a first-born son, but his younger feckless brother was his parents favorite whom they indulged, while letting him make his own way in Gaborone with hardly any support at all. He had to become streetwise and learn how to survive in Gaborone with very little.

While childless, Andrew has a longtime and much older girlfriend who is a prosperous, well-paid accountant, with houses of her own—she lets rooms to two of the other prophets. Having recently won the church's beauty contest, dressed handsomely in his best smart suit, Andrew boasts of his title, Mr. Eloyi, and pages of his album are devoted to his pictures, trophy in hand, surrounded by the most beautiful women in the contest. He likes a city bar where he can drink wine, never beer, and never gets drunk. He prides himself on being able to live on less than other prophets, because he knows his way around the city. His income he estimates at roughly 3,000 pula a month, including about 400 pula from a part-time taxi job, driving a regular customer to work in his girlfriend's car, and an irregular income from his "surgery" or "consulting room" at home.

Spending the day with Andrew gives one the feeling of being plugged into a high-volume switchboard, with endless incoming calls though relatively few outgoing ones. He is, like other prophets, constantly on his cell phone. A compulsive locator of others, especially the four prophets closest to him (Joshua, Matthew, Obed, and Reuben), he keeps very busy confirming arrangements, checking on what is happening in the church and with the other prophets and his patients. Patients call him frequently, book an appointment, and consult about their problems in conversation. He says that, according to the tally on his phone, in the roughly three years since he bought it, he has sent more than 6,000 messages, and received 16,000.

When we had an appointment, he would call me to remind me to be on time, though on his side he felt free to delay or respond to patients or even disappear: he knew I could and did wait. I must confess, however, to more than a little irritation at his use of his favorite and glorious golden robe, the one with all the glitter, to command my car, when I was about to leave a church service with him. He would install his robe, carefully and neatly folded, in the front passenger seat, and go off, suddenly, without a word, ever busy, on some church errand. I along with a carload of others would wait until someone would leave the car to hunt for him—he never made excuses on his return, but always smiled graciously.

During an earlier schism in Eloyi, Andrew left and took the opportunity to become one of the leaders of the small, splinter church. Somehow, he made his way agilely back to Eloyi, however, against the will of the Gaborone pastor-general, who wanted him to remain suspended but is now reconciled with him in the new Conollius church.

At the height of the crisis in Eloyi, Andrew told me the bishop and prophets would leave the church and that I was one of them and must come with them. Agreeing that the archbishop is a holy man, perhaps holier than the bishop, Andrew said that the archbishop "does nothing for us, the prophets, but the bishop is always helping us and looking after us." In his view, the bishop wasn't given the respect and honor, *tlotlo,* due him in his own church.

Andrew now speaks of himself as Boitshepelo's "right-hand man." In the new church, he is chairman. A strikingly pious man with street smarts, Andrew is ambitious and, I believe, looks to becoming a church leader himself eventually, or at least a very prominent pastor.

PROPHET MATTHEW

Of all the prophets, the youngest, being in his early twenties and perhaps the most immature, is Matthew. A southerner from Mochudi, near the capital, Matthew is short, baby-faced, and with the look of a choir boy in his favorite white robe and white crossed miter. Unmarried, he says he "will wait till the Lord tells him he is ready to marry." Outside the church, and even in the presence of his current, steady girlfriend, he often has roving eyes, on the lookout for the prettiest girl passing by. Always very short of money, he is the one among the prophets who badgered me constantly, without peace, for gifts. His hustling tamed me into giving him something almost on first sight, if not small sums of cash, then food or other gifts, such as the new pair of girl's jeans, which he prefers because of their tight feel and display of his body.

Prophet Matthew himself has been taken, as it were, under the wing of the most entrepreneurial of the prophets, Reuben, who is a northerner, not Prophet Matthew's home boy. Reuben, like Matthew, is himself the son of a diviner, and this continuity is common among more than a few prophets. Outstanding as a dramatic witchfinder and exorcist—the one who fearlessly bursts forth with the hidden and most dangerous-looking witchcraft knives and snakes—Reuben is rich and very successful. He owns a Mercedes, which he drives recklessly on long-distance journeys, fast enough to burn out the tires; his healing practice in South Africa is booming; and usually being there, he lets Matthew stay, freely, in the rooms he rents from Andrew's girlfriend. Although Matthew is yet to gain a certificate from the traditional doctors' association that includes *sangoma* mediums—as Reuben has, and proudly displays on his wall—Matthew, too, has become skilful in the traditional practice of incision to cut away witchcraft substances. For such incision, he demands high fees, saying that he fears it is dangerous to life, above all his own. What Matthew does is Christianize this anti-witchcraft practice by preparing himself in prayer in the wild on a hilltop, remote from people, and then praying over the patient before the incision.

Matthew loves Gospel music. Reuben's collection of Gospel DVDs from South Africa is large and splendid, so much so that Matthew plays and watches a selection when holding a private diagnosis at home. For Matthew, the music has the same effect as Eloyi church music (and he is a very gifted tambourine player)—it gets him in a spiritual mood. He has a ready answer to Andrew, his partner in a diagnosis, when Andrew seriously complains that the Gospel music is enjoyable but a distraction from hearing the Word. "Listen to the person, not the DVD," Matthew insists.

It is Reuben, about three years ago, who fully lifted up, *tsholetsa,* clarified, *ranolola,* and unwrapped, *phutulolela,* Matthew as a prophet in the making.

Matthew was not ill, he says. Instead, he was seeing visions, including bolts of lightning, and not only seeing but feeling the painful troubles of others on his own body. It all began even earlier, before the death of his father. As a diviner, he gave his son a warning: Matthew had not the gift of divination but *neo ya semowa,* the gift of the Holy Spirit. In response, Matthew entered a splinter church that had broken away from Eloyi, the Church of Heaven, and then under Reuben's influence left it for Eloyi. Now in renewal of his faith and spiritual power, Matthew makes regular ascents to the highest nearby hilltop to be away from people and in touch with his angel.

The Case of the Renter and the Duped Child

As a prophet, Matthew pays special attention to the way people suffer because they or innocent others are duped. He also goes to very great lengths to show the spread of an illness across the body. An example of this is in the following diagnosis he offers at church during a weekday morning set aside for diagnosis and prescription, but not a main service. The patient is a worried-looking middle-aged man, a villager by origin and now living in a rented house in the city. Prophet Matthew begins with a call to a brief prayer, and then he examines the patient: "Cup your hands, sir, we will see. Lord God, mighty King, I appeal to you, Sir." He asks the patient, "Old man, where do you come from, whose place is it?" The patient at first misunderstands the question. "It's my mother's," he answers. "Or do you mean the place I rent?" Prophet Matthew seeks to locate the patient's main yard, in the village or the city: "Where you are living. Whose is it?" "It belongs to a certain woman named Kuru," the patient answers. Prophet Matthew pursues this. "Do you rent it?" he asks. "Yes, I rent it," responds the patient.

Having established that the patient is not the owner but a renter, who may have trouble with the owner, Prophet Matthew closes in on his story's trail. He now lets the patient know of the guidance from the Holy Spirit that makes the prophet ask and go on the hunt in his journey. In accord with that, he reveals the spread of disease in the body of the patient, while manifesting that with strong gestures on his own body. He speaks very rapidly, gushing ahead with his eyes shut most of the time:

> It is said I should enter where you live. It is said I should look for medicine inside a plastic. You are not waking well. You are going about with cold which enters your joints, and you have pain in your belly. This illness spreads, it enters your heart. Your belly gets full and

> swells up. It is as if you can tell people you are being killed in your kidneys. You are made tired, when you relieve your bladder, and you are caught by numbness, *bosisi,* that goes to your feet, the very soles of your feet.

The patient agrees, "It is so, Sir."

Prophet Matthew continues, "You say, the place where you stay is whose? The girl about so big [gestures for the height of a small child, four or five years old], whose is she?" "She's the grandchild of the yard's owner" is the patient's reply. Prophet Andrew reports more of his vision

> I see you turn your back there. But I see that little girl follows you. It is not good. She is being used. You know it's not good in your yard because that child is being used. It is said I should press hard, *gatelele,* saying that this child can *tswalela,* shut off (block), your lives in your yard. Do you hear me?

The patient answers compliantly, "Yes, I am listening and understanding."

Prophet Matthew reaches his conclusion and ends the diagnosis:

> I see it is said that this child is at a crossways with you and she comes and goes in the opposite direction. She is the one they say is closing off your lives. She is being used. You are not living well, sir, you go about with pain in your head. It says it is as if you can shed many tears.

Turning immediately to another patient, Prophet Matthew later dictates a prescription for this patient to a volunteer secretary, who transcribes it onto the church form. In the next chapter, in discussing the Case of the Victim of Ingratitude, I analyze Prophet Matthew's approach closely, and in Chapter 8 I consider his prescription for this patient. First, I want to complete my account of the prophets' own lives.

PROPHET JOHANNES

Johannes, a prophet in his mid-twenties and slightly older than Matthew, exemplifies the itinerant prophet who comes to the Gaborone branch on a visit. Now based in Francistown, the country's largest trading town in the north, he is unmarried and not permanently employed, though sometimes he works part-time as a bricklayer. He successfully attended Shashe River School, has a Cambridge certificate, and speaks English fluently (his mother tongue is Kalanga). Whenever doing piecework keeps him from church, he prays to God for understanding, but he does sometimes suffer nose bleeding because of his neglect of the church and prophecy.

Prophet Johannes uses cinematic imagery when he describes his experience of diagnosis. We discuss it in English and Kalanga, and in the following résumé of his description from my notes, I use quotes for a word of his in English. In diagnosis, Prophet Johannes tells me, he sees moving images. Scenes flash by. It is all in fragments. When he "rolls" in whirling dance, it is to concentrate, "to focus." There are so many fragments, they have to be put together, and he needs to focus to get to the truth. And his aim is the truth, he says. One reason patients deny the truth that he tells them is that sometimes they don't recall things, even familiar things. It might be a casual meeting with a dog, long forgotten years later and never understood in its true meaning. He has to make the true meaning clear. When he sees a vision of fire, it is not the same as ordinary fire; instead, it is an image of the attack burning up the patient from within.

Prophet Johannes does his best to give me a sense of the intense state of his being with the Holy Spirit. What he feels in his body is vicarious pain, the patient's pain but even sharper than in the patient, and it acutely alerts Prophet Johannes to trouble. It can be an affliction already bothering the patient or one that is about to come.

With a fellow prophet, who shares his rooms in Francistown, Johannes sings and records church music in duos, occasionally joined by his sister. Johannes is the one who composes the music and lyrics. The CD I bought from him for 50 pula has a mechanical back-up beat provided by a Zimbabwean recording studio. Admitting that I find that beat monotonous and off-putting, I suggest to Johannes that he might do well by getting prophets to ring bells and play tambourines for the back-up. "No," he tells me, "that will never sell in Botswana." It is already hard enough to make the CDs, he says, because out of the 50 pula all he keeps is 2 pula.

A strikingly tall northerner, especially by contrast to southerner patients who are often rather short, he ordinarily has a gentle, amiable manner. As a prophet, however, he is sometimes fierce and overbearing. His license to talk to an elder aggressively, without the polite respect due him, comes from the Holy Spirit. The Holy Spirit demands that he speak out boldly to rescue the elderly patient from his ignorance of the true nature of his troubles.

Johannes made his own choice to join Eloyi, and not the church of his parents, when he felt he was a responsible person, at about the age of sixteen. At the onset of his being filled with the Holy Spirit in prophecy, he had no illness, but felt disturbed and uneasy, though he managed to continue at school without interruption. Earlier in his youth, his grandfather, a well-known *sangoma* possessed by healing spirits, died. This *sangoma* grandfather then appeared to Johannes in visions and still does, but not as an afflicting spirit, even though his grandfather is not baptized. Johannes express pride in his heritage, rather than rejecting the *sangoma* tradition as an evil coming from a denied past. Even more, Johannes is also proud to tell me that he went to the Francistown diviners and herbalists' association for a test, passed it, and is now waiting for his certificate to be signed. He knows that the archbishop condemns all that and is against bringing the church together with "traditional healers." The church is under threat from them, he sees, because they are jealous of the church winning patients in ever greater numbers, and they do everything they can to block the church. But he feels he must be true to his own spiritual visions and the good spiritual guidance he still gets from his grandfather, the *sangoma*.

A *SANGOMA* HERITAGE, THE WOMAN PROPHET BOIGELE, AND REFORMATION

In my view, Johannes is, like Matthew, Reuben, Andrew, and Joshua, at the forefront of a new generation of prophets for whom reformation is something of a return. The new generation is reversing the break made by the Apostolics' founding fathers. For these founding fathers, to contact the dead and their powerful essences is disenabling and disempowering; for the new generation, contacting the spirits of the dead is empowering and enables a Christian mission—the very counteraction of the fabrications of the *sangoma* and *moitseanape,* occult cunning and expertise.

There is a riposte, also Christian, of course. In Archbishop Jakoba's own scolding, young prophets like Prophet Joshua and Prophet Johannes are dirty and polluted, having become, in his damning word, "*Sangomanyana,* Little *Sangoma.*" As the archbishop sees it, "These Tswana things are not compatible with, *thokana* (in need of), the work of God." Purity is paramount for the archbishop in accord with the idea of the holy, *boitshepelo,* that includes *itshepa* (the pure, sanctified), and trust (*tshepa*).

In the light of the prophets' Christianizing of a *sangoma* heritage, I want to add a qualification to my remarks in the second chapter about the prophets' masculinizing of the prophetic domain in Eloyi. Before the church split in two, I saw in Eloyi at the Gaborone branch no exception to this rule: there were no women prophets, and the young men had effectively excluded women, above all the old women who formerly prophesied in the past. But in an early service in the church of Conollius, I came upon

Boigele, visiting from the church in Mahalapye town and dressed like a prophet in a rich blue robe and a red cap, or fez.

Barely twenty, Boigele is a remarkable young woman, most striking in her build. Boigele is, in a word, Junoesque. Or, in the choice phrase of Botswana's celebrated novelist Alexander McCall Smith, "she is a woman of traditional build," big-boned, well over six foot, athletic, and a very substantial presence in every respect. Brought to meet her in church by one of the prophets, I was amazed to hear her introduce herself, with great pride, saying, "I am a prophet."

Boigele's father, a Kalanga-speaking northerner, is a very famous and successful *sangoma*. From him, she inherited the ability of a *sangoma*, but the Holy Spirit turned that ability from evil to good, she explained to me. Her father now accepts that she has herself turned into a prophet. Like any other prophet, she feels the patient's pain, she diagnoses its cause and source, she relies on her visions to locate the patient's dangerous setting, and she prescribes the remedy or needed treatment. Even more, she excels in her capacity as a "sniffer dog," like a *sangoma* successful on the trail of hidden witchcraft. But—as prophets say about women who would be prophets—she does cry out. Despite her big build and large, strong bones, she can hardly bear the burning of the Holy Spirit inside her or the fierceness of contact with uncovered witchcraft substances.

At the Conollius service, when I first meet her, Boigele rushes out of the church and runs with the other prophets. She sniffs about until she finds "a bullet" a "medicine" originally bought from Durban and intended to attack the church. On her return, quite stiff with it in her frozen grasp, Conollius' new bishop (formerly pastor-general in Eloyi's Gaborone branch) takes it from her, for destruction by burning. Boigele reveals what is further needed in her eventual prescription of materials for treatment. These come in a plastic vial, as I am shown, clearly labeled "pure sea sand" and "from the ocean," "pure salt water." As I understand it, the bad import calls for a good one, also a purchase but instead from a pharmacy that sells the needed materials. However, as befits a woman, even an exceptional one with the needed big bones and substantial build, Boigele, although an acknowledged prophet, does cry out when she suffers being a sniffer dog.

This leads me to a further point about this apparent exception to a masculine rule of prophecy. I understand from gossip that Boigele's conversion into a prophet has been something of an exchange in that other prophets, some said to have been her lovers, have in turn learned from her about *sangoma* practice. My point is not merely that this exception does uphold the masculinizing rule—given Boigele's crying out, her exceptional part can still be explained away by the young men in command of the domain of prophecy. My point also is that the masculinizing goes ahead along with Christianizing, in this case a process that includes and, in practice, even needs a woman such as Boigele—it is the process of Christianizing a spiritual heritage, namely, that of the *sangoma*. Whereas rejection of that heritage is the mission of Apostolic founding fathers, it is accommodation with that, as an original spiritual heritage, that prevails in reformation for the third generation and its vanguard of streetwise prophets. Reformation goes forward by turning back on itself.

BISHOP (LATER ARCHBISHOP) BOITSHEPELO

The patron of these reformation prophets, Bishop and later Archbishop Boitshepelo, is a middle-aged district council driver. He owns a modest car and lives with his current partner in a small house in a working-class neighborhood of Gaborone. Having no taste for flashy clothes or designer labels, by contrast to most of the prophets, he wears a respectable dark suit for formal church conferences and meetings apart from church services. When relaxing on rest days, he favors the casual clothes of youth, including camouflage trousers. In South Africa, as a young man, Boitshepelo worked mainly as a security guard in the mines. There he became more familiar with the practical organization of the industrial world, and he came to admire both bureaucratic routines and modern methods of management. He also gained great skill in carpentry and building, which stood him in good stead during the 1980s construction boom in Gaborone and, of course, in building his new church.

Apostolics draw my attention to the difference in the lifestyle of the assistant bishop, his younger brother Sekai, who is responsible for Eloyi's town in Pikwe. He owns a couple of Mercedes, said to have once been government ministers' cars, is a very successful businessman, and owns a popular bar, known as Bishop's Bar. But he is a more reserved, less accessible man than Boitshepelo; few Apostolics know his cell phone number, they say. At a wedding for Prophet Obed, I found him to be somewhat aloof; he kept to his own table and got up only to pose regally for a photo with Prophet Andrew. Several of the prophets, who admire him greatly for his spiritual powers and sermons, jokingly call him "boss," behind his back, in part because in church he wears a military style robe with epaulettes and three stars, affecting the appearance of a general and commander.

Hanging on the walls of Boitshepelo's living room are iconic portraits of Jesus, the archbishop, and the bishop himself, gloriously robed in gold, vestments fitting, indeed, for a bishop. The iconography resembles that on the prophets' walls, with one significant exception. The bishop's walls have, in addition, two icons of Adam and Eve with the tempting apple and the seductive snake in the Garden of Eden.

It is, of course, an iconography of human weakness faced with the temptations of sin, especially of the flesh. Knowing some of the moral accusations against the bishop—that he abandoned his second wife, leaving her to his father's care in Tsetsebjwe (where I met her in 2005); that he now lives with his partner, allegedly in adultery; that his own cousin preaches against him, if indirectly, in sermons about "men going about wantonly with women"—I wonder what is the personal significance of the Garden of Eden icons for the bishop, but I do not dare to ask.

Although a bishop and later archbishop, Boitshepelo has much in common with the prophets, and yet much that distinguishes him above all. One thing is most remarkable, for me at least. Boitshepelo's hands are extraordinary. Shaking Boitshepelo's hand, I find it memorably large and strong and yet gentle, soft, somehow surprisingly fleshy.

I must say more about that for two reasons, both to do with contact, which I want to discuss in some depth. The first reason is holy spirituality, the great significance of laying on hands among Apostolics. Warmth in intimacy is the second reason, given the special art of the open caress in shaking hands so much enjoyed by many people in Botswana. It is never an abrupt grip, but a long consensual welcome, as it were, taking each other's life trustfully in hand and making very touching contact. Boitshepelo excels in the public contact, as much in that art of the open caress as he does in the laying on hands. Boitshepelo is, in the richest sense, a handler—he handles the people he manages, especially the prophets, keeping in touch with them despite the dangers or even the dirt they grasp.

What is more, Boitshepolo's reputation for laying on hands with prayer, like the reputation of many other Apostolic bishops, is legendary. For example, one story, well-known in the church, is about a man of the Zion Christian Church (ZCC) whose son was charged for murder, after a witnessed attack. The ZCC man rushed to Boitshepolo and appealed successfully to the bishop to pray for his son. It was in response, Apostolics say, that the post mortem showed the cause of death was not at the son's hands, despite the attack. One point of the story is that Boitshepelo was immediately accessible; he acted right away. It is a point that reflects, in the eyes of some, Boitshepelo's great strength, and in the eyes of others, his weakness, which is unmanageable by others in the church hierarchy and the executive committee. Boitshepelo is famous for acting spontaneously, according to his own judgment; it is often without consulting others who think he should take advice from them first.

If regarded as impetuous and willful by some, Boitshepelo is widely admired for being the man of the people who is accessible to everyone in need, any time of day or night. He is never out of contact. His cell phone number is widely known; he answers it constantly, as I found, repeatedly interrupted by its buzz, when trying to film him. When it comes to building his new church, he works by the sweat of his brow, hammer or saw or plank in hand, right along with everyone else, and for longer. His favorite word of address, especially for the prophets—and I bring a great smile to his face when I use it for him—is *mogalona,* mate or home boy (someone of ours).

Boitshepelo is not a man who fastidiously withdraws into purity, as does his archbishop father. On the contrary, he seems to revel not merely in human contact,but even in contact with waste or, more strongly, in dealing with the nasty things that might pollute him. His archbishop father never handles such things; he avoids even being present at exorcisms and the digging up of charms. Boitshepelo is fearless and, what is more important, is seen in the eyes of everyone around him to be fearless in his contact. Most strikingly, and without hesitation, he uses his own hands directly to draw out the evil, dirty things from the hands and mouths of his sniffer dogs, the prophets, during the highly dramatic exorcisms. With his perceived gift in prayer comes the recognized gift of powerful contact.

The schism in the church has divided Apostolics in their approach to Boitshepelo as a handler. Some have continued to seek his contact; others avoid it. The most dramatic show of this divide was at the Sunday service when the bishop resigned. Usually, at the end of the service, everyone joins the line for the bishop's blessing and laying on of hands. In a display of distrust at the resignation service, some of the *bomme batona,* the great mothers, the elders who are the most prominent women in the church, did not join the line and avoided contact with the bishop. One of the women told me that she now felt that the bishop was involved in handling too much dirt. Angry at this insult to the bishop's dignity, the pastor-general confronted some of these women outside church and threw the insult back by accusing them of being not only polluted but even more trapped in the evil of the church's enemies, "You are in the dirt of our enemies."

So far, my account of the bishops has presented the difference between the priestly purity seeking of the father and the pastoral contact management of the son. But there is an aspect of their difference that both might

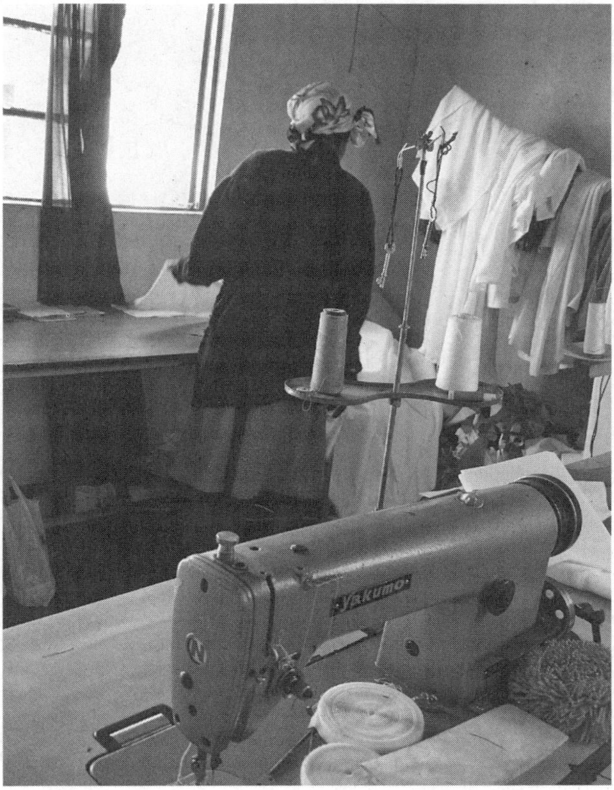

Figure 10. Bishop's seamstress preparing robes.

well say is spiritually the most profound, namely, that of charisma and trance.

The archbishop is seen by Apostolics, during diagnosis, to be visibly enduring the burning fire of the Holy Spirit within his body. He gasps and, according to my observation, hyperventilates seriously. His body language, manifesting the suffering of his patient in himself, is powerful and charismatic. The point is not that the archbishop is a prophet like any other, but that his somatic practice—his entry into trance, his evident experience of transcendence, his body language and realization of empathy with and knowledge of the other—is exemplary. The rest of the prophets follow his example in their practice. Even further, and along with his command at the top of the church hierarchy, the archbishop brings together in his person the prophetic and the pastoral.

His son the bishop prays, dreams, and has visions, but he never enters trance and never gets wholly taken over bodily by the Holy Spirit. However much he whirls in dance with prophets, he is not one of them; if he experiences euphoria, it is not seen to be their ecstacy. A pastor *par excellence,* rather than an ecstatic, he is not a person like his father who has the exemplary and encompassing spirituality.

Despite all that, or perhaps in part because of it, there was ambiguity or even open doubt about Boitshepelo's authority while he was Eloyi's bishop. Not Boitshepelo, but his younger full-brother Sekai was the first in their generation to be appointed by their father to high office in the church hierarchy—in 1985 as Assistant Bishop. Sekai is, and was, a much more favored son and, in his father's eyes, has more exceptional spiritual gifts. Many of the prophets, too, admire him greatly for his *dikgakgamatsang* ("wonders," "miracles"); his portraits, more even than Boitshepelo's, adorn their walls. One prophet told me he has seen the green circle on Sekai's back—it is a sun, and it shows his power, the highest. The assistant bishop's name, Sekai (meaning "Example"), came to his father in visions, one of the signs of the cross on Sekai's flesh and the other vision having holy paper marked "Sekai" and borne by five doves. His father never had any doubt about Sekai's appointment as assistant bishop.

By contrast, Boitshepelo's own appointment was at first special to him and not spiritual. It was to act as his father's right-hand man in the role of church administrator, an ad hoc role not formalized in the constitution. As church administrator and also his father's first-born son, Boitshepelo acted in such matters as registering ownership of church land. In the case of church headquarters in Mahalapye town, he registered it in his own name—a prudent choice, at least for his own interest, as it now appears. Boitshepelo and Sekai worked closely together and without quarrels for many years building up the church—their co-operation was in great amity and Christian fellowship, both insist. Eventually, the archbishop sent Boitsephelo to Gaborone to be in charge of the city branch.

But how and when did Boitshepelo become a bishop? Or was he a bishop at all? Boitshepelo's own son put this question to Assistant Bishop Sekai himself. It was at a final meeting of Eloyi in Gaborone called to resolve the church crisis, if possible through reconciliation. Aggrieved and openly upset, Boitshepelo's son rehearsed the rumors that his father had never been ordained by the archbishop. Rather than giving a direct answer, yes or no, the assistant bishop answered, "We are the ones who sent him to you," and left it at that. And that, for Boitshepelo, when he heard it, was the final straw, making him a bishop who is or perhaps is not a bishop; he announced publicly his already well-prepared decision to leave Eloyi and found his new church, Conollius.

In the next chapter, I show the importance of Boitshepelo's innovations in the church. I trace the course of the schism among the Apostolics and give my account of how they pass through an ordeal full of moral uncertainty and anxiety about lapses in faith. My argument highlights the usefulness of Gregory Bateson's idea of schismogenesis in the analysis of schism as a process within a much longer term and continually changing process of Christian reformation.

4. Escalating Crisis

Faith and Trust "under Destruction"

SCHISM AND POWER STRUGGLES

Witchfinding and demon exorcism have made Eloyi famous, popular, and, of course, very controversial. The reputation gained by this Apostolic church in the media is sensational. This has been an important factor for the growth of the church on a vast scale, especially in the 1990s and most recently during the church boom at the height of the current AIDS pandemic. It is, however, not Eloyi's village-based archbishop but his city-based son, Bishop Boitsephelo, who has led the growth. Bishop Boitsephelo traveled tirelessly across the country in organizational campaigns, and still does. He introduced innovations in the church and won the reputation for being what the media call a "popular witchbuster," "for people across cultures."

For the prophets, being in the vanguard of Boitshepelo's campaigns while in Eloyi has meant being in the vanguard of struggles for power. It is, however, power that has to be appreciated in at least two contexts of value and innovation. The first is with regard to value in spiritual authority, honor, *tlotlo,* and personal virtue[1] and the second, with regard to iconoclasm and recast cosmology.

In this chapter and the next, I trace the escalation of a crisis, leading to a schism in the church, and show how power struggles are seen in each of these contexts. My account documents the making of the schism as a highly public event and yet an event that shakes Apostolics in what they hold to be a deep, innermost truth of their lives, their faith in their church and as Apostolics. The fear they express is *kgelogile,* turning aside, backsliding—to become lapsed Christians. There is a much-repeated hymn sung when exorcists pile up the heap of uncovered demonic charms, things of witchcraft, and materials of *bongaka ya setsho,* traditional healing:

Come back to the church. God wants you.
God wants you. Come back to the church.

For Apostolics, the greatest power, *thata,* is the Power of the Word of God, *Lentswe ya Modimo,* which calls, above all, for faith, *tumelo,* and prayer, *thapelo,* if it is to be effective in anyone's life. The sense of a loss of faith and of a shortfall in prayer, in the face of hostile and evil attack, weighs more heavily on certain Apostolics as the crisis escalates. But some, if deeply distressed by feelings of betrayal, of loss of trust in people who were closest to them, are consoled—God still guides them, they affirm, and they pray as ever, with moral passion and fervently, to *Modimo yo o Senatla,* God of Heroic Power. The power struggles become ever more struggles for Power.

Enemies accuse the prophets of being tricky street kids wrongly turned into prophets by Boitshepelo. Can the Holy Spirit have street smarts? The accusations against Boitshepelo himself are felt to strike deeply at his honor, *tlotlo.* These include adultery, unholy sacrifice, misuse of church funds, false prophecy, and sinful breach of biblical commandments for priestly purity. The accusation he himself says is most wounding—he claims it drove him in the end from Eloyi—was that he was not a bishop, never properly installed. Worse still, this attack on his *tlotlo* is being spread in gossip by his own brothers. Committee members also accuse Boitshepelo of bringing the church into disrespect; they are aware of criticism which members of mainline "respectable" churches make that Eloyi turns to superstition in exorcising demons. For one of the most prominent of the prophets, Joshua, these accusations and family quarrels within the very heart of the church are very deeply distressing. At a Bishop's Special Conference about the church crisis, Joshua complains, "I find my faith leaving and wasting away on me. *Tumelo yame e tsamaya e e mphelela* . . . We are shocked breathless and things get mixed up."

To put this moral crisis in a frame of analysis, I want to give my own view, somewhat abstractly, and then continue my account in more depth. In my own view, certain principles underlie endemic conflict within the church. Four principles are most salient. The first is patrimonial. It is a principle that turns the church into the patrimony of its founder and, in turn, his family. It is expressed most approvingly by the archbishop himself when he says, "This church is mine," and when he controls and distributes church goods and appointments himself, favoring his family, perhaps with some consultation with his inner circle but without being guided by the church more widely.

Most trenchantly opposed to this principle are the members of the church's executive committee, who insist upon a constitutional principle, whereby the church is the church of its people and has to be governed by their elected representatives, according to a formal constitution. For such advocates of this principle, patrimonialism is, to use their battle cry, "nepotism."

A third principle is pastoral. The bishop stands for this principle in much of his practice in that he sees himself as holding a holy and pastoral appointment within the church hierarchy. In accord with that, he seeks to take his guidance from God and, above all, directly, in prayer. In accord with that also, he reads and glosses official documents, such as the church constitution. Finally, there is the prophetic principle under which the inspiration by the Holy Spirit and the angels prevails among the prophets.

If negotiable much of the time, in the crisis these principles become the contradictory priorities over which people fight, passionately. It is not my view that the principles are held as absolutes. On the contrary, even during the crisis, extreme advocates of one principle make some allowances for others, while fighting for their own principle to be dominant, or at least highly valued in mutual accommodation.

Among the Apostolics in crisis, there is also tactical action for advantage. One tactic is to lend Jacob the guise of Esau, to use a favorite biblical example of the archbishop. To illustrate, in his new Conollius church, Boitshepelo makes one prophet, Andrew, his executive committee chairman, and he is confident that the prophet is his ally in principle as well as practice for keeping the executive committee subordinate to the church hierarchy. It is a tactic the old archbishop also used in Eloyi, until forced to concede to elected representation.

The bishop's predicament is pressing in the crisis. He finds himself opposed on two fronts. On one is the archbishop in his assertion of patrimonialism and leading others of those most prominent in the hierarchy to undermine the bishop's authority. Making much of constitutionalism on the other front are the executive committees, both for the branch and the church as a whole, led by their chairmen, including the former chairman who is still suing the archbishop as well as the bishop, in the High Court, for abuse of office in breach of the church constitution. In response, the bishop's tactic is strongly co-optive, most importantly on the remaining church front, apart from his own pastoral front. The bishop turns to the prophets for a united front, and he co-opts them even further by giving them appointments, such as that of a deacon and the executive committee chairmanship. He also promotes his loyal pastor-general to being a bishop, but when he apparently tries his tactic on executive committee members, some rebuff him, insisting that their loyalty to their church is not in trade for office, or anything else.

ESCALATING FAMILY QUARRELS AND PUBLICITY

The family quarrels from generation to generation have shaken the hierarchy, intensely and with more and more publicity. To document this from the viewpoints of different participants, I quote at length first from a newspaper report and then from the bishop and the archbishop, themselves. On this basis, I then open out the issues of charismatic spirituality, religious authority, organizational innovation, and litigation in the power struggles.

Under the heading "Eloyi Church Leaders in Bitter Row" and in an article by Ditiro Motlhabane, the *Midweek Sun* reports:

> Eloyi Christian Church leadership is embroiled in a bitter war of words, which has threatened to drive a wedge between the general membership. Following months of internal bickering, with strong worded letters flying back and forth between the leadership, the executive committee of Eloyi has been summoned to a meeting at the Ministry of Labour and Home Affairs on Friday (October 12) by the acting Director of the Department of Civil and National Registration, Mabuse Pule.
>
> Secretary General of the Eloyi, Botho Ragele Thibile, invited Boitsepelo to the central committee Aug 25th at Tsetsebjwe 'to address some situations which require immediate attention'.
>
> 'In accord with your position (*maemo a gago*) we request that you attend the meeting, because your advice is very important', wrote Thibile under the chairmanship of Joseph Jacob [Boitshepelo's half-brother].
>
> Bishop Boitshepelo replied spitting fire and dismissing the whole executive committee of the church. He ordered the committee to suspend the meeting until a special conference he was calling on September 1, 2007 and to disband with immediate effect.
>
> He told Thibile that he does not have the powers to summon him to a meeting because in his view such powers only rested with one Kekwaletswe. Boitshephelo in his letter accuses Jakoba's sibling of neglecting the maintenance of the church only to appreciate his point late in the day.
>
> Sources inside the church allege that Boitshephelo has repeatedly snubbed attempts by the church leadership to call him to order and misinformed the Ministry about the goings on in the church. (*Midweek Sun*: October 10, 2007:1–3)

This extract reflects the media interest in coverage of Eloyi as a sensational subject of reader curiosity.

The following is part of the angry letter the bishop sent to his half-brother, Pastor Josefa, as the disputed head of the church's newly elected executive committee. This letter was read publicly to the Gaborone congregation:

> To Pastor Josefa Jakoba,
> First I send greetings to you, sir. I have received your letter. Now I am saying I am notifying you that I will not be able to come to that meeting you asked me to attend. The reason is that you are not the Chairman of Eloyi Church. The Chairman is Kekwaletswe, as shown in records at the registry in the Ministry of Home Affairs. I want to let you know that you are recklessly putting on the speed so that you will wind up butting against trees.
>
> The other thing is that meeting you called me to should stop instantly.
>
> You should also dissolve what you claim to be the church committee, right away . . . There is to be no meeting until the conference I am calling for the first of September. Josef, you yourself are too young, and cannot manage the church business. Stop writing me letters. I want you here on September first at the church's special conference. Again, I want to inform you that I am the Bishop of Eloyi Church and beyond that, this church that you see all over the country everywhere, it was made by Bishop Boitshepelo. All the pastors and prophets you see were installed by Boitshepelo. I would be wrong to attend a meeting not called by the Mr. Kekaletswe's committee.
>
> The September conference will go ahead whether you come or not, in accord with the Church Constitution. From today onwards, I will shoulder the responsibility of the church until I enter the grave, regardless of who says what. I am tired of having to provide for the maintenance of Eloyi Church. When I speak saying things are getting spoiled, I am taken very lightly. Finally, you must realise that particularly among the sons of Jakoba I point the finger at you. You are among the first to get lost when troubles start.
>
> That is all, I am Boitshephelo Jakoba of the Church of Eloyi.

Shortly afterward and at the height of the crisis, the archbishop spoke out angrily, while I was filming him with my assistant, Njebe, and his wife, Martha:

> This little boy, my son Boitshepelo, has that little spirit of babble and turmoil, *bokebekebe*. Some days ago when I instructed him to stop his plans for a special conference, he refused and said he will deal with

> whoever doesn't come to the conference. This church is mine. I had only sent him to go and help people. Now he is using extortion to get his way. He tells himself that because there are a lot of church members in Gaborone, he is now boss. I see him as fighting with the church. He thinks he is a Little Head, a big shot. He doesn't know I can talk with the government people to arrest and detain him. I have never seen a child do what he likes in front of his parent. I don't know what this little boy thinks he is in front of me. I am told he lied to the Government that the [church's] general conference was not successful. But the hall was full to overflowing. He's been with Kekwaletswe as National Chairman [the former head of the executive committee]. Now their committee has been voted out. We've a new committee headed by my youngest son, Pastor Josefa [half-brother of Boitshepelo], who works in the far west. Recently when we phoned him, we found Boitshepelo had written him saying he doesn't know what my youngest son is in the church, and that my youngest son will butt against a tree. We don't know if he will bewitch him or do what. I scolded him recently and he snarled.

Defending his own reputation, at the time of the split, Boitsepelo explained to me and my assistant, Njebe, how offensive he found various accusations against him as part of a campaign to undermine not only his authority but even his branch of the church, "I was told right to my face that I had anointed street-kids, *bobashi,* as prophets in the church at Gaborone, and that this branch should be closed down and scattered."

The Bishop's Special Conference gave Bishop Boitshepelo a platform for telling his side of the disputes in the church. Sober in his dark suit, the bishop addressed the conference for nearly two hours in one stretch. He rehearsed the church quarrels in fine detail, at once very passionately and very deliberately—a much-practiced orator, his speech is usually slow; his sermons, patient and measured. At one point, he seemed overcome with emotion, when he told of the attacks on him from within his own family: his half-brothers' malicious gossip denying his ordination as a bishop. In the end, the conference response disappointed the bishop, and he decided to abandon Eloyi.

Bishop Boitshepelo's conference tested his support among the Apostolics. Many came who lived in Gaborone, but he failed to attract others widely, and he did not get strong backing from the church as a whole. Before holding his last Sunday service, Bishop Boitshepelo resigned. In an intensely moving sermon, with a parable from Jesus' last words to his apostles, the bishop urged his congregation to take heart, renew their faith,

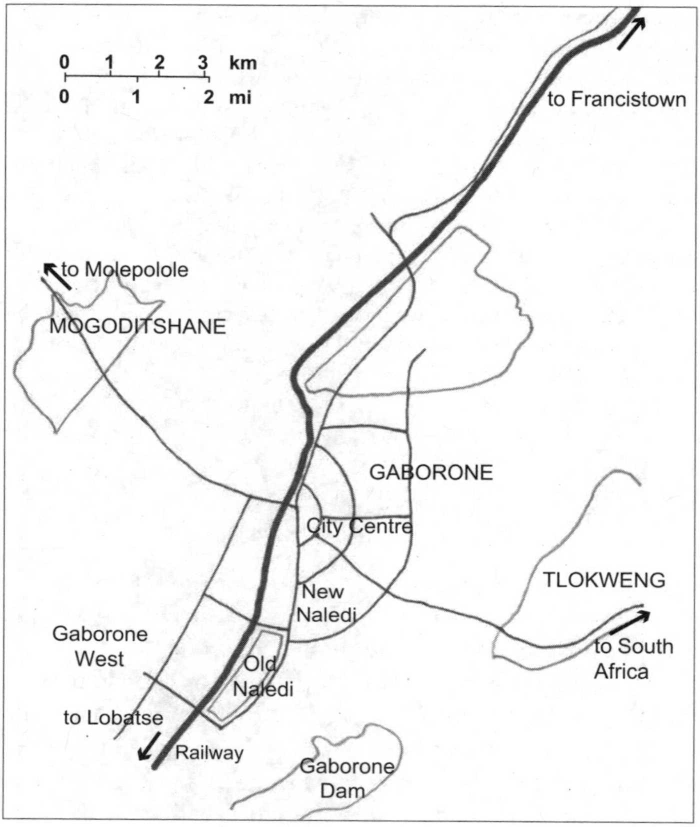

Map 2. Gaborone and environs (Courtesy of Frederick Klaits. Reprinted by permission.)

and not let the church's quarrels destroy this Gaborone branch itself. That might happen, if he were to remain, he feared, and in his sermon he promised to hand over everything, even his very robe, to the branch's new management committee.

Eventually, he wrote to his younger brother, Assistant Bishop Sekai, with a bare trace of the old fellowship between them:

> To Bishop Sekai,
> I greet you in the name of Jesus Christ. I am myself living well in the name of Jesus who loves us all. Being your elder brother, Boitshepelo, I am writing to say I see it is very important that I direct the following words to you, sir. I am resigning from your church of Eloyi. This will be from the first of October, from then on I will no longer be a

> member of Eloyi Church. . . . You may ask yourself what are the reasons. The reasons are that you indicated many times that I am nothing in the church. You and I, in the future, will only meet because we are born of one mother. I thank you.

VISIONS AND DEVASTATION: INTERPRETATIONS

Late in the bishop's last service, Prophet Joshua revealed an ominous vision of a threatening evil attack:

> I see an elephant standing, and its left tusk is broken, completely out of sight. The one on the other side is half broken. In the bishop's car, sea water needs to be put in. It is so, Mighty One of Life. Listening, I see a powerful wind stirring the car. I am astonished. There is a whirlwind in the car. A cyclone is at work. It is said we have to treat it with sea water. Hallelujah.

For the congregation, the bishop immediately gave the prophet and his vision public support by offering this interpretation:

> Hallelujah! Our people, we thank you. What has been said is by the Spirit. It is true. Truly, I dance to the Elephant totem. Seeing it standing like that, well, it is my totem that's being shown. I am of the Elephant. It is so. Amen. When it is seen with broken tusks, it means something has not gone well. Amen.

The bishop said nothing about his car. He commented on that only later in the light of subsequent events. His remarks, which he also elaborated later, primarily focused on his totem and the elephant; in his own words, after the schism:

> The elephant with one tusk missing, and the other only a half, well, that is my father Jakoba. Today he remains only with my brother. I Boitshepelo am not there.

Four days after the vision, Apostolics were bruised but escaped severe injury when a gale destroyed their building. It was a flimsy structure, originally meant to be temporary. Apostolics then built the new Conollius church elsewhere, completing it in a week. On another site, as I mention in Chapter 2, the Eloyi church was earlier razed to the ground, without warning, this first time by a bulldozer under a city council scheme to rid the area of unregistered buildings and settlements. For the church building and its contents, Eloyi has never received any compensation from the Gaborone Council, and it has been trying to raise enough funds to buy a plot of its own for a permanent building. The building materials were a donation or, in part, a loan from the Gaborone branch pastor-general, who is a rich building contractor and remains a loyal, trusted friend of Boitshepelo. The pastor-general himself became the bishop of the new Conollius church, and he rescued his building materials for it from the razed remains; he also provided sturdier, prefabricated walls.

The ironic twist—making the victim of destruction, its agent—is that when the Apostolics enter a yard for a destructive exorcism, one pastor usually warns that they are coming "like a council bull-dozer."

Apostolics responded in very different ways to the devastation of their church. Survivors, church servants who ran for their lives to escape the crashing roof and walls, told me, on the spot, about the scream by the landlady of the church's rented plot. The landlady was herself often accused of witchcraft by the young prophets, and she was heard to scream, when the gale hurled corrugated roof sheeting in her direction, "They are fighting among themselves. Now they want to kill me." One of the servants blamed the destruction on witchcraft by church leaders. Another thought that the bishop had already taken the holy ash away from the church, but if he had left it, it would have been spoiled. As for himself, he said,

> I am at home again. I am with the Lord, praying with the Lord. Everything is good. I am not lost. But others who do not keep themselves clean and pure, *itseka,* they have not kept the church sacred, *ga ba ilele kereke.*

Unshaken in his faith in the Lord and in the angel of the church, who attends to the good against the evil, this church servant blamed the destruction of the church on the failure to revere it and keep it sacred.

This is the question that worries Apostolics: Is the church still sacred after the destruction? And what about its contents, most importantly the holy water? I return to this question in Chapter 6, when I discuss prayer, intercession, and blessing.

Seeing the ruin with me soon after the gale, Prophet Joshua volunteered this: "Pillars of the church are fighting, Bishop Boitshepelo and Bishop Sekei. Their fighting brought down the church, it does not come as witchcraft from outside."

Later, in a rare sermon of his, given in a temporary tent for the new church of Conollius, Prophet Joshua publicly found solace in the Bible, after he had grieved that his faith in the church might be wasting away. His bond with the bishops, including their father, the archbishop, runs deeply from his own childhood, and he said he read in the Bible a revealing truth about love, for the church and for its father and his sons, despite the break between them:

> This church we are in, you should love it, and it will love you. I read John chapter 1, Romans verse 3. It says, 'Who is it that can love the Son and not love the Father?' Who is it among us who can do that? I read it, when my heart was grieving sorely, *pelo yame ele botlhoko thata.*

Bishop Boitshepelo himself takes the destruction to be a proof that he is in the right. He claims the moral high ground and is not troubled by the disaster. For, unlike others in the hierarchy, he is following God's guidance. The destruction is an omen for the bishop:

> *Ntlu ele ke sign ya gore kereke ya Eloyi e ka tlhantlhamoga ga ba ga sala gole lebala, ga ele gore dilo dingwe ga di dirwe sentle.* This house is a "sign" that Eloyi church can be shattered to pieces and be left a mere clearing, if some things are not done well.

The bishop's use of the word *lebala*—a clearing, a bare open space, a mere plain—conveys his understanding that as a house of God, a church must be a holy place built up by people to contain them and their services for God—such a holy place cannot be open, a mere clearing. With this understanding, the bishop found even more truth in Prophet Joshua's vision, and he elaborated it, after the fact of destruction.

"That wind of the vision," the bishop told me, "is the very wind that did take the church, for the church is the vehicle I have been driving." His gloss, as truth interpreted after the fact, is a rereading that nicely matches the present, if not revealed earlier. The bishop turned the car of the vision into a metaphor; it is a metaphor that he unpacked as his actual vehicle, the church that he drives.

The bishop went on to explain to me the error in the ways of his father and brother by contrast to his own:

> My brother and others [including his father] used the church on Wednesday, and preached about our disputes in my absence. But hardly a day then went by. Thursday the building was razed to the ground. To my knowledge, according to my guidance from heaven about that church —and I was told—disputes about the church should not be discussed within its walls but outside it. That's why I called the conference, but they stopped people from coming to it.

Listening to the bishop, his partner was herself concerned about the meaning of the destruction and asked him, "Heaven showed that situation before it happened, but never showed how to prevent it. Now I am asking, 'Did heaven saw that fit to happen?" In response, the bishop hedged and avoided too strong an answer: "My answer is that heaven can show a thing but not disclose the answer for it."

Later, at a service of his new church, Boitshepelo credited the young prophets with other visions and revelations about the vehicle he drives, his church:

> They said, "Slow down. Let your tires cool. Things are still mixed up behind you. This load we're carrying, well, we don't know it for what it really is [an allusion to witchcraft and demonic attack]." Amen.

The driving image speaks forcefully to the prophets, who love cars and speed, and, of course, the bishop as a driver by trade.

Not surprisingly, one politicized and morally justified reading of certain visions invites such readings of other visions, as the church leaders jockey for the moral high ground, where lies the Power they seek. Accordingly, enraged by his son Boitshepelo after the schism, the old archbishop used a vision against his son and his son's new church—it is a vision long said to have been a family secret, and thus all the more awesome and, in this case, damning. The archbishop revealed his vision first to intimates and then, apparently, in a very public sermon in Mahalapye town at a major conference. His vision let him know his son's rightful name, Otlhabane, He Has Fought, the name actually true to his son's character. Not holiness, as in Boitshepelo, Holy Place, but strife, Otlhabane, He Has Fought, is what his son brings the church.

The old archbishop blamed himself for ignoring this ominous vision. I was told he mistakenly desired to become himself named "Father of Holy Place," Rra Boitshepelo. The Tswana saying is *Ina lebe seromo*—"A name has its infected sore"; that is, a name is ominous, bearing the evil. Giving the true name would be a self-fulfilling prophecy in itself.

In the same sermon, the archbishop spelled the vision out further with a complaint about his son's appropriating the name Conollius. If for others it marks a return to the original way of the church, for the old archbishop it is another part of his son's fight for things that do not belong to him. Greed is the sin of his son, the archbishop declared. He accused him of the wrong of treating his father as if dead by already presuming to be *mojwa buswa,* the eater of the estate. This accusation, for Tswana, amounts to a father's curse.

The property at issue is the very land and original town headquarters of the Conollius church, and in turn of Eloyi, in Mahalapye town. The plot was registered in Boitshepelo's name at the Land Board early in the 1990s, for convenience at the time, or perhaps prudently on Boitshepelo's part in the light of his present needs. But his father has disputed the ownership, arguing that the plot was given decades earlier for the church by the subchief in the presence of witnesses; it was before the establishment of the Land Board. A tribunal is to hear the dispute, and it festers in rivalry between Eloyi and Conollius.

At the risk of an aside to my main argument about contested value, honor, and church goods, I want to comment very briefly on the significance of the original site. Mahalapye, the town where the archbishop took refuge when he had to flee religious persecution in his home village, is central for the country. At the Registry of Societies, Boitshepelo registered his Conollius Apostolic Church with its headquarters at Mahalapye, not at Gaborone, which remains merely a branch, as it were on the periphery. Boitshepelo could have chosen to recenter, making a break with the past for the sake of a holy place, a *Boitshepelo,* that would be his in name and his in its centrality in the city. Instead, he displaced his father in a move that spoke of restoration, a return to a true church, a highly moral act and not a takeover in greed.

THE SPLIT AND THE MORALITY OF MONEY

Immediately before the Apostolics split, the morality of money in the church becomes increasingly contentious in that accusations of greed began to fly thick and fast between opposed sides. Against the bishop, members of his branch's executive committee spread stories of his wrongful fee charges for treatment; for example, that he gets a police officer to pay 3,500 pula for treating the policeman's own body, 2,500 pula for his girlfriend's treatment, and 1,500 pula for the policeman's car. Committee members also spread the suspicion that the bishop is withholding or using certain church funds for his own purposes or gain, and that he intends to run off with Eloyi funds to a new church. On these grounds, the chairman got the local fundraisers and the treasurer to withhold from the bishop all subscriptions and concert funds immediately before the schism. The chairman gossiped, also, that the bishop was trying to draw people away from Eloyi by promising them offices in his new church; but people are refusing, because, they say, "We are Eloyi people, not Boitshepelo's people."

The bishop, on his side, objected with his own complaints about greed. He spoke bitterly about having to resist his father's pressure to hand over most of the branch funds. These are from a reserve raised to buy a city plot for 55,000 pula and there construct a new and permanent church building.

The Eloyi branch chairman let it be known that the bishop wanted to buy the plot in his own name. He could then take it with him to a new church; the chairman delayed the purchase to avoid that. The archbishop had his own priority: housing hundreds, if not thousands, of Apostolics on Passover at his village headquarters in an abandoned, vast warehouse of the Botswana Marketing Board. The Board now wants the church to pay its large debt for the warehouse, and the archbishop is demanding that the city branch, being well off, has to meet most of the debt, irrespective of his son's plans.

While more acute and extensive in the church crisis, such struggles over the morality of money among Apostolics had proceeded against a background of suspicion and quarrelling for at least a decade. What the crisis did was to bring the background to the fore, especially in the elaborate raking up of historic grievances in certain disputes involving the national and branch executive committees and the bishops. At least one of these is currently in litigation in the High Court. It came after an earlier High Court decision, restoring a national executive committee against the bishop's wishes. Oddly enough, a basic rule was never brought into the litigation: the constitution calls for election to the executive committee by secret ballot at the annual conference, but no secret ballot has ever been held, and committees somehow elect themselves and their officers, or are appointed by the bishops.

LITIGIOUSNESS, CHURCH, AND STATE

Later I say more about church litigiousness and the state. At this point, I simply want to stress the festering in the crisis of longstanding struggles over control of church funds and property. These struggles, like the other power struggles, are also moral, and they call into question the authority and honor of bishops.

It is striking that the assertions and, in turn, the counterassertions escalate in a reach for authority beyond the church's own. Each side lobbies to get backing from the state by turning to the government's Registry of Societies as if it were an authorized agency for dispute settlement and church regulation. Rather than shunning the state, the church embraces the state in confidence and confidentiality. The lobbying fits a broader, longstanding trend in relations between the state and civil society in Botswana. I want to comment on this general trend in order to bring the Eloyi example better into relief.

The general trend is highly litigious and politicized. It reaches all the way to the High Court, and it is a costly trend, in time, money, and effort, implicating state officials and lawyers in the affairs of nongovernmental organizations, from churches to unions to cultural or ethnic and leisure associations.

One might take this trend to be merely democracy in action, Botswana style. But to leave it at that, or even to suggest that the trend is the real democracy of everyday life by contrast to the appearance of democracy in elections and party politics, would be a mistake. There is of course a great debate about democracy in Botswana, and this debate is almost an industry in itself, for scholars, the media, and a broad public. But leaving that aside, I argue that for Apostolics and, indeed, inclusively in Botswana for spiritual or faith-healing churches, the need is to shift the focus of our analysis from democracy to democratization.

By democratization, I mean the process in which there is active intervention by officials, claiming state authority, who seek to re-create civil society and nongovernmental organizations in a democratic image of the officials' own. It is something of a mirror of officialdom, or rather what officials hope is their best practice—among other things, being publicly accountable, in accord with written rules, modern, efficient, and, above all, well documented. More specifically, for officials in the Registry of Societies, the campaign of democratization had got going by the early 1990s, the time of the modern, newly renamed Eloyi church, in full boom. In that period, the Registry formalized constitutions; it pressed for detailed annual reports, especially on funds and meetings; it demanded that church leaders have formal training and that they understand and uphold practices of good governance. Having reached a peak, with considerable success, more in church aims and rhetoric and less in other practice, the campaign has been somewhat on the retreat, though not completely, in 2007. This retreat is, in part, due to the fact that Registry officials, overreaching themselves beyond their remit in law, had come under expert attack from lawyers.[2] Eventually, the Registry had to admit it is meant to be an archive, open to the public; it has no authorized powers to settle disputes or intervene in the regulation of registered societies, although it agrees to offer mediation subject to the consent of the interested persons.

For our understanding of the escalating crisis in Eloyi, an even more specific review is useful. The stream of correspondence in the Registry has been considerable, a fact which is in itself significant. It is an indicator of the fierce commitment to constitutional legalism which Apostolics share with so many of their fellow citizens in Botswana. It is also a reflection of

Apostolics' belief that they can get justice by going to law; that their determination to fight publicly for their cause is right—they are not quietists who wait upon the Peace of the Lord. Not surprisingly, the correspondence resonates with the superabundance of suspicion and defamation in the moral and political arguments among the Apostolics. For example, in a letter of 8 July 2004 to the Registry, the head of the national executive committee complains,

> It is a disappointment to find that some documents sent to your office including returns are missing in the file and nobody was able to account for the whereabouts. I am afraid that there could be a deliberate tampering with the file to cause confusion as it was previously attempted by some people.

Unaware that the Registry documents are open to the general public, members of the executive committee suspected a breach of confidentiality; they complained that the bishop knew their deliberations because he had access to their confidential minutes. In fact, being wiser in the ways of public administration, he had simply gone to the Registry and openly filled in the request form, which the Registry then added to the numbered church documents: he exercised his right to consult the documents the executive committee was obliged to file.

So great and so finely detailed is the stream of correspondence that anything beyond a brief dip into it would drown my main argument. For this reason, my review is brief. The following rehearsal of Apostolic funding grievances is a representative extract from a letter of 8 November 2003 by the head of the executive committee. The author is a son of the archbishop's older brother and thus close enough to be within the historic range of likely rivals among relatives. He is one of the most influential, tireless critics of nepotism on the part of the archbishop himself and his family.

> Since 1994 annual subscription fees have been paid into the Church funds (assets), but to date the Church has neither any monies nor fixed assets. The annual subscription fees have since 1994 been collected and handed over to Jacob Keiphile (Archbishop) for his personal private use.
>
> No records of such monies have been kept. Other funds raised by the membership of the Church have gone missing and no proper investigations have been made to the effect. Failure to carry out the investigations was extenuated by the mere fact that [Archbishop] Jacob's sons (family) were involved in most cases. In addition to this one Isaac Jacob [a son of the archbishop] has been the chairperson of the youth committee for many years and has failed to either have his

> committee producing a financial statement or any report of their activities. On the other hand no monies have been handed to the Church treasurer for the period. The youth in our church hold concerts throughout the country and are therefore our sole source of income apart from collection of monies from members and annual subscription fees. At the conferences he has promised that he will in a short time make the financial statement and other relevant reports available, but never fulfilled his promise to the membership of the Church. This has also been brought to the attention of the church hierarchy and his father (Archishop) but no action has been taken over the years.
>
> Mostly the above matters are happening because Jacob Keiphile (Archbishop) believes that he personally owns the Church, and, further perceives that he can do what he finds suitable even if the others are not parties in agreement with his decision. (Registry of Societies 2003c)

In addition to trying to get the government to intervene for the sake of proper regulation of a registered Society, this head of the executive committee, like some of the others after him, tried to assert, as the governing rule, that the church is the not the church of the bishops but of all the Apostolics.

EXCLUSION, HUMILIATION, AND THE CONTESTING OF THE PROPHETIC DOMAIN

The Gaborone branch chairman insisted on this rule, immediately after the two churches began rebuilding. The church of Eloyi is not Jakobo's or his family's church; he is merely the founder of the church, he warned me, rather dramatically. His all-too-obvious intent was to teach me a lesson for appearing to take the side of the bishop and his prophets. The chairman stopped me from filming the rebuilding of Eloyi at its new site. Asked about future permission, he told me that he is a man of letters—he is a salaried clerk in Customs—and that he will write me one, which of course he never did. For the rest of that fieldwork, I accepted my exclusion from the Gaborone branch of Eloyi and very happily continued my filming with the welcoming Apostolics of Conollius. Martha, my assistant's wife, has remained a devout Apostolic in Eloyi, and I kept track of Eloyi in crisis through her and others in the new as well as the old church, and also through the government's Registry of Societies, its correspondence, and the minutes of church confrontations at the Registry.

My exclusion from the Gaborone branch was a minor, though typical, event in the larger moment of crisis. Faced with a searing schism, the old church withdrew into itself. There was a heightened sense of threat and attack in the war of good and evil. The felt need was to protect boundaries and boundedness. It was all the more urgent to deal with the enemy, once the unrecognized enemy within the church.

For some leading Apostolics, formerly of Eloyi now of Conollius, the crisis became full of bitter experience, when they suffered rejection, were accused of betrayal, and were degraded in humiliation. One prominent target was Prophet Joshua. He tried to attend Eloyi as well as Connollius, but his old church fellows stopped him from watching the measures they took to protect and bless the church, especially its four corners and boundaries; when he came to take part in the sacrifice to sanctify Eloyi's new church building and celebrate its completion, Prophet Joshua was rudely driven off, which offended him deeply, he told me.

Felt to be even more degrading was the treatment Eloyi Apostolics gave Saulo Solomon, the former pastor-general for Eloyi's eleven far-western branches in Maun. Saulo is something of a charismatic legend. Still a prophet, his reputation for exorcism is outstanding; he is much admired by prophets. He dares to risk his life and limb leaping onto roofs, despite having to convalesce from leg injuries suffered in a car crash. He was chairman of the national executive committee until ousted for being "incompetent"—hardly the reliable pastor but truly the erratic prophet who comes and goes according to inspiration from the Holy Spirit. He very rarely turned up for committee meetings on time, if at all, and the committee was stultified under his chairmanship. This left the bishops free to run the church unchecked, which I guess is why they wanted him to be the chairman.

When Saulo tried to come to that burnt offering, he, too, was rebuffed. Even more painfully, he was made to understand the strength of the fear in Eloyi that he would sabotage the sacrifice by making it unfit and not holy. Belittled, he was dismissed as a "Whose-Guest," that is, somebody or other's guest—someone of no account. Worse still, he was actually expelled physically from the church. Never had he been so badly treated, and he revealed his distress publicly and very dramatically immediately afterward, when he sought to be accepted in Conollius.

While he was seen in serious torment by the whole congregation, he whispered into the archbishop's ear, what amounted to a confession full of self-revelation. Nearly all of it was drowned out by the increasingly loud music—perhaps sung protectively by the congregation led by the prophets—and finding it beyond the sensitivity of the microphones on my camera, I brought very close my digital voice recorder, set for speech primarily. The end of my film *Holy Hustlers* shows that and the three of us, in rapt attention.

The confession was at his very first service in Conollius. Following the way of prophets, he began with a vision from his trance of a deeply puzzling journey. It was long and rambling; for my immediate interest, I give a relatively brief summary of his narrative and then quote his distressed cry for help, for a touch of the bishop's hand, for his prayer, and for song from all the Apostolics calling to heaven on his behalf.

In brief, what Saulo recalled is a very anxious vision. He told it with a good deal of uncertainty; he remarked repeatedly that he does not know what events mean, or where he really is even when he recognizes places oddly out of place, or what is the meaning of the speaking in tongues that he hears. He spoke from his trance of himself being amazed, as prophets usually do in expression of their wonder in the presence of the Word, but he conveyed that he is struck dumb and doesn't know if he can really talk of the *kgang,* the issue and matter of concern. "I don't know what the Word, *Lintswe,* wants to guide, *kaela,* me to." On the journey he and the pastor-general witness the bishop striking something to the ground hard enough to release snakes and a tarantula spider. Fearless, the bishop sings a favorite hymn to children who spring up elsewhere suddenly, "Ye who love Jesus come nearer." But fearful, Saulo and the pastor-general flee in his car, abandoning the bishop. Their car runs on rims, not properly on wheels, and takes them to a place where no one accepts them dressed in their robes. The bishop arrives with his robes dragged along, hanging out of the open back of his car. "I am a person who understands dreams from here to Mahalapye," Saulo said, "but I don't know what God was guiding me to."

Saulo went on to rehearse more of his dream, in part in anticipation of an exorcism later that day, and then poured forth, on the verge of tears,

> I am sick at heart. I can hardly think. When I entered here and looked at the bishop, my heart was broken. I went outside the church. I don't know why, but maybe you heard me say I want to hold the bishop by the hand. I don't know if I am allowed. I want to touch his hand. But when I look at him, my heart gets broken, and it is very painful. I don't know what is happening. I want you to put me in your prayer, you Eloyi people, I mean you Conollius people.
>
> I beg you to sing, when the bishop may come and pray over me so that the trouble in my heart will come out.

In response, the bishop prayed and laid hands on Saulo while the congregation sang, rejoicing in the Lord. In turn, Prophet Joshua offered an assuaging vision—that Saulo is immunized against poison; that scorpions are after him, but because he is immunized, he will well survive.

In the schism the very command of the prophetic domain is being contested, driven in opposite directions from one church to the other. In Conollius, with even stronger backing by Boitshepelo as archbishop, the prophets assert themselves publicly more than ever. They shout the Word out loud, in explicit euphoria at becoming what at a Sunday service they themselves call "a team," after the example of the Zebras, their much-admired national football team.

It is as if they are agilely passing a ball from one to the other, during a Conollius diagnosis. They take up loudly broadcasting a sufferer's troubles and, in turn, carry the séance forward, especially against resistance or doubtful responses from the sufferer. When one prophet flounders too much, or is felt to need support, another intervenes or even a supporting congregant may intervene, sometimes with a song at first, before one prophet or another resumes the revelation of the Word. Prophets sometimes admit their floundering by expressing spiritual distance and appealing for support to approach the angels; "Angels are far, we need to draw near."

Privately, after filming the impressive teamwork, I dared to ask one prophet if the prophets are ever rivals or jealous of one another. He replied that the church itself is too new to have rivalry, and anyway, now prophets do stand solidly together.

Being assertive in Conollius at church, prophets have become even more entrepreneurial and assertive in hustling outside it. Some increase their private sessions, and two hold them jointly, mainly for prosperous yet troubled women with good incomes, including civil servants in the upper middle-range. One prophet has also recently come to act as a banker for a few others. In cooperation, they fulfill a contract with a physiotherapist whose professional-looking office, with a welcoming secretary and well-appointed reception and treatment rooms, is in a smart part of the city; she sends them patients and they receive hers. Her fee she pays in a monthly check—for 1,900 Pula, the month I saw it—made out to the prophet, who deposits it, then cashes shares for the others who lack an account. The prophet gradually let me know the details and see the office, after first mentioning that several of the prophets are "doing errands" for the physiotherapist.

In Eloyi, by contrast, prophets have come to be more on the retreat. They try to assert themselves without the bishop's backing but face a bolder executive committee, elected by the rump congregation of the Gaborone branch. They are stopped from speaking out freely and publicly, in any one's hearing, when filled by the Holy Spirit at church. They can no longer publicly broadcast the Word about sufferers' troubles, about who is attacking them and how, or utter their prescriptions for public knowledge. Instead, prophets are forced to go back to whispering, once the main approved practice in the church. Their whispering is kept even more under control in that it has to be made to a pastor and in turn by him to the sufferer. The committee's demand, ostensibly on behalf of the congregation, is for confidentiality, and providing that, in effect, subordinates prophets more to the pastoral hierarchy in Eloyi.

The contesting of the prophetic domain raises issues for analysis that I consider further in Chapter 7. There I discuss diagnosis, prophetic utterance, and the making of uncanny yet uncertain, humanly fallible knowledge of the Word. This present chapter provides the context for that discussion by illuminating the personal ordeal in the Apostolic schism and the process of making it as a public moment in church history. Prophets find they cannot span both sides of the schism; they have to choose welcome on one side and on the other, rejection, even suspicion about their spirituality and charisma. In the escalating crisis, apart from their elaboration of exorcism, they hardly contribute to the organizational innovation among the Apostolics—that comes primarily from struggles within the church hierarchy. Their creativity is in church guidance through visions of occult threats, through warnings of enemies and of the ominous war of good and evil in their midst. But the crisis does put their command of their own prophetic domain at risk. In the old church, they are given less support from the hierarchy and the branch committee and they are more strongly subordinated to the old archbishop's authority. In the new church, with the backing of the new archbishop, and thus the hierarchy as a whole, prophets become even more assertive in their hustling—in public teamwork during services and in their private enterprises for personal profit. In the present chapter, I argue that the prophets' engagement in struggles for power has to be appreciated in at least two contexts of value and innovation. Having discussed the first, value in charisma and religious authority, in (*tlotlo*) honor and personal virtue, I turn in the next chapter to the second, innovation in iconoclasm and recast cosmology.

5. Schism, Innovation, and Continuity

INNOVATION, ORTHODOXY, AND COSMOLOGY

If much welcomed by the young prophets, Boitshepelo's innovations while still in Eloyi brought him into head on opposition with his father, the archbishop. Boitshepelo himself argues that he has had to innovate to suit city conditions, conditions not faced by his father in the countryside. He tells his church at a founding service:

> First, you will have to fill a form and write your feelings and then sign. You will bring a passport size photo that will be attached to the application form, marked with the church stamp, and filed. Every member will have their own file.

This innovation, deliberately modeled after a modern hospital and biomedical routines, introduces paperwork, including prescription forms and identity cards, and along with that certain other people-processing procedures. Boitshepelo innovates as, among other things, a modernizer and a church master builder.

Another innovation of the bishop's is animal sacrifice during the day as well as the night. It is against established church practice and, his father insists, against the Bible. But challenged by Boitshepelo, his father fails to cite chapter and verse for biblical authority. Prophets welcome this innovation, because it increases the supply of ash from burnt offerings and is sometimes more convenient for city dwellers, having an urgent need and too busy to spend the whole night at church.

To each of these innovations, the old archbishop objects righteously, and very strongly in the case of sacrifice. He acts passionately in defense of his spiritual authority as the archbishop and, with no less moral concern, as an aggrieved father faced by the denial of his paternal authority.

He encourages Apostolics to come to him for sacrifice at the village headquarters, rather than to his son in the city. When it comes to the paperwork and procedures, he conveys they go against the personal, immediate encounter with a suffering other in the presence of the Holy Spirit. I say more about—vicarious suffering, empathy, and bodily mimesis—in Chapter 8.

For their part, the prophets take on the innovations zealously. Although they still hold face-to-face séances during church services, in the presence of the whole congregation and for a few subjects at a time, the documentary and biomedical routine innovations allow them to handle large numbers of people who come merely for prescriptions. In certain sessions at church, the prophets streamline their final examinations and diagnosis. Given the patients' forms and pictures, they dictate to a secretary the prescriptions for treatment.

On church stationery, the prescription form has these headings:

> Patient's surname, First name, Date, I.D. [the number of the national identity card], Home village, Ward, Headman, Next of kin, Prescription, Consultant [the examining prophet], Signature, Secretary, Signature.

An example, which I discuss more fully in Chapter 8, is the first prescription given by Prophet Joshua for Martha, the wife of my assistant, Njebe:

1. She should bathe, while five red candles are lit around her. All her joints should be sealed with the image of a moon.
2. Her bed should be tied with a red cord and a cord of many colors, crossed.
3. She should be prayed over with long tapers and a red cord fastened around her body.
4. She should be bathed with boiled river water.
5. A bottle of the water should be kept for her pillow.
6. A many-colored cord should be tied around her loins, doubled.

"The image of the moon" in the prophet's prescription above is revealing. In Eloyi, Apostolics see the image within their church's orthodox cosmology. Overturning that in Conollius, they remove the image of the moon from its place below the image of the sun within a whole body of heavenly imagery, as I show in Chapter 2. There I unpack the heavenly imagery more fully, as a basis for my present discussion in which I appreciate iconoclasm in Conollius, and some of the reasons for that.

ICONOCLASM, AESTHETICS, AND SCHISMOGENESIS

It is remarkable and highly significant that the most visible change in Archbishop Boitshepelo's redesign of his new church is in the cosmic cosmology. Star and sun, as the past celestial images, shared with older Zionist and Apostolic churches, for purposes of charisma disappear from the Conollius vestments, as they do from the church and its material presence. Such imagery no longer serves in the transfiguration of Apostolics in Conollius. What Archbishop Boitshepelo keeps is his own identification with the gift of the moon, and he makes the moon a church-wide emblem for the ordinary members. There is no sun around any longer to indicate a rank higher than his own.

Instead, bars or stripes mark seniority and standing in the new church, somewhat the way they do in modern official uniforms, in the army or a hospital. Boitshepelo is eager for his church to be even more up-to-date and modern than Eloyi. He now has the mosaic of a cross centered inside the dance floor of his church, instead of the old one's red circle for the sun of Eloyi. In breaking out of Eloyi, the new archbishop has been determined to free his church not only of his father's authority but of his father's heavenly ranking of charisma. For certain prophets, it is a welcome end to invidious distinction. Cosmic categories no longer subordinate their charisma. In Gregory Bateson's terms, the schismogenesis starts from intense rivalry, but it proceeds toward increasing differentiation: schismogenesis that generates the schism exaggerates the distinction of one church from the other (Bateson 1958:285).

The introduction of new church robes for Conollius—the most visible exaggeration of difference—heightens the contrast to Eloyi dramatically. It displays the unmistakable change in church identity and perhaps says something otherwise unspoken. For Conollius, the new archbishop is inspired to choose robes for the most senior of his Apostolics that are rather bland and gray in background but edged with white and red stripes. On one side of his miter is a moon and on the other, a cross—still an undeniable index of his spiritual gifts. The new caps for the baptized who are ordinary members or servants bear the red emblem of the moon or the cross, matching his. Their gowns, like their caps, are a warm yellow with a tinge of orange and have copes, red with white edges. There is differentiation by seniority, but the old divide by gender is effaced—men and women of both ranks wear the same costume. One might say that the new archbishop manages to please somewhat opposed interests at once—on one side, that of the mothers of the church, who are now on the same

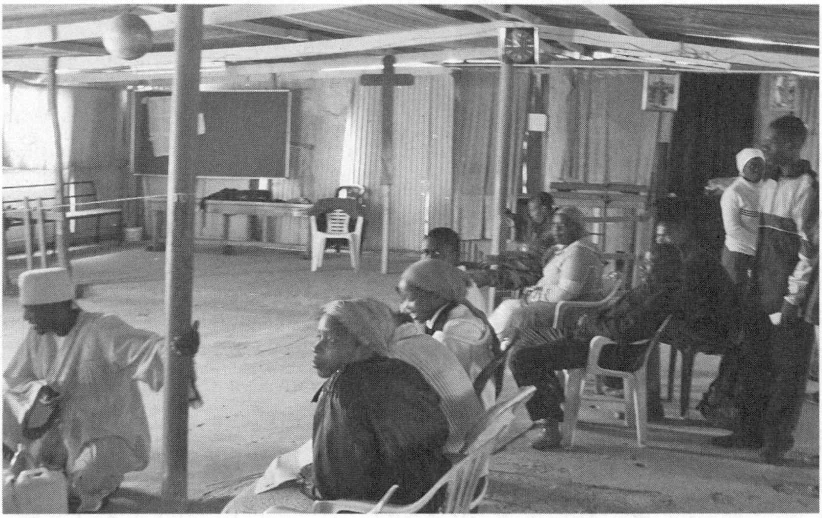

Figure 11. Servants with patients waiting for treatment.

senior footing as the men, and on the other side, the young men who as prophets are allowed even more prominence and command of their domain of prophecy. The new style is consistent with his penchant for the standard and the uniform: as exemplary in such order, he admires modern hospitals for standardized, uniform routines in the mass turnover of patients in the city.

Archbishop Boitshepelo could hardly have found a greater contrast in distinction from Eloyi's colorful richness. That was the brilliance so greatly favored by the prophets for morale and power boosting, for the glory of God and their own glorification, and, of course by me for the spectacular, cinematic force it brings in the camera. I must admit to being disappointed by the boring new robes; I much missed the old ones, though the church music and the vibrant whirl of dance on the church inner circle continued to be hypnotic. As one might expect in schismogenesis, there is virtually a principle of difference emerging in the schism: what is spectacular in Eloyi is somewhat toned down in Conollius. Another aesthetic is in the making.

I felt this toning down, also, in the illumination of the churches and even in their realisation as interior and holy spaces. Candles and candelabras at night give a wondrous light to Eloyi's Mogoditsane branch; they are colorful according to a color code that I discuss below. It is away from city-supplied electricity, and apart from evening concerts for fundraising, I never see bulbs lit by the church's costly generator.

Eloyi's interior, at the city branch church, is significantly elaborated as a holy and healing space, after the model of both a church (Apostolic and also Catholic or Anglican) and a hospital. Somewhat after the example of a Catholic or Anglican church, there is a sacristy, and Apostolics kneel when first approaching their plain cross (Protestant and not Catholic). Facing the congregation is the cross, above a lectern and a raised dais, with an alcove to which the bishop retires for prayer and contemplation. Near that alcove hang icons, portraits of Jesus and the archbishop, and somewhat to one side, the church's powerful crystal ball. On the bishop's right is a table with its bench for the prophets and sometimes also pastors and servants.

At the very center of the whole church, on the floor, is the holy circle for the prophets and others whirling in spiritual ascendance and transfiguration—once a brilliant red circle, now faded by the force of so many dancing feet. This holy circle is on the model of other holy circles, widely found in southern African Apostolic churches.

Behind the circle, and toward the back of the church, during weekday treatment sessions, there are very busy spaces filled with drums of water, bottles and basins, and lines of waiting patients. These treatment spaces are called "the dispensary," after a hospital pharmacy. While in use, the dispensary is cordoned off by white thread, in place of the red one usually around some of the area—to keep people from wandering about in it during treatment. Beyond it is another space, called "the theater," again after a hospital—the operating theater. It is a small chamber used for the incense bath, in privacy, when a person is nude, having the whole body vaporized and smoked.

For the protection of the whole church, outside on one very tall pole flies the yellow church flag, and on another emerges the cross drenched in red.

Eloyi's village headquarters is more simply a church, after the Apostolic model. It has none of the hospital-like spaces, no pharmacy, no dispensary, no theater. Around the sides of the church, in Gaborone as in the village headquarters, hang the significantly colored cloths and protective strings of wool, iconic for the wool and the veins of the Lamb, Jesus.

In contrast to this elaboration and richness in Eloyi, devoutly furnished over years, Conollius is bare, even Spartan. Its church still has a readymade look about it. Although its roof and timbers were built on the site, it is largely pre-fabricated, at least in its well-bolted walls (unlike Eloyi's rather flimsy corrugation), and was constructed very quickly,

Figure 12. Archbishop with Mothers of the Church at headquarters.

within a week. There is no lectern or dais; there are no hangings; and perhaps most striking, there are no candles—the illumination is by neon lights, again a leveling away of wonder, perhaps only temporarily, since Conollius has now moved back, after my fieldwork, to the old site, away from electricity.

That said, I must qualify my impressions, first about interior space and then about the means of lifting the spirit in both churches. Very important for both is the enclosure of holy space within a holy place. The church is a built space. It is not open or out in the wild away from where people live together. Its doors should usually be shut, and, ideally, Apostolics should not come and go freely during services, above all during a night-long vigil from 10.00 pm to about 4.00 am, around dawn. The church is meant to be stronger, more spiritual and with greater blessing, by containing holiness within its walls. The enclosure has some resonance with that in an older tradition among ritual healers in southern Africa, for example, among Xhosa who shut their healing in and close all openings, doors and windows, to "prevent evil from outside coming in" (Burhmann 1981:189).

At the height of the church crisis, a gale destroyed Eloyi's building. Later, I discuss the significance that has for the schism and how Apostolics

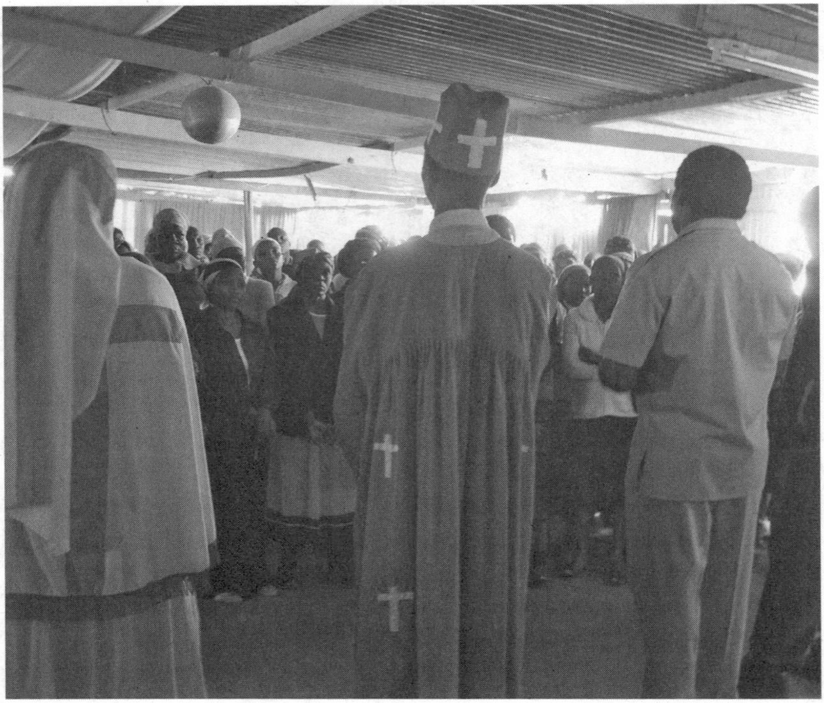

Figure 13. Bishop reporting at city church on his tour.

explain it, from different viewpoints, against the background of their shared understanding of holiness in its containment and enclosure.

What is not toned down in either church is the distinctive vibrance, the strength of the music. For in both churches, as among other Apostolics, the strong clapping, the rhythmic ringing of the hand-held bells, the urgent striking of the tambourines, the rising song in call and response—all that passionate outpouring so lifting of the body, swaying along with the spirit, is not mere music. As the bishop tells me, spirit is strong, so too must there be power and strength in response to meet spirit.

Musically strong, the Apostolics are being with spirit, in strength. Other churches like the Methodists and Catholics fail in prayer, because they don't clap hands and, with their hands, make bells and tambourines ring out to the Lord, the bishop explains to me. By contrast, even apart from the main services and in the almost daily treatment sessions, both Apostolic churches, Eloyi and Conollius, come alive with spiritual resonance, at the very least in the humming and prayers of church servants on their caring missions of healing and protection. Apostolics are disposed to be transfigured and with Spirit in the sound of their hands and their voices, in the very movement of their whole bodies. That shared disposition for the transfigured subject, in sound, body movement, and dress also, continues both to set Eloyi and Conollius apart from certain other Christian churches and to limit the Apostolics' schismogenesis.

CONTINUITY THROUGH SCHISM AND SCHISMOGENESIS

In all this reformation, through schism and schismogenesis, the Apostolics are not "making a complete break with the past," of course. Perhaps most important for prophets is the Apostolic continuity in regard to angels and the dead. Each prophet claims to have at least one angel with whom he usually speaks and reports in Tswana, although he may turn to others, according to the patients, and use their languages, Kalanga, Zulu, Ndebele, and so forth. Prophet Joshua tells me,

> Different as we are, our angels, too, are different. Some are heavy or powerful. Zulu, Ndebele, or Venda angels are very powerful, and when one of them speaks in you, he overpowers the hard condition in the patient before you.

Even in Conollius, prophets do sometimes whisper in confidence. But in both churches, when speaking in foreign tongues, prophets do not, as it were, speak in tongues; they do not babble or pour forth sounds, meaningless yet somehow all the more significant. In both churches, *ranolela* (to make clear, to translate) remains the avowed purpose of prophets telling the Word.

In both churches, at certain times, prophetic appeal to the Word of the angel can be authoritative for the whole congregation. For example, after my fieldwork, I was told over the phone, in 2009, that Prophet Joshua heard his angel's Word, unhappy with Conollius' newly built site and calling the Apostolics to return to the old Eloyi site, abandoned by both churches. Now back again, Apostolics in Conollius give this angel's Word as the spiritual reason for their return.

As for the dead, they weigh heavily in Conollius as in Eloyi, but not, in either church, as ancestral spirits, *badimo*. Traditionally, the ancestors as *badimo* are arbiters of obligation and subjects of offerings; their just anger has to be appeased by, among other things, a rite of blowing away wrath with water. If in a new Christianized form, the rite of aspersion persists. But in both the churches the dead are merely a dividual burden. The concern in their burdensome arrival is primarily pollution, significantly a traditional concern also. What worries the living is said sometimes to be that the dead were never baptized, and so remain restless ghosts. Or having been great witches in life, the dead fail to get into heaven and burden the living with troubles. With still others, the contact is so recent it has to be sprayed away. The means to rid the living of the burden of the dead, cleansing the pollution involved, is a *semama,* a usually green whisk.

The Apostolic rite Christianizes the Tswana traditional use of the *semama* against pollution from the dead, commonly at funerals. In the Christian version, the *semama* is made with green but sometimes white wool; it is an evergreen branch in the traditional rite. The replacement upholds an explicit principle of the Apostolics: rejection of plants and herbs for occult purposes. What their principle allows them to keep is the name of the means for the rite. After all, the old name still fits the purpose, as I spell out immediately. Taken for granted, and not in perceived need of reform, are the logic of transforming dividuality and certain associated notions of being dead or alive.

The dead are black. Being composite with them, permeated by contact, brings the living into blackness, *sefifi. Sefifi* is, as mentioned earlier, the occult condition of darkness and "bad luck." The fit condition of the living is greenness, *butalo*—quintessentially among Tswana the much-longed-for greenness of spring, "when the country comes alive." "Greenness" also means being wholehearted. The Christianized rite, like the traditional one it replaces, restores greenness, while making the dangerously dividual person a wholehearted, living individual. The Apostolic cultural selection along with significant rejection refreshes while it reforms, another instance of reformation being a remix of the old and the new.

For both churches, Apostolics agree on healing by color. Their agreement is significantly a matter of common sense about iconic resemblance, common sense that is shared by many people in Botswana and more widely in southern Africa—it is not distinctively Apostolic. For example, in iconic resemblance, conventionally green is verdant growth, and black, the dead. Green is used for a desired condition, and black is avoided, because it is for a rejected one; both the usage, for growth and fertility, and the avoidance, for its opposite in death and disease, are common in many Zionist and Apostolic churches (West 1975:177). The color is sought according to an iconic resemblance to a desired condition, and what is marked is the iconic difference from the alternative, the color for the opposite, rejected condition.

The aspect that is distinctively Christian, for Apostolics, is the spiritual cause. It is the spiritual cause, according to the church, that makes the color work upon an affliction or ill-being. In conversation, a prophet or another Apostolic will take that cause for granted and talk of a color working or say it "combats" something. For some patients, the color seems to be magical, the same as traditional charms and medicinal substances, despite church understandings, and the magic of color is a problematic issue, as is the magic of other things. Prophet Matthew's argument, given more fully at the start of Chapter 8, illustrates how problematic magic is.

In brief, there is a difference, due to the Word. There is ordinary water, a mere thing, and holy water, which is effective when "attacked" by the prophet's voice and stored in a holy place, Prophet Matthew argues, and even more to the point, finds he has to argue with an awkward patient, as I show more fully in Chapter 8.

For devout or faithful Apostolics, accordingly, it is not the color in itself that is effective in redress or healing. Each color must be used, Apostolics insist—and take much pious care to uphold ritually—with strong faith and wholehearted prayer. I infer, moreover, that the color is not intended to be an index, something in a causal relation. Instead, the intent, at least among the devout, is to have an icon for conveying desire to the Holy Spirit, perhaps most commonly the desire for protection from enemies who fabricate affliction and disability. It is conveyed in the silent language of things because, being icons, they are unmistakable in their simplicity. The power is in the Word and the Voice, not the thing.

In common and like many similar churches in southern Africa, the Apostolics use mainly a triad of green, white, and red, and to a lesser extent yellow as a variant for white and for red, brown, or orange. Their material is protective yarn of wool tied around the waist or other afflicted part, or candles, church cloths, and vestments.[1] The continuity is in accord with the enduring orientation toward personhood—dividual and individual—and it is grounded in cultural understandings and idioms widely accepted in Botswana and elsewhere in southern Africa: it thus cuts across the schism.

In this consensus across the churches the following is the color usage. Red, if bright, evokes the good, vital flow of blood, and, while healthy, it is very powerful and can be dangerous. The person who is *madi mabe*, bad blood, is evil. If the color is brown, it is not as good or powerful as bright red. White is milky and pure; it is specifically spiritual in being iconic of the robes in other churches, and it invests one with *nonofo ya thapelo*, the capacity of prayer; hence, it brings "luck," blessings and protection, protection even from the other churches[2] Yellow is somewhat to white as brown is to red, but it is valued against bile. The final color in the triad, green, is the one I discuss above and about which Prophet Matthew says, "Green combats *bolwantsha,* all things that are not good." Having the colors mixed up, for example intertwined in yarn, at once manifests and, with prayer, eases the condition of being confused or muddled. A main source of confusion, Apostolics insist, is going from one traditional diviner to another (or being attacked by someone who does that). Each diviner gives "medicines," *miti,* herbs and other substances, which get mixed up, mixing the person up. Bringing the colors together around the person, with a prayer, counteracts the occult confusion, reconstituting it as a holy Christian combination blessed by an Apostolic, such as a bishop or even a servant, in a state of holiness.

In this and the previous chapter I have traced how the escalation of the crisis leads to a schism in the church. I convey the tone of the power struggles, their felt qualities in rather painful experience and dissonance, and I also show what are the continuities and discontinuities that define or redefine church cosmology through the schism. My account has documented its making as a highly public event. I locate the schism in a certain context of state intervention, because even government bureaucrats get involved, and their aims and participation have to be appreciated along with those of the charismatics. Despite the schism and schismogenesis, however, the sustained cross-church consensus is considerable, and I return to this in the following chapters, when I discuss prophetic utterance in diagnosis, in the giving of prescriptions, and in the revelations during services.

CHRISTIAN REFORMATION, MORAL PASSION, AND VICARIOUS EXPERIENCE

Applying a processual view of reformation illuminates the repeated schisms so strikingly endemic among Apostolic churches. It is hardly novel to say that schism in the churches comes with struggles for power. But power struggles take many forms, some deeply grounded in spiritual or moral concerns. In some, for the Apostolics themselves, power is subsumed by Power, the Power of God. We have to ask, across generations, what is the power for or against and about?

More specifically for church schism, with regard to Christian or other local understandings of virtues such as purity, dignity, honor, and respect, we have to ask, How does moral passion enter or alter the power struggles? And how do the power struggles relate to iconoclasm and religious innovation in cosmology? Furthermore, given that Christian faith is itself contestable and often highly vulnerable, especially in Apostolics' own perceptions of the lapse in faith, how and in what forms does it survive schism?

My own responses to these questions owe much to Frederick Klaits' deeply considered study of a shebeen queen (bar owner) turned prophet in Botswana's capital city (Klaits 2010). In the same city, Apostolic holy hustling is an endeavor of unemployed, urban, and masculine youth. I have continually found it good to think with Klaits' ethnography of something remarkably different and yet profoundly related in Christian practice among the urban poor. For the context in political economy, which I do not address in this book,[3] I refer the reader to Klaits' study, which gives fresh insight into change among the urban poor in domesticity, kinship, sexuality, marriage, and housing activity. By way of acknowledgement, and to highlight certain salient implications of Klaits' ethnography, I want to comment on it at some length.

Death in a Church of Life reveals the force of mothering, careful intimacy, and moral emotion in the lives of members of a very small and intensely bonded Apostolic church, Baitshepi, during Botswana's time of AIDS. The church is based within Naledi, a high-density neighborhood and once a poor squatter settlement in Botswana's capital city. Perhaps uniquely among churches of the spirit, Baitshepi has former shebeen queens for its founders and bishop. "Indeed, from their point of view, the church may be a transformed shebeen [bar]" (Klaits 2010:155).

Klaits enables us to grasp how he came to understand, through repeated fieldwork over nearly a decade and a half, Baitshepi's distinctively maternal ethos and nurturing practice in Christian fellowship, "spiritual kinship," in the bishop's terms. His rapport with the bishop is open, strong, and sensitive, an affectionate bond across recognized difference. It is productive of Christian ethnography, uniquely, though not exclusively, focused upon the biography, conversion visions, and other religious experience and teachings of a shebeen queen turned Apostolic bishop.

Klaits shows a transformation of intersubjectivity: that the Baitshepi church recreates subjectivity and moral agency within recast relationships. In this Apostolic church, there is a striking contrast to what the church literature often foregrounds for Pentecostals. Baitshepi Apostolics create "reconfigurations of ancestry" "to remake relationships of blessing," rather than "make a break with the past," seek a rupture with kin, or efface ancestrality.

Instead, in accord with mothering and the bishop's movingly expressed inner vision of God housed in every one, members feel the need to strive for a caring sociality with others. They want to be freer of aggression, more compassionate, more consoling, more peaceful. No longer must they be tied to divination, to blaming others for witchcraft (and thus projecting hostility), and to attributing illness to elders' grievances, just anger, or ancestral wrath, *kgaba*, though, as the bishop put it, "Ancestors live in you" (Klaits 2010:193).

Baitshepi members must put their faith in redemptive hymn singing, prayer, and water, blessed to be holy and cleansing. They must not turn to substances, that is, the treatments trusted by other Apostolic churches, including Eloyi, that oppose traditional Tswana medicines by using variants as material substitutes.

On Baitshepi's horizon is love, as shown in conversations, among other things, about "promiscuity" and sexuality and through the church's resonantly translated hymns and sermons. The bishop says that love is a seed planted by the Word within the person. But never in easy reach—and the fear of jealousy and resentment is great in the church—love must be realized in conscious, deliberate memory work. Love calls for the spoken, caring, and faithful word, no less than the mere deed, so this lucid ethnography shows with a remarkable wealth of fine observation at funerals, church services, and in everyday, casual encounters.

Through close textual and historical sociolinguistic analysis, Klaits unpacks basic terms of relatedness in Tswana semantics—in actual usage—above all, for the changing social realities of faith, sentiment, and personal agency. I follow his approach in my own regard for the semantic fields in Apostolic prayer and prophecy. Similarly, I attend to his linguistic arguments on the comparative and theoretical importance of Christian Apostolic utterance in Botswana. Speaking the word of God is salient in what Klaits acutely conceptualizes as "religious valorizations of intersubjectivity" and "linguistic ethos."

This brings me to Klaits' leading contribution to the cross-cultural appreciation of empathy.[4] Given the importance of vicarious experience as divine in Christian passion, one might expect a high regard for empathy in the anthropology of Christianity and other Christian studies. Yet in this regard Klaits' contribution is exceptional, and not merely for Africa. His contribution on intersubjectivity speaks significantly also to the wider theoretical interest in the anthropology of the senses. Klaits accounts, with culturally specific understandings, for the moral passion with which Christians voice and take on the part of the socially significant other, often but not always a fellow church member, while they attend to suffering, bereavement, joy, or even ecstasy.

My own account of prophecy in Eloyi and Connolius shows that Apostolic prophets are specialists in the realization of compulsive mimesis during ritual. The ritual itself, compared to that of Baitshepi, makes the body more vicariously an instrument of the Voice—the interior of the other is mirrored, painfully and even with searing force by Spirit, in the body of the suffering prophet, so that the other, the patient, has to become conscious of interiority, sometimes in ways that the patient, in resistance, is unwilling or slow to accept. Sacred mimesis comes in this ritual from without; it is an imposed compulsion to undergo a spiritual passion; it is not, as in Baitshepi, simply wholeheartedness, which is the love from heart to heart, as it were, an intersubjectively desired communion between the interior of one person and that of another.[5] In Chapter 1, I showed how prophetic practice engages with both mimesis and also empathy that is revelatory, free of the other's misrecognition of self and situation.

Apostolic prophets have a spiritual mandate for subjection, for remaking the subjectivity of the other, powerfully, sometimes by bullying. Their practice confronts malevolence head-on, where the quietist commitment of Baitshepi favors avoidance. Where the former shebeen queen of Baitshepi leads in feminized *agape,* the love of the divine in humanity, the unemployed young men of Eloyi gloss Christianity in the light of their very different experience—they impose their charismatic understandings of the human condition according to masculine street smarts.

There is a rich literature on masculinity in Africa, and the vulnerability of young men in the present time of AIDS has now been insightfully documented and closely analyzed (Simpson 2009).[6] But the literature on African churches is only beginning to open out our understanding of the part young men, at once vulnerable and also assertive, now play in remaking Christianity. Intentionally or not, young urban men as charismatics rework in Christian practice a common and widely held stock of ideas about the invisible world and its fabrication, about the dead and the ancestors, about the body under occult attack, about the management of intersubjectivity, and about the material means to reach well-being.[7] Their Christian creativity raises the issues of syncretism and antisyncretism to which I return repeatedly throughout this book.

PART II

Wondrous Narration and Somatic Revelation in Prophecy

. . . . .

Prophets intercede with the Word on behalf of suffering and needy Apostolics through prayer, *thapelo,* diagnosis, *tlhatoba,* and prescription, *tshebetso.* In this second part of the book, I discuss their intercession primarily during church services and in private consultations at home. My analysis brings into relief distinct semantic fields—one in their rhetoric of prayer, another in diagnosis—and certain common yet variable forms of prayer and prescription. I also consider the movement in performance from one ritual mode or linguistic register to another.

The moving image is significant for prophets. Their visionary experience is cinematic. In this second part, I show how and in which respects they share that significance and cinematic experience with their patients. I highlight the birth of prophecy from divination, and their continuity in tandem with each other. My account also carries forward my argument about reprise and the long-term in the process of Christian reformation.

In Chapters 6, 7, and 8, although I document in some detail the streetwise content of prophetic counseling, my main interest is in dialogics and in rhetoric, in the prophets' use of persuasive and ritualized language. I illuminate its idioms of politeness, its force, its forms in dialogue, its narratives of fabrication, and the particular types of response it evokes from the Apostolics who approach the prophets in seeking God's help. In addition, I address subjection, and show how it is a linguistic accomplishment of the prophets as holy hustlers who exert leverage on their patients.

Diagnostic practice is epidemiological. Prophets make manifest, on their own bodies, the answers to such questions as "What is the course of a disease?" and "How has it spread across the body?" and "Has the body lost control of itself?" Toward the end of Chapter 8, I discuss such somatizing more fully, when I turn from my present interest, verbal language, to body language, to the somatic and empathy.

6. Personal Nearness and Sincerity in Prayer

FAITH IN ARGUMENT, IN A SEMANTIC FIELD, AND IN DOUBT

Prophet Matthew and a patient get into an argument when they come to the ruin of Eloyi's church to fill a prescription. It is the day after the gale brought the building down. Rubble is everywhere. Even a Bible lies in tatters. The destruction itself is awesome, I feel. The patient wants fresh water, blessed by prayer and with holy ash. Against that, the prophet insists that the church water in an open drum is still holy; that any water is still ordinary water until it is blessed, for it is the Word, evoked in the prophet's voice, which attacks and is effective:[1]

> Water is just ordinary water whether there's anything to put in it or not. But when I enter and attack it, *tlhasela,* with my word and voice, it will do the work it's meant to do fully, *ka botlalalo.* Do we understand each other, sir? The water and all the things in this church are very good, *disiame thata,* better than anything coming from outside.

The patient is uneasy and raises doubt. "Maybe the pastor-general has come already and poured it out," he suggests. "But you have faith, *tumelo,* in the water from here?" Yes," Prophet Matthew replies, with a mocking laugh. "And you yourself are the problem." "Let's go and draw fresh water," the patient suggests unsuccessfully.

Instead, Prophet Matthew demands the church water for himself. "Give me the water," he says. "Bring it here. I'll bathe with it." The patient becomes defensive, asking, "What do you mean?" "Give it to me," the prophet demands, and goes on to belittle the patient's faith. "I will take it for myself," he says. "I'll give you the one you want, because your faith is very little, *tumelo ya gago e potlana.* I can see you."

Rising to the provocation, the patient challenges the prophet, "Whose faith?" "Yours. You don't have faith," Prophet Matthew says dismissively. The patient gets even more defensive, and asks, "Faith?" "Yes," replies Prophet Matthew. "It's very great," the patient objects. Prophet Matthew denies this. "It's not there," he says. "Your faith is very little."

In the face of this damning judgment, the patient caves in and wants to prove his faith. "Yes," he says, "I will bathe with it." But he is too late, for Prophet Matthew is about to hustle and teach him a lesson: "No, you said I should take it for myself. You yourself want the clean one from the pump." The patient tries to get round Prophet Matthew by accepting that the waters are the same, "They are just the same. What's the difference?"

Prophet Matthew lays the law down, "The difference is this one is inside the church. It has spent the night in the church being blessed, *segofatseng,* as always. Do you follow me?" "Under destruction," the patient interjects. Again Prophet Matthew lays the law down, "This water is under *tshegofalo ya Morena,* the blessing of the Lord, no matter that the church has been destroyed. It is water inside the church, the place for *itshepileng,* becoming holy, and it has *itshepile,* become holy." The patient walks away from the ruin, laughing and admitting defeat by the prophet, "You know you are difficult, a bruiser." "I'm not," says Prophet Matthew triumphantly. "I want things that go by a procedure, *lenaneo,* which is straightforward, in a straight line, *ditlhamaletse.*" The patient makes his final riposte, on his way out, "They can't cope with you, even in the rough neighborhood of Naledi."

Prophet Matthew laughs at this banter over his reputation for being streetwise and himself goes off, but carrying a bottle of the holy water and confident in its effectiveness. Prophet Matthew's own view immediately after the destruction of the church is that it is temporary, and Eloyi will rise, rebuilt again.

Procedure, *lenaneo,* that is straightforward, in a straight line, *ditlhamaletse,* is the regulation the streetwise prophet wants to uphold: the procedure that goes straight, according to the way of the church and the Holy Spirit. Procedure, in my view, is a matter of widely shared and much-invoked common sense in Botswana, both in the city and in the village. The high degree of litigiousness, which I discuss in Chapter 4, is also linked to the considerable value put on upholding procedure: it is an agenda in itself, and, as a civic and not merely Christian virtue, it is continuous with justice and due process in law.

This conversation between prophet and patient pitches an argument over holy water against a background of many shared understandings.

These are entailed in a whole semantic field of virtuous terms. Included are:

the straight-forward, in a straight line, *ditlhamalalo*

being in harmony, *utwana*

truth, *bonnete*

trust, *tshepa,* especially trust in the Lord

tsepha Morena (being upright in the Lord)

rely on, *ikanya*

making holy, *itshephileng*

holiness, *boitshepelo*

the pure, sanctified, *itshepa*

blessing of the Lord, *tshegofalo ya Morena*

faith, *tumelo*

dignity, *seriti* (shade)

having heroic excellence, *senatla*

gravitas or weighty competence, *nonofo*

care, *pabalelo*

compassion (understanding suffering), *kutwelo bothoko*

pity, *tlhomoga pelo* (be moved with compassion, as in the removal of a thorn from the heart)

Such highly significant terms, within the wider virtuous field, inform the meaning and practice of prayer as pleading and intercession, *rapela,* among Apostolics.

Strikingly absent, and marking the limit of these terms, is sin, *dibe.* Prayer as intercession is free of the confession of sin. If, in such prayer, Apostolics seek mercy, bent, weak, and humble before the Almighty, they do not beg as sinners in moral torment (cf. Robbins 2004). Nor is self-examination about sin a precondition of their prayer. Apostolics, at least in public, make no explicit mention of the sinfulness of either the intercessor or the subject of intercession. They seek to be in a straight line, *ditlhamalalo,* to realign themselves with power, or rather Power, but their prayer does not demand that the person become a more self-conscious subject.

Spelling out at least a part of that virtuous field of terms in intercession enables us to appreciate better a ritual process—that is, not only Apostolic prayer itself but the move during a consultation or service from prayer to diagnosis. As I mention in the Introduction, entailed in diagnosis is a semantic field of slippery entrapment terms, and these are used by prophets in exposing the reality that the familiar world has a dangerously deceptive appearance. The virtuous language of prayer reaches above and beyond that field of slippery entrapment toward the exalted in upright excellence. Or, rather, it is only after the prophet engages and reengages with the straightforwardly virtuous that he can and does speak of the deceptive and the tricky.

Faith is one of the central terms in this virtuous semantic field, and it is faith that is held by Apostolics to be fundamental for effective prayer.[2] Yet, as the conversation between Prophet Matthew and his patient shows, it is faith that is also highly problematic. When seeking healing and well-being, an Apostolic is sure to claim to have great faith and to feel abused, even in spiritual or occult peril, if his faith is challenged. Is the Apostolic's faith great or small? Is it the full faith in the Word and the church, or something short of that, suffering from doubt, *pelaelo*, perplexed and perhaps misguided even, as in this argument, about holy water, as if it were a potion or like a traditional medicinal substance? Has the Apostolic strayed from the path of the Lord, turned from Jesus and lapsed from faith in the church to rely on traditional doctors and their medicinal substances? Such questions, which continually worry Apostolics, are as revealing of common Apostolic predicaments and existential concerns as are their specific answers in particular cases of prayer and intercession.

This is how Apostolics sing of their concern and their hope in faith:

Baetsa dibe ba bantsho.	Doers of sin are black.
Ba sekene ka tumelo.	They cannot enter in faith.
Batho kena teng, ka bosweu	There are people in white,
Ka tshepo le ka thapelo.	in trust and in prayer.
Se teng, sediba sa Moeng.	It is there, the well of Spirit.

Prophets tend to pray briefly, with a simple gesture. They cup their hands in the appeal of a supplicant before God, and they sometimes ask their patients to use the same posture. By contrast, the archbishop usually begins a diagnosis in a humble posture at his church altar by kneeling and prostrating himself before God and with his back to the Apostolics. Sometimes, he keeps his great staff in hand, and rises with its support. At first, the archbishop prays at some length, covered by his red cope and withdrawn from this world. Later, in the course of diagnosis, he often returns to prayer.

For example, before a diagnosis for my assistant's wife, Martha, he prays,

> God in Heaven, oh Father! You Powerful Savior, Lord of Excellence! For You are the Lord of Exceeding Power. Benevolent Overseer, God of Life, God of the Heavens, Powerful Star, Surpassing Excellence of the Heavens. All things are in Your Power. Save, Oh Father, for the Powerful Name. For all things are in Your Power.

What the archbishop recognizes above all in such prayer is the great might of God in heaven above and, at a distance below, the frailty of mankind, and drawing on a stock of praises for God's supreme capacity, he asks the God of Healing, Christ Son of God to save and be benevolent toward the supplicant Martha. Also assumed in the archbishop's prayer is Eloyi's cosmology of the heavens: its Powerful Star, Sun, and Moon that the Apostolics of Eloyi manifest in their vestments, according to their rank and spiritual gifts.

Immediately before this diagnosis, and following an earlier one by Prophet Joshua, Martha makes her burnt offering of a goat in the archbishop's presence at church headquarters. Martha kneels and puts the imprint of her hand on the goat's forehead, and the pastor-general prays:

> God, Our Father, God of the Gospel, God of Healing *Molemo*, Christ, Son of God, Rock that Falls and Rises again, your daughter is kneeling below you, at your chest, Overseer, to stamp this goat in your name, according to the verse read with your gospel, you the healer. Here she is, Sir, God of Compassion, *kutwelo bothoko*. Heart of Pity, *tlhomoga pelo* [*tlhomola*, pity as in pulling out a thorn], Christ, Son of God. Receive her hand in your Mighty Name, God our Savior, *Poloko*, Capable and Heroic Overseer, *Senatla Mookami*. Here she is, Sir, to cleanse all her overwhelming sicknesses in your name, Our Lord. The turmoils, *dikgoberego*, agitating her soul should be cast off, *diapolwe* (undressed), by means of the blood of this kid in your name Jehovah. May you undo the contact, *moamolole*, that has touched her. It comes from your power, Capable and Heroic Jehovah. I am raising it above (hanging the kid above, *pega*, hang up) in the hands of the healing angels, *matsogong*, to bring her nearer to the greatness of the heavens. Following the commandment we read, Christ Pillar of Life, your child has fled to you, our Savior. Have compassion, Capable and Heroic Savior, in your mighty name, Father. She raises it up in the altar today in your chosen name, God of the Heavens. At this time, let your hands reach her so that she may be saved in your name, our Savior Full of Compassion. Amen.

Even before the pastor-general finishes, the congregation breaks into this song:

In Life, in Life, Hallelujah, in Eternal Life, Hallelujah, you will live.

God is above in the heavens. Below is the supplicant. Dressed in dirt, she must *diapolwe,* be undressed by the sacrificial blood; in harmful contact that has to be undone, her very condition of turmoil makes her remote from God. She must be brought nearer, being cleansed and redressed. The intercessor on her behalf, the pastor-general, pleads in God's mighty name as Jehovah the Father and as Christ the Savior: may God reach out His hands to her, receive from the angels the offering in her hand as it rises up in smoke from the altar to heaven above, be compassionate, and save her from evil. Such sacrifice is, of course, not communion, which is reserved for the Church's annual Paseka. Instead, this sacrifice is a Christian version of exchange in ancestral sacrifice; it takes something bad away and gives something good in its stead: it brings individual salvation from Christ the Savior in a cleansing exchange of the disabled life for the one that is enabling, full of potential for birth. That said, I must stress that the prayer presents the intent of the sacrifice from the orthodox perspective of the praying pastor-general. The same sacrifice, from the perspective of someone, like Martha's husband, who watches without faith in any Christian church, is not so far removed from an ancestral sacrifice, if at all.

This prayer resonates with another prayer for Martha, offered by a prominent city pastor, this time for her husband, Njebe, also, during an exorcism at their yard. They are seated on their bed, their heads bowed in respect, and the city pastor prays over them, lifting his great staff in benediction:

> Benevolent God, you Great Savior, God of Glory, we present your people before you, father. Revive all their goods dressed in your glory of the Holy Spirit. Let your merciful compassion follow them, Father. You yourself, by your power, dress them in well-being and blessings, Father. Drive out evil from all of theirs, Father. Let all their goods be dressed by justice and righteousness. Pillar of heaven and earth, our Father of Redeeming Light, let your eternal glory descend from heaven. Father, we pray to you, shelter them under your protection. Let enemies and all evil, Father, be dispelled far away from them, *baba le bosula bothe, rra, di kganelwe kgakala le bone.* We beg you father, care for them, extend your good hand and hold them fast, *huparela,* under your wings. Warm them with goodness forever. You God of Jacob and Isaac, work with your capacities beyond all doubt, *belaelang.*

On behalf of Martha and Njebe as the supplicants who are suffering, the pastor appeals in virtuous terms for care, warm comfort, compassion, for benevolence, well-being and blessings, for shelter and protection, for justice and righteousness, for redress, and for evil and enemies to be dispelled. Let God's eternal glory descend from heaven to bestow these virtues upon the supplicants below on earth.

While similarly addressing God and Christ by drawing on the common stock of mighty and benevolent praises for divine capacities beyond doubt, each prophet, like the archbishop, the pastor-general, and the city pastor, makes his prayer a personal creation of his own. For example, before a private diagnosis at home (which I discuss more fully in the next chapter), Prophet Matthew prays, "Christ, Son of God, bring this person of yours nearer, and save her, King of Heaven, You who loves us to live." At the same time, in tandem with Prophet Matthew, Prophet Andrew prays, "Good Father, Lord of Heaven and the Son! Be compassionate, You who rule with the Sword of Spirit." During a church diagnosis, Prophet Joshua addresses God, "You, Overseer, Son of David, Great Pillar of Life, Mighty Pillar, Overseer of Life." Later at the same service, but separately during another diagnosis, Prophet Johannes prays, while vigorously laying hands on a sufferer, "God of the Israelites, Heroic Power of the Jews, King Full of Peace and Glory, Jerusalem the Mighty, Heroic Power of Heaven."

Prayer is transformative, for the congregation along with the prophets. For, as prayer is felt, seen, and heard, it is an experience of movement, away from others and nearer to God. Praying, bishops and prophets alike shut their eyes. They are seen to withdraw from the space around them; they are reaching into an interior space toward God and the angels in heaven above. It is a moment that calls for the greatest concentration, because a prophet is preparing to hear the Word of God and the angels.

A prophet may not always keep to the orthodox way of concentration. For example, at one such moment of transcendence in the first home consultation mentioned above, Prophets Matthew and Andrew bicker. Prophet Matthew insists willfully, against Prophet Andrew's irritated objections, on playing and glancing at a Gospel DVD, because, like Apostolic church music, it "really sends" him. But distraction, at that moment, is the last thing a prophet wants, Prophet Andrew unsuccessfully tries to make clear. From time to time, later during the diagnosis, his look betrays his continuing complaint: he likes Gospel, but not when hearing the Word. "Listen to the person, not the DVD," Prophet Matthew demands. His demand has force, because he insists upon the intersubjective listening *theetsa,* attending, that matters in diagnosis—the listening to the person by the prophets, by the person herself, and by the Holy Spirit, who, in turn, makes all listen truly.

Putting on a robe dresses the prophet in glory and, prophets hope also, in Power. They dress and redress, with that glorious and Powerful purpose in mind. But it is prayer that transforms the prophet in his own eyes and in those of his patients or congregation into an intercessor near and with God, now ready to go on to diagnosis. Listeners usually bow their heads and cup their hands in respect and in the hope of receiving good from God.

It is worth saying that after a church service including diagnosis, the one to give the final prayer, closing the service, is usually not a prophet but a pastor, preferably a pastor-general. His final prayer is much longer and more elaborate than a prophet's, and it resonates with a sermon, as shown by this last prayer given by the Gaborone pastor-general:

> In the name of the Father, in the name of the Son, in the name of the Glory, Lord. We are on the trot, we are disappearing from view, while others are watching. People are becoming anxious. It is like the time when people said to Moses, "When we were in Egypt, you spoke toughly to the Egyptians, saying The Lord to whom we pray is called Alpha and Omega. But today we are in the great desert, a treeless place. Moses, you are asked to explain to us now what is the name of the God you are praying to." Moses said only one thing. He said the God of my prayer is El Shadai, the God of our Bishop Boitshepelo, the Great Lion of the Creation, Lord of Care, Lord there is nothing we can say. You are the one who knows. Let your will be done. Let it not happen in evil. Let it be only good.
>
> Lord, King, Lord of Youth, Lord of the Holy Spirit, look over the four cardinal directions of the earth. Look at Eloyi, let them all hear the Word being shouted, saying Eloyi, forward with Power, Amandla (in Zulu, the rallying cry in South Africa). You are full of glory and respect. Lord who sits in the Great Parliament of Heaven.
>
> Lord of Jacob, Isaac, Father, we pray to you.

The pastor-general's prayer registers the moment of crisis. If the present be a time of plagues and suffering, as it was for the Israelites in the past, then God can be appealed to and, as in the past, let God's will be done for good: forward with Power.

At the conclusion of an exorcism at the bar of its popular owner, the shebeen queen, the pastor-general prays similarly. Again by reference to the Israelites in the desert, he compares the shebeen queen, now exorcised of her demon, to Hagar. Without recalling any sermon, the pastor-general appeals to the benevolence of Christ, who sacrifices his own life for others:

> Oh Mighty One, hear, oh natural Power from Heaven, Lord, El Shadai of Heaven, the one sitting in the great Parliament of Heaven, in the

> great dreadful passage. Master, we recall Hagar in the great desert when she danced the hymn of strangers on a journey. You benevolent one, who sacrifices his life for others, we are standing at the gate of the village of the great sunset. We call your name, you overseer, saying let your will be done, Lord, as it is in heaven. Lord, go with those who are going and remain with this house forever and ever, in the name of the King and in the name of the Holy Spirit. We have finished, Great Lion of the Universe. Amen.

Invoking the powerful names of the King, the Holy Spirit, and the Great Lion of the Universe, the pastor-general asks protection for the house being exorcised and all who come to and go from it.

In these examples, the terms of address invoke Power, while appealing to God's goodness, glory, peace, compassion, love, support for life—and a favorite allusion is to God's chosen people, the Israelites, and Jerusalem.

The appeal is for closeness to God in the future—the condition from which all good flows—according to the Biblical fulfillment of God's promise in the past. The primary aim is overcoming distance: the felt need is to bring Apostolics and God nearer.

In Chapter 1, I argue that it is through reformation that Apostolics confront the changing moral and metaphysical problems of alternating personhood. In the rest of this chapter, focusing on the importance of prayer in such reformation, I want to clarify certain shifts in Apostolic prayer in the light of two of their expressed and pressing concerns. The first is their concern for the rejection of ancestral prayer. A second concern is for the human frailty in lapse of faith by Apostolics.

There is a third concern, which I mention briefly to convey more of the Apostolics' existential anxiety in prayer. "Sometimes things happen and we pray for them to be solved," Bishop Boitshepelo told me, "and sometimes we don't pray for them but they come and happen." If Apostolics pray in hope, they also pray in uncertainty; their prayers sometimes fall short, but why they do remains beyond their understanding, they recognize, being known only to God. Of course, prophets, too, share in the existential anxiety that they have become distant from God. As I mention earlier, Prophet Joshua finds there are times when bearing the troubles of so many people overwhelms him and makes him feel far from God. It is then that he turns from his powerful red robe to his white one, to be re-empowered with the gift of prayer. In white, he feels himself "dressed in the glory of the Holy Spirit."

In my analysis, for the sake of clarity, I conceptualize shifts in Apostolic prayer by reference to a significant triad of intercession. It is the triad of intercession that constitutes prayer as an intersubjective act of care, *pabalelo*. I begin with ancestral prayer, then turn to the Apostolic in order to show how the triad of intercession shifts from the ancestral to the Christian version.

Included in the triad of intercession for ancestral prayer are, first, a troubled sufferer as the subject of intercession, second, a pleading agent as the intercessor, and third, the dead as the spiritual objects of the intercession. The living and the dead are perceived to be together in an order of descent, in which a living senior generation mediates with the dead for the juniors. It is taken for granted that the intercession calls for avowed amity and benevolence on the part of the intercessor, a senior relative, even when praying along with significant others, including nonrelatives living with the intercessor. Only with that avowed condition of benevolence, understood to be internally cool or white hearted in peace with the subject, can the intercessor's appeal to the dead succeed. It is usually a plea for the dead to go away, rest, and stop troubling the subject. This act of care has the intent of providing comfort and assuagement, easing the troubles of a "child," and it is usually accompanied by the blowing of water to disperse *kgaba*, the wrath of the dead, and to restore their protective shadow over the living (Werbner 1989:28–29).

The triad of Apostolic intercession, seen against ancestral intercession, is a counter-triad. Apostolic intercession is foregrounded against a background that so worries Apostolics that they sometimes convey an anxious concern in their prayer. "We do not pray to you like one without faith and trust in all the paths on which you go, oh Lord," sincerely avows Prophet Andrew. He expresses the same concern further: "I am not pleading with you like someone who is *tsietsang*, cheating and not in good faith." The anxiety he and other Apostolics share is about doubt, *belaelang*: the possibility that there are lapses in faith; that some Apostolics turn also, and alternatively, to those who cheat and trick, the traditional doctors; that because they are led astray from God's paths, some Apostolics deceive themselves as much as others by turning back, temporarily, to ancestral prayer, and then they seek prayer and cleansing by holy water in the church. There are Apostolics who try to maneuver their spirituality pragmatically. Apostolic prayer at once registers that as deception and counteracts it in demands for sincere, wholehearted and exclusive faith, for complete faith (*badumedi ba ba lefatsheng*, the faithful who are complete in faith), for faith beyond doubt, *belaelang*.

Apostolics expect empathy, *utlwa bothoko*, during prayer; that the intercessor feels the condition of the subject and has the spiritual and holy Power to make that condition known in the distant heavens above. It is with God and the angels that the Apostolic intercessor pleads. But the dead are not the object of prayer, although they are still burdensome. Instead of providing a protective shadow, the *seriti,* the essential shade and dignity of the dead, felt in substance, merely weighs down the living. From the dead, the living bear *sefifi,* the substantial burden of darkness, of "bad luck."

Apostolic intercession provides care for the troubled subject in *dikgoreba,* turmoil, in contact with dirt, and whose body is not at peace. The intercessor has the spiritual gift of prayer recognized by the church but need not be the subject's relative, and usually is not. Where subject and intercessor primarily belong together, Apostolics expect, is in the church. As Prophet Joshua conveys at the height of the church crisis, to find the church collapsing into disarray with fighting between its very "pillars," the bishops who are full brothers, is to feel one's faith leaving one and wasting away. Prayer, like faith, is not a matter for the individual alone. The church is the context for faith and prayer as intersubjective realities.

7. Diagnosis, Reconnaissance, and Fabrication

DIAGNOSTIC STORYTELLING AND THE APPEARANCE OF THE FAMILIAR

Diagnosis drives the movement in prayer onward. At a major service, prophets start to diagnose only after the congregation has warmed up, clapping and singing with great enthusiasm—their work throughout the diagnosis is to bring the angels nearer through the attractive, joyful vibrance of congregational music. For example, during a diagnosis, and obviously struggling to find his way, Prophet Joshua calls out for congregational support in song and dance, when he remarks, "Angels are far, we need to draw near." Some of the singing is antiphonal, with call and response, the intent being to bring everyone together and, as Prophet Joshua puts it, to raise "the morale." Even further, antiphonal singing invokes the coming of the Savior and the approach of God:

SOLO: Jesus is coming, hewhu hewu (loud humming).
CHORUS: We are going, going, going to see the King.
Going, going, He is coming.

Other churches, like the Catholics and the Methodists, fall short, the bishop tells me, because they fail to clap and they sing too softly, but Spirit is strong and powerful and demands strength and power in response, as in all church work.

During a diagnosis in church, the prophet often shouts, drowned out or interrupted by the joyful singing and vibrant clapping of the congregation. Even so, in some moments, the congregation sees or hears most, perhaps all, of a diagnosis, and a hush often comes when a prophet cries out a vision important for the whole church. Often during diagnosis, the prophet's speech comes in a torrent of words, and it is not usually civil. The harangue overwhelms the listener; ordinarily, it would be regarded as ill-mannered, totally unacceptable, especially in a youth addressing his elders, when respect calls for slow, measured, polite, and deferential speech.

To bracket and authorize their speech, prophets repeatedly say, "It is said," indicating that the speech is reported from the Holy Spirit. Every diagnosis is full of such citation idioms, which also serve as disclaimers—the prophet himself is not to be held responsible. Sometimes, a prophet will offer an apology for appearing overbearing. He will say that he is not quarrelling, but is driven to act and speak by the Holy Spirit. In using a disclaimer, a prophet follows the established convention—"It is said"—whereby diviners externalize responsibility; they attribute what is said to an occult authority, that of their divining lots.[1] The difference is that prophets Christianize this long-established convention for external responsibility by using it in the name of the Holy Spirit and other Holy Beings.

Inspiration by the Holy Spirit also licenses the prophets, in moments of diagnosis, to tell patients' fragmentary, often shocking life stories. "Story" is, indeed, the very English word Prophet Joshua uses for his narration. He finds it wearying and a burden to have to reason, *akanya,* through so many different stories for so many different people, he tells me. Prophets hear each others' stories, some of which have topics or objects that become favorites, running like fads through them. The elaboration of a story varies somewhat according to the occasion. Rarely does a prophet get the opportunity to tell the diagnostic story at as great a length during at a service as at a home consultation. Sometimes the story gets interrupted at a service and remains a mere introductory fragment for elaboration on another occasion, possibly in a special morning devoted to prescription. The home consultation provides the occasion for very full, detailed, and lengthy diagnostic storytelling, as I document later.

Most commonly, a prophet begins the diagnostic story by taking the patient through the enigma of arrival. Patient and prophet go together, as it were, on a visionary walk. The prophet reports he is told to go about and, *reetsa seemo,* listen to the situation. The prophet's narration revisits a site, usually a yard in a home village and sometimes, but more rarely, the patient's city yard. It is a site familiar to the patient and yet uncanny and occult for the prophet. He conveys that he sees somewhat darkly or partially at first; that he knows the site's location and landmarks—a ruined house, a corrugated roof, a vacant plot, a path, a river, a certain tree, a nest with odd eggs, a bedroom with a colorful mattress or pillow—but barely, just enough to ask the patient questions about what he sees. In this way, prophets establish a shared milieu as puzzling and yet strangely fabricated, and then they take the visionary walk forward, culminating in exposure: the familiar is a mere appearance.

What prophets say turns patients' everyday things, familiar places, and intimates into something else: enigmatic, hiding intrigue and occult aggression, and not to be trusted at face value. Prophets speak in shocking images of fire, acrid stink, bullets, whirlwinds, snakes, creepy crawlers, tool kits full of knives, Vaseline jars with black mixes, dolls, odd pillows, and mattresses, all of which are much worse and more dangerous than they appear to be, because they are, *dirisiwa,* fabricated maliciously and the malicious fabrication is hidden or occult. The prophetic imagery of malicious fabrication captures opaqueness; life is not transparent. The natural attitude is under attack by the extrasensory attitude.

To develop my argument in more detail, I give two cases of diagnosis in church by Prophet Joshua. The first case is presented very fully, and the second, more briefly, in an extract.

THE CASE OF THE FABRICATED CONTAINERS

The first diagnosis made by Prophet Joshua is for a couple of patients, middle-aged strangers from a village near the city. Immediately before the diagnosis, at a big and well-attended Sunday service, other prophets carried Prophet Joshua into the church after he sniffed out and grasped witchcraft bits on the church roof. He arrived comatose in trance. Still inwardly overcome, he sweated profusely, stood and swayed in recovery, tottering then leaning for support on the bishop, until he shouted wildly in awesome revelation: the doll, the doll. In the hearing of the whole congregation, Prophet Joshua announced this first fabricated object of his vision and asked God, then the husband in the couple of patients, about it, while delivering this interior monologue:

> Hallelujah! Our people, there's something like a doll, a teddy bear. Who is using it? Whose is it? There's a doll going with a bullet inside it. Who is using it, sir? Ohh.

The husband was frankly puzzled. "I don't know."

Prophet Joshua pictured the first fabricated object, the doll, in more detail and then went on to the second, a house being built, which the husband did recognize:

> It's a white teddy bear. A white doll. Who is using it? There's a hide and a thing fabricated of a white doll. There is a house being built and it's not completed. Where were you building it, our father?

"At home," the husband acknowledged. Prophet Joshua pursued the site. "At your yard?" he asked. "Yes," the husband agreed. On an agreed track, Prophet Joshua resumed, reporting the authority of the Voice; his interior monologue followed a whole set of possibly familiar yet fabricated objects and containers, a bullet inside the doll and a tool box, perhaps wood or tin:

> The Voice says, "We should stop at an unfinished house." And I ask if there's a doll inside. I see it going with a bullet in it. It is put inside it like this. There's a bullet inside the doll, when you look at it. It's inside a tool box. Is it made of wood or tin or what? What is it? What's it got in it and whose is it?

Still in agreement, the husband answered, "It's the trunk of my spanners." Prophet Joshua praised God, and reported more of the hidden, fabricated objects, including a hide also, which were going or working, secretly and dangerously:

> Hallelujah! Its going amazes me. It is said that we should go and listen inside it. There is another hide. It is going inside the tool box. Do we understand each other well?

Prophet Joshua then addressed the wife and husband in turn, about a nasty acrid stink perhaps from fire, the next fabricated thing, and then appealed for explanation by the Mighty God of the Heavens. "This situation first. Our mother, you get the smell and its fumes overwhelm you." Turning to the husband:

> Does she ever ask you what is stinking or burning? There's a smell that gets into her, time and again. Mighty God of the Heavens explains it so. Before it happened this way, the clothes got burned. Whose are they?"

The husband was unsure. "Do you say clothes?" he asked. "Yes, sir," Prophet Joshua replied. "Fire burst and nearly burnt the clothes. What caused it, mother?" She answered in recognition, "At my brother's place, there was a fire that nearly burnt clothes."

Still on track with the cooperative couple, Prophet Joshua again reported the higher authority, the Great King of Peace, for his interior monologue, and he went ahead to reveal the spread of disease or affliction all over the patients' sleeping bodies. Asleep, they were unaware of what was happening; their bodies were being taken over by the things going all over them, without their knowledge.

Getting this revelation and dealing with the fabricated objects through direct contact is something of a hard, wearisome struggle, Prophet Joshua told the Apostolics in a torrent of words:

> Yes, sir, the Great King of Peace says we should go and tell it like that. I don't know how it goes. For this concern has been laid on you. At night when you sleep, things go all over your body. Where you live, when I ask, it is said the bullet stayed in your pillow. I ask how come? It is said, "The things were coming together." It took me a long time, calling this bullet to come nearer to her from there, and it wore me down. When I ask how? It was said that I can't split up. It is said, "This bullet stays in the pillow." When I wrestled with it, I felt it burst in her body. When I asked, it was said, "It is now reaching her. Catch it before it gets into her body." The Great Doctor of Life went on saying that. Do you understand, our father?

The husband nodded silently, and Prophet Joshua hunted the next fabricated containers, a bed and a Vaseline jar: "The Great King of Life amazes me. First, we are seeking a bed with a red mattress. Where do you use it? Let me say it's red with a design of trees. Where do you use it?" The husband answered, "At our yard."

In accord with that, and under reported guidance from the Great Star of Life, Prophet Joshua hunted and questioned further, raising the need for exorcism, to rip open the mattress:

> Sir? Is it the one you are using? It's said, We should tear it apart. There's a Vaseline jar. Do you know Vaseline? It's a jar, this size. It's going inside the mattress. I ask the Great Star of Life, Oh Lord, why is it like this? It's said, "We should tear it apart, and look for the big concern that is like that." Do we understand each other well? In your bed it's colored cream, mother. Great King says we should tear it open underneath. I ask, "How come?" It is said, "Below the mattress base." I see a cream cover, and it's said we should tear it. I ask, "How?" It is said, "There's a closed knife that's moving." It's wrapped with a blue cloth sewn together. When I ask, if it's a church cloth, then it's said, "Yes." This concern was so told. Do we understand each other well? And truly, where do you come from, at home?

The husband replied, naming the nearby village, "We come from Mochudi." It is Prophet Joshua's childhood home, and their dialect is one he actually knows well. Prophet Joshua had in mind, he went on to reveal, the image of a house in Mochudi, which is amazing in its concealment and which has two persons buried in it:

> I was amazed. I asked the Peaceful Heavens of the Holy Ones. It is said that first we should go into a house which has a concrete step in front. Hallelujah! Who was buried in that house?

"Two young children," the patient answered. Visibly overcome, his face showing grief and suffering (watching this on a DVD player, he himself draws my attention to that, later), Prophet Joshua shouted, "Hallelujah," and he fainted away. The Apostolics sang out loudly, "It is so, my Lord. He said so, my Lord."

Pastors wrestled with Prophet Joshua, bearing him up in his trance until he recovered consciousness. Then he announced that the patients are the victims of deliberate occult aggression:

> The two of you have troubles created deliberately. It is said I should explain this to you. These things were made deliberately. The Voice of Peace spoke thus. Do we understand, our father?

The husband agreed silently. The diagnosis came to an abrupt end. Prophet Joshua rushed off to another patient at the back of the congregation. He told me later, upon watching my footage of his whole morning service, that he found himself overcome by the Holy Spirit calling him to another sufferer. The expectation was that the couple would return soon for a full prescription and to arrange for an exorcism.

This diagnosis is fairly limited as reconnaissance before exorcism. It is straightforward in that the prophet rehearses what he finds and discovers, *fitlhela,* from his journey in an occult hunt, and these findings mainly elicit acceptance from the patients. The patients are warned they need exorcism in their yard at home. Part of the reason for the brief limit is that short consultations are usual at a busy Sunday service, when a good number of patients seek to consult the prophets. Church members complain there is not enough time for them to be diagnosed, and even that too many strangers are being given preference in diagnosis. In response at a major church service, prophets are themselves under pressure, as in this case, to go more quickly from one patient to another. The diagnosis becomes well-focused on what prophets and many of the congregation alike look forward to expectantly: more exorcism, more destruction of fabrication.

THE CASE OF TROUBLE BREWING

Let me illustrate further by giving a very brief extract, necessarily out of context, from another diagnosis by Prophet Joshua in which his patient was a stranger, a man in late middle age, living in the city but with a village home in the countryside. Prophet Joshua began with his interior monologue:

> This hut was knocked down by a Tswana whirlwind, a whirlwind sent by witchcraft. I don't know if beer was being brewed inside it. It was taken by the wind on top. The Voice of Spirit goes on saying this. I am amazed and asked the King.

In direct dialogue, Prophet Joshua addressed the patient, "You are supposed to enter into an invited gathering. What is it?" The patient responded with a denial, "I don't know anything about it." Prophet Joshua wondered aloud about his vision and put his own questions:

> Is it a ritual cleaning of the shovels after a burial? This is supposed to come in the future? But it's not for joy. I don't know if it's the distribution of an estate after death. The Voice of Spirit says so. Or it's the laying of a tombstone, or what?

Prophet Joshua visualized a hut destroyed by the lightning of witchcraft. Perhaps the hut was a kitchen for brewing beer, but he admitted he did not yet know. His admission of ignorance is a shifter in the dialogue with the patient; it leads on to a question for the Holy Spirit but it also elicits a possible response from the patient. The questioning is circumstantial and oblique in that it is directed at the patient by way of at first asking the Holy Spirit, in the interior monologue. Prophet Joshua used a disclaimer, "the Voice of Spirit goes on saying this," which authorized the utterance as God's, not the prophet's. The prophet's own attitude was amazement in the presence of a wonder and in God's Presence, and he sought further understanding by asking the King, and in turn the patient, about the occasion for the beer brewing.

The patient was in denial. He was not hooked by the allusion to such a familiar occasion; that did not fit his concerns or a target he had in mind. Like most patients, he seemed stunned and kept his own voice low. Like most patients, also, whatever his doubts were, he was not very assertive or ready to answer a prophet's question, in turn, with his own questions. As is usual, he kept his eyes staring ahead, as if dazed or hypnotized. He followed the tendency of patients to keep on saying "Amen" and letting the prophet get on with the diagnosis.

Undisturbed by the patient's bewilderment, Prophet Joshua forged ahead. He went on wondering aloud, hunting from space to time on the trail of his vision by going from the setting, by a hut, to a possible moment for the occasion. Perhaps the time was in the future: hence the reason for the patient not knowing it. What the prophet did know was ominous for the patient. The patient was made aware that his ignorance of the future is dangerous, because it may well be a matter of death, not life. The prophet admitted he was yet to discover what the death implied—if it was a matter of the distribution of an estate or the raising of a tombstone.

In such diagnosis, revelation comes through imperfect knowledge, and it is about imperfect knowledge, as prophets recognize explicitly. It is a matter of fragments, of seeing flashes and catching fleeting images, not a whole vision at once, prophets say. They find themselves having to make a discovery with the patients' help to make sense of the given visionary bits. They become aware of having the experience of a flash forward, of significance lost at the beginning and found only on a return in conversation at the end of the diagnosis. They sometimes comment on that experience by expressing an admission of early error or misunderstanding and remarking that it has turned into enlightenment. They use a good deal of ex post facto reasoning, as they gloss initial fumblings or uncertain knowledge to make that part of the true revelation in the light of things that come out by the end of the séance.

In conversation over a lunch with Prophet Andrew and his girlfriend, I dared to raise the controversial question of such glossing. My opening came when Prophet Andrew rehearsed his view that women are not able to be prophets. He recalled our seeing a woman running amok like a sniffer dog, but not finding anything and having eventually to be restrained, during a recent exorcism. It was her imagination, he told me.

Exclaiming "imagination" myself, I told him that in my opinion maybe 80 percent of prophets' examination is guesswork. Most of the time, they get it wrong in telling a patient their prophecy during examination. He offered me the usual comeback, that the patients themselves don't know, because it has happened earlier, and patients forget. Still bold on the issue, I gave the example of the last week, when Prophet Andrew told a woman one wrong thing after another—first, her admitted case of dispossession of an inheritance was three years back; second, her father was a miner; third, and so on. Against that, she quietly corrected, her case had been earlier this year; her father was a policeman. I asked, "Wasn't that imagination?" He looked at me, looked at his girlfriend, gave what I call his "natural smile"—very broad, ear to ear—chuckled, and said no more. I perceived that, as he sees it, with a patronizing measure of good humor, what is still beyond me is the understanding of miracles. Nor do I truly hear the Word.

Prophetic knowledge comes and goes in diagnosis, and prophets say they cannot remember it later. As Prophet Joshua puts it, when we watch and discuss my footage of his diagnosis of a woman patient's suffering, "Spirit is instructing me the reasons I tell her, but afterwards I forget. I finish talking to her, and her film I've been seeing passes away."

Sometimes, the patient volunteers a dream for comment. For example, Martha told this dream, toward the end of a diagnosis by the archbishop:

> I'm bothered by a dream. I dream something's coming out of my mouth. I pull it out and it is long. Before I entered Eloyi church, I used to pull it out, but it was hard. It was fragmenting in bits. Since I entered the church, I dreamt it three times. And I was pulling it and it was coming out easily.

The archbishop gave Martha no detailed interpretation but conveyed that it all had to do with her being entered by the Holy Spirit, which she mistakenly took for an illness.[2]

Very often, there is a shift from the prophet to the patient in the burden of finding the significance, if any, of the visionary bits. The prophet admits he has a glimmer, seeing only partially. He uses expressions such as "I don't know if it's . . ." and "it amazes me," drawing the patient in with questions about something glimpsed. Even the rather muted contradiction of the prophet by the patient turns into a matter of the patient's own confusion, which the patient has to work through and thus get a sense of discovery in a quest for truth. There is, in James Fernandez's celebrated phrase, "edification by puzzlement" (1982:512–13).

Earlier, in Chapter 1, I suggest that prophets draw upon a certain semantic field during diagnosis when they *fitlhela* (discover, find out, expose) that the familiar world is a dangerously deceptive appearance. This is the semantic field of slippery entrapment terms, the one I mention earlier being *matemeka,* the precarious and unreliable. Prophets also speak of the following:

mathaithai, puzzling mazes

marara, inexplicable things

usa tlhaloganyo, beyond understanding (without a plan)

tlhaloganyo, a plan or scheme (a malicious one, in this usage, but also understanding and mind, in other usage)

moitseanape, occult expertise or the traditional occult expert (also, in earlier usage, a soothsayer or diviner)

maretswa, slippery tricks

meleko, ordeals and hurdles

mathakathakanya, mix-ups and entanglements
mafaratlhatlha, tangles
matswakabele, morass
malepa, intricate and puzzling knots
ema emisa, an impasse
matshwenyego, worries and problems,
ga sa itsagaleng, an unknowable way
seemo singwe, another situation (oddly different)
ka tsela ngwa, in an odd, perverse way
tsietsang, cheating each other, not in good faith
boretshwa, mischievous knowledge
rontsha, (*rontshiwa,* passive form) sabotage, maliciously cause something to be unfit for its purpose

Using these terms, prophets see themselves as having to contend with clever tricksters, above all the Tswana doctors who are *bofitlha,* fond of hiding things, who *dira,* fabricate and *tlhakanya,* cause things to be mixed together, and who *thebetsa,* block or frustrate others in their lives. Where such tricksters hide things, prophets tell the truth, by Holy revelation, they convey.

My impression is that while the archbishop also uses some of these terms, such as *matshenyego* and *meleko,* the semantic field as a whole is far more greatly elaborated among prophets in terms of slippery entrapment. As a whole, this semantic field resonates with the prophets' experiences as streetwise city youth, who are wary of tricksters. But it also resonates with awkward straddling, with patients' own unsettling predicaments in being urban villagers who keep one foot in the city and another in the countryside. There is a forceful art in diagnosis by which the prophets bring the semantics of entrapment to bear on the objects and dilemmas of everyday life. Using this art with leverage on their patients, the prophets create stories and elicit assent, or try to elicit it, from the perspective of the victim of tricky malice or ingratitude which, if suspected, is somewhat hidden or unrecognized.

In order to document and further analyze such artful, leveraged narration, I turn now to two cases of diagnosis held privately for women patients by two prophets, Andrew and Matthew, working together in Matthew's room. The contrasts between the two cases bring into relief some of the significant variation in diagnosis, according to the predicaments and responses of the patients.

THE VICTIM OF INGRATITUDE

My first case comes from a home séance held by Prophet Matthew and Prophet Andrew for an Apostolic widow in her mid-thirties. A member of Eloyi at a branch in Botswana's far west, she came to Prophet Andrew on her visit to the city, and at their request I brought them to Prophet Matthew's home in the Mogoditshane suburb. She was a junior civil servant, whose clerical job was in Maun, the western district capital at some distance from her home village.

My impression is that the prophets regarded her as somewhat naïve, short on street smarts, certainly not as wise in city ways as they are. As Prophet Matthew dressed himself, dancing to a Gospel DVD seen on the monitor, the patient was so taken by the prophet's robe and his seductively swinging, with-it style that she asked if she could wear his robe for a photograph; he agreed, patronizingly. The fact that she walked with a slight stiffness was also salient in the consultation.

Knowing who she was, a widow with a job away from home and a relatively good, if not big, salary, the prophets were aware of what might be her likely predicament, as a woman straddling town and country. For such straddlers, perhaps most problematic, at least in moral terms, is what I would call migration ingratitude.

Migration ingratitude arises in the perceived inequity—perceived from the migrants' view—between the straddling migrants and their significant others in their places of origin. As the straddlers perceive it, they give as much as possible, without stint, and yet the value of their giving is not appreciated; the recipients are not grateful. Women as straddlers commonly want to be known for generosity toward less prosperous kin, whom they support by sending remittances back to their home village. Usually, they also build a house there or, at least, get a plot ready for building. Straddling town and country puts them under certain moral and financial pressures, which the prophets regarded in this consultation. Migration ingratitude worried their patient. Counseling the victim of ingratitude in a streetwise way is part of the holy hustling in such diagnosis.

One reason why Prophet Andrew was cooperating with Prophet Matthew in the consultation is that Prophet Matthew was skilled in incision, the Tswana healer's practice to remove witchcraft substance and occult matter. It is a costly operation, which both prophets knew the patient could afford, which they were eager to perform for cash, and which, by the end of the consultation, they convinced her she needed.

The consultation room was small and crowded. The prophets sat on a bed; their patient, opposite them on a chair next to me, and being myself somewhat cramped, I filmed them with my camera almost in the doorway, but at enough of an angle to have them all in view. The prophets took turns, after praying simultaneously (see Chapter 6 for their prayers and disagreement over hearing and watching the Gospel performers on a DVD).

Prophet Andrew began the diagnosis, saying, "We should listen to each other closely. Agree with what you understand. Reject what you don't. I prayed hard and asked." He told the patient that mutual understanding between them is essential, so she had to take an active part—to agree or disagree according to her own understanding. She needed to know too that what he was about to tell her comes from his having prayed hard and asked the Holy Spirit about her condition, how it has spread. Then, after a brief interior monologue, he described this for her—pain on her left side, which goes numb—while showing it on his own body. If she listened and attended to herself, *itheetsa,* she would feel that pain, because grief is breaking her heart and has been doing so for at least the past five years, since her husband died.

The patient responded by saying that she knows she has an illness but can't really say where it is painful, though last night she didn't sleep well, and she had trouble lying down.

Prophet Andrew made entrapment their primary concern, from the start. He immediately announced, *boitseanape bomwe,* a certain matter of occult expertise, working inside her. It was to make her suffer until she entered her grave. This matter was later revealed by Prophet Matthew, during his turn in diagnosis, to be a human hair coiled inside her, specially fabricated and needing to be removed by incision.

First, after an exchange between Prophet Andrew and the patient—questions and answers about the time of her late husband's death—Prophet Andrew resumed the journey of his interior monologue and told what he sees of her natal village. The prophet fumbled, then recovered his way. He appeared to get the number of her siblings wrong. Corrected by the patient, he explained away his mistaking them for nine, instead of ten, "When I ask why I count you as nine, it is said those still alive lack mutual understanding, *kutlwano.*"

More circumstantial and local details were revealed as the prophet spelled out his interior monologue. He saw a horn wrapped in plastic; it was fabricated to serve a scheme, *tlhaloganyo,* for blocking the good things from her life. He saw her wanting to build on a plot that is still to be used, and she agreed with his vision, saying that she had just now started building on it. Having made headway, Prophet Andrew addressed a brief prayer, "Mighty Judge, Lord of Life," and let Prophet Matthew take over.

Prophet Matthew started with a short interior monologue on the Spirit's command for him to rush to her home village. Before he continued the monologue of his journey, he asked her about who she lives with at home: "It is said that I should leave you first and run to your home," he said. "Whose place at home are you staying at?" The patient replied, "At my elder sister's." Then Prophet Matthew went on:

> It is said that I should stop and listen to another situation, *seemo singwe* (a situation that is odd, somehow other than what it should be). If you listen to yourself, *itheetsa* (attend reflexively, pay attention close to yourself), you will feel you have a pain in your left side. You wonder, "Why do I have this numbness?" It is said that when you get hungry, this thing shows up. It is said I should look for another situation, in which you have been fed with a human hair. You had an affair with its owner and he is now dead.

Prophet Matthew showed her condition by gesturing on his own body:

> It is said that it is eating you up inside. You would cough and your coughing is going to be very high. You would have a severe pain in your chest. It would be as if you would spit blood. I go and ask the Mighty One, "What is this situation for?" It is said, "It is for the human hair. It is eating you and it has been there for some time." When you cough, you find that you have been made on the inside, *ona wena o diretswe ka teng* (you have something fabricated inside you—i.e., you are bewitched). You can have your body cleansed, but your things would still scatter all over the place, until you'd feel like crying. You'd be saying, "I don't know what I've done to whoever it is." You could end up giving up hope. Do you hear, my mother (polite form of address)? It is said that you have been worked upon inside you.

The patient listened silently and with a look of intense concentration and concern. Her reflection gave Prophet Matthew a moment's pause, letting Prophet Andrew take over. His next hunting was somewhat off the mark, from the patient's view. What he related and asked about—a girl, perhaps a close relative, dying oddly and leaving the patient bereaved—she denied, saying she knew nothing about that. The fumbling was awkward, as I see it, and Prophet Matthew soon came to the rescue, in the occult hunt, by better locating the scene and the agent of, as it were, the crime, that is, the witchcraft against the patient.

Prophet Matthew took her on the track in this way:

> It is said I should go along the road and count each yard until the seventh. In it is there a person who is a Tswana doctor? Even more, he is someone who mixes things up, *o tlhakantse*. He lives on the side of the road. How are you related?

The patient replied, "He is my brother." "By your brother, what do you mean?" Prophet Matthew asked. The patient answers, "My elder brother." Prophet Matthew then asked, "Is your elder brother a doctor?" "I hear people say that," the patient replied, avoiding a direct contradiction of the prophet, "but I have never seen him healing." Prophet Matthew continued, "He is fond of hiding things (an allusion to the penchant of doctors for witchcraft)." The patient stuck to what she herself knew as against what people say, "People say he is a doctor, but I have never seen him heal, *alafa*, not even once." She went on to match the prophet's monologue journey to the actual way to her home. The prophet's yard count, the last being seventh by the path, fitted her brother's yard, then her own yard; she said, "But by the way you speak, it is my elder brother's yard, then comes mine. The path you speak about is the one he stays near."

Prophet Matthew, having stirred her suspicion, now took care to deny any intent to meddle and drive brother and sister apart: "Me, I don't make people break with each other, Mama. Do you understand?" The patient agreed, "Yes." Prophet Matthew insisted, conclusively, "There is a certain situation (another situation) that is not right."

In the immediate pause, Prophet Andrew took his turn, on the track of the occult expertise. He drove the oddness of her situation home, while he reached her feeling of frustration, of having had to put others so much before herself that life is slow, passing her by. The patient had to realize that her situation was fabricated for her deliberately by the malicious cunning of an expert at witchcraft:

> There is *boitseanape*, occult expertise that was fabricated against you deliberately. Your life, it's as if it's a wheel that turns around but in you, it's a wheel that's not living, one that goes slow. You can be quick to help other people and slow to do it for yourself. That's the way it's been worked out against you. Now you are very quick to do other people's business, but fail to do your own. Do you realize that?

The patient agrees, "Yes."

Following Prophet Andrew's mutual understanding with the patient, Prophet Matthew then took the diagnosis forward by pursuing the trail of the fabrication, of the material means of the witchcraft. It was a black mixture in a Vaseline bottle (a favorite standby of Tswana doctors that they would say is a remedy, not as in the prophet's view, poison). Gesturing on his own body, Prophet Matthew imaged the patient's painful symptoms, shooting up and through her back:

> It's that there's a medicinal substance made in a Vaseline bottle and it's black. If you watch yourself well, you'll find when you wake up in the morning, your chest is shining. You've been smeared with that at night while sleeping. They make a cross on your back. When you wake up in the morning, you start being tired almost fainting, as if you could go on sleeping. It's as if you do not sleep well at night. You have a pain in your lower back. The pain starts stabbing you so much you feel it can shoot right through your back. You feel a lot of heartburn. On one side of your head you have a headache. On the other side, you feel so tired, it's as if you are about to have a stroke. Isn't that so Mama?

The patient answered, "Yes."

Given that agreement between the patient and Prophet Matthew, Prophet Andrew then took up the issues of treatment and exorcism in her yard, after questioning her about how she divides her time between Maun town and her village. He warned her she needs both prophets to come to her yard and exorcise; that her legs will so fail her that she will want a hospital massage. This so rings true—and a sharp eye can see her stiffness in movement—that the patient told of how her legs failed her at a funeral and she collapsed.

The diagnosis passed into the patient's moment for emotional release. It was her moment for heightened conviction: she was reaching some higher truth and insight about her life. Overwhelmed, the patient poured forth her feeling of amazed agreement; she was the victim of ingratitude:

> I am just amazed. You see when someone tells me that I do a lot of things for other people—it's true. I can't deny that. I was asking myself what caused it. The man you have been talking about isn't my mother's son, not of both my parents. He's my father's son. I ask myself, "After all the things I am doing for him and other people too, why should they do that to me?"

Prophet Andrew then advised this victim of ingratitude with a bit of streetwise understanding on help and getting a good return for generosity to others:

> You should give within limits, not too much. I don't want to say you should stop helping people. But it is causing you troubles. Some of your help goes to where they are not worth it. Do you get me?

Prophet Andrew gave her a long, searching, and significant look. Then the prophet addressed God, before urging his patient to be more realistic about the people around her. Otherwise, she would continue to be taken lightly and not given her due, when she needs it. Ingratitude is dangerous for the victim, who needs to be wised up. He clarified the diagnosis even more:

> Oh, Mighty Judge! The other concern that he (Prophet Matthew) explained is that there is charmed medicine you are being rubbed with every night. It's put you in a condition where even if you do a person good, they turn against you, *nyatsega*. People can manage to take you lightly in everything. You see? You yourself, if you have problems nobody will help you.

The patient challenged the prophet, "So how will you help me?" Prophet Andrew answered her challenge, "There are only two things. First, you have to get that thing (of *sejeso*, the oral poison) out of you." "Yes, I understand," the patient interrupted, "but what should I do now? About that thing you said that is rubbed on me during the night, do they still rub it on me while I'm here in Gaborone?" Prophet Andrew replied, "That thing, well, there's nowhere you can get away from it." "Is there anything you can make for me that I can take away?" the patient asked further. Prophet Andrew insisted, "No, there is nothing that can go and remove those things. It's only us, and we can go and take it out. First, here, we can take out the oral poison, *sejeso*."

The patient asked, "Who will take it out?" "This man will take it out," Prophet Andrew answered, referring to Prophet Matthew, who had left the room for a moment.

The patient was worried, asking, "Is it painful?" "No, it's not painful," Prophet Andrew claimed. "You only need a razor blade. And he does it. When it's open, he sees everything. Do you understand? He can take it out." The patient was worried and uncertain "You said it's what?" she asked. Prophet Andrew replied on behalf of Prophet Matthew, and gestured to show the coiled hair, "He said, 'It's human hair. It's coiled hair inside you.'" The patient tried to get it clearer, "What did he say it does?"

"What did he say it does?" Prophet Andrew turned the question back. Distressed and wound up, the patient herself rehearsed her painful symptoms, "Is it the one that makes me feel lazy? You know what it is? I am struck by shame. My head just aches and aches. Is it because of this hair?"

Prophet Andrew's answer focused even more on the witchcraft stuff of the hair coil, the medicinal substance, inserted with the occult expertise of a doctor, who mixes things up, maliciously, and makes people feel they are not blessed:

> It's the one that mixes many things together. Even the bad luck you tell people about is because of this hair. You can tell people that you are not blessed, *segofale,* with things you try to get in life.

The patient vented her feeling that she is being exploited, yet God knows she doesn't have to be forced to be generous:

> I get a surprising amount of money. I get serious money, but at the end of the day I don't know where my money goes. And to say that I give generously, even God knows I give to my family.

Prophet Andrew concentrated on rehearsing her needed treatment, "I mean that's so. There are two things: you can be helped at Maun and at your village. However, this oral poison of the hair, we can deal with it now." "Where," the patient asked, "will I get the blade?"

Having hooked the patient in their shared understanding of her situation, Prophet Andrew got to the issue of payment. "We can buy it," he explained, "but the problem is he doesn't like doing it for free. He fears doing it, because he says it kills. He only wants to do it for cash." The patient is startled, knowing church policy on free treatment. "What? She asks. "How does he do it?" Prophet Andrew put it bluntly, "Only for cash." The patient asked, "How much?"

Prophet Andrew made it clear that it is expensive, and that he himself doesn't like doing it, but he feels he is forced to help: "He does it for four hundred. Incising and smelling out, it's something I don't like. But there are other things that can force you to help a person." By the end of the diagnosis, it is agreed that the prophets will treat the patient the next day by incising to get at the witchcraft coil, and later they will go to the patient's home village.

Given the close regard for the patient's specific circumstances, this diagnosis is, in many respects, a typical example of doubled dialogue. Rich in the semantics of entrapment, it is effective and persuasive, for both prophet and patient. Understood as a journey, it is the finding of concealed hurdles, such as the failure of reciprocity, of good actually being requited by evil, through deception, and, in turn, the finding of the way past the hurdles. Finally, the move is toward hope with the promise of the right treatment, according to the Holy Spirit.

There is also, of course, a good deal of body language between patient and prophet, especially in the prophet's somatic presentation of the patient's illness and suffering. But that raises issues that I take up separately, in the next chapter.

My account of the diagnosis brings into relief the fumbling and the tacking back and forth, with more or less collusion between prophet and patient. With that in mind, I want to add a qualification to my remarks about the perceived importance of the senses of sight and sound for understanding in diagnosis. I left out smell, or rather the capacity for supersensory smell that prophets have as sniffer dogs. It is this capacity that prophets trust when they appear to others to be fumbling, or rather hunting here and there but not yet quite on the track—they are sniffing about in cinematic reconnaissance, as they do bodily when searching wildly through a yard during exorcism. Prophets are not put off, or driven to become cynical charlatans, simply because of failure along the way. Prayer on their behalf by a pastor in exorcism reveals their prevailing attitude:

> In the name of the Father, the Son and the Holy Spirit, we beseech you, Great Pillar of Heaven, be full of pity, you Pillar. Let us take out all things that were hidden.

Accepting human limits, prophets know they cannot succeed without faith. They have to trust in their appeal to God, because ultimately it is God who uncovers the hidden, fabricated objects of their occult hunt.

THE CASE OF THE MIXED-UP CIVIL SERVANT

A second home diagnosis brings out significant differences in the practice of prophecy when a prophet, such as Prophet Andrew, speaks to someone who is, in his view, smart, city-wise, and a woman of the world. Her sister, an Eloyi member, brought the patient to Prophet Andrew, who had never met her before. Like the junior civil servant in the first case, this patient, too, was recognizable, in the prophet's eyes, by her age, appearance and bearing, her speech and manner, even her expensive perfume: a woman about forty years old, a relatively senior civil servant, perhaps in charge of an office, self-assured with higher education and a house in the city, and a poised, attractive woman who has had many lovers. She is strikingly thin, smartly and expensively well-dressed. Noticing that she was reluctant to be filmed, that she hides her face from the camera, with her broad hat, I assured her that I will not show the footage publicly and that I will protect her identity.

Prophet Andrew greeted the patient, respectfully, "How are you doing, Mamma?" "I'm not well," the patient replied. "You see me, I'm not here well. I should be at the office." Prophet Andrew acknowledged this, "Yes, Mamma." She continued, "My things are all mixed up. I want you to fix them up for me."

After his opening prayer, which I give above, Prophet Andrew alerted the patient to the need for mutual understanding through careful listening to each other. Then he offered his interior monologue. In it he told an ATM (cash machine) story, speaking with first-hand knowledge, since he is one of the few prophets who keeps a bank account with a cash card. His story about the money being short at the ATM resonates with well-known experience in Gaborone and, most importantly, the likely experience of his patient, who is an elite and salaried single woman working in the city. Regarding her as a senior and responsible office worker, he spoke to her on a shared plane of modern knowledge in the city: he too knows about hospital scans, computers, and viruses, and, as it happens, he does have two computers at home, which give him trouble. On that shared plane, he drew a comparison. If she were not a person but a computer, he would say she herself needs to be "reprogrammed."

Introducing his story, he reported he is under guidance from the King of the Voice of Prophets "to do a scan" on the patient. It revealed her condition in its inner reality along with its outer appearance. He recounted her physical complaints and hardships—her loss of weight, her too quick, hard-throbbing heart, as manifestations of internal trouble—her grief at heart, her panic in anxiety. He reported that he asked on her behalf about this and was told—and he apologized in his report for having so rudely to invade her privacy—that he has to scan her wallet. Her panic is about money. Even on payday, she finds at the ATM that she is short of her cash. She fears someone is stealing from her. Having completed the story in his interior monologue, he asked the patient very politely if he was oppressing her, weighing her down with a false story. He wanted her to agree or disagree.

The following is Prophet Andrew's interior monologue in his own words, and the patient's immediate response:

> Let's listen to each other, our mother. It was said I should look at you and do a scan on you. You are a person who has been troubled in your heart. It is said I should explain it to you like that. And it has already taken from your body, losing weight. This body is really not yours. If you got on a scale to weigh yourself, you'd see that day after day you are losing weight. It is said I should explain this matter so, and not

> hide it. You heart throbs quickly, and when you touch it with your hand, it beats hard inside you. I pray hard and ask the King of the Voice of Prophets. It is said you have a long time now with this complaint about the hardships of your life. When I ask, "How come?" it is said first I should open out your wallet. Money does not stay with you. You should forgive me for speaking in this way. It is that when you work, the day you go to the ATM, and you want to take out your salary, the money is "short." You yourself get shocked. You say, I have been ruined, and someone is stealing in my yard. What's happening?
>
> Tell me, if I am saying something that doesn't exist. Do you understand me, Mother? Am I oppressing you by saying something false? Say if you agree, or disagree.

The patient began to answer, hesitantly, "It's recently I went to see what was happening in the bank." Prophet Andrew immediately interrupted her to make her realize what she is truly up against: serious occult entrapment and witchcraft. He went on assertively with his interior dialogue; and in response to his questions from that, about her family and bereavement, she gave brief answers:

> Do you understand me, mother? You are up against occult expertise, *boitseanape*. It is said to be working right in you. There are two deaths which involve you; they are close to you. One is a little child's death, the other a grown-up. How are you related?

The patient answered, "One is my father, and the other my brother."

Prophet Andrew continued:

> It is said first I should speak so. It is said they *amila*, touched, your feelings. But these two deaths have not happened well. One of these deaths got you into an impasse, *ema emisa*, trying to find out what killed the victim. Whose is it?

The patient replied, "It's my brother." The memory of the brother's death moved the patient, and sensitive to that, Prophet Andrew offered a disclaimer, "It is said I should explain the concern, *tlhaba* (affair), in this way. I shouldn't hide it. It is the truth." Touched by the prophet's words, the patient reflected on her father's death as well as her brother's and the family's efforts, though in vain, to find and deal with the right person to blame for the deaths, "Truly, even my father's death was just like that. But we stood up, *ra eme,* and did something."

Prophet Andrew pursued the story of her becoming the victim of much occult expertise that has put her out of tune with herself and the world—things are actually not going on well as usual:

> It is said first of all I should attend and listen to you very hard. It is said very great occult expertise is involved. It was worked against you. Do you understand what I am saying? It is said there's a great deal of expertise involved. It's working as we are talking, live. If you were not a person but a computer, I would say you need to be reprogrammed, yourself. You are out of tune. You are not in the program because you've got a virus. You should be cleaned up and reprogrammed. Do you understand me? Forgive me for speaking so.

The patient understood and acknowledged the truth in the prophet's words, "I understand you, very well."

If sure-footed so far, Prophet Andrew now fumbled, or temporarily appeared to do so. He reported that the patient's life, in entrapment terms, is *matemeka,* unstable and precarious. But he misses what the patient claimed was the simple truth about her own fidelity, at least during her marriage:

> It's that your things are not going well. It is said I should speak so about this concern. I should not hide it. When I ask, it is said your life is *matemeka,* unstable and precarious. Even a man, you are failing to tame one and stay well with him. Where is your man?

At this question, surprisingly, at least for the prophet, the patient laughed loudly and, apparently, with much pleasure, "I don't know where he is!" "Did he sneak away silently?" Prophet Andrew asked, somewhat awkwardly. "No," the patient insisted firmly, "I am the one who sent him off. He was already useless, *mosola,* and we were fighting. And I saw that . . ." Prophet Andrew interrupted apologetically, "You should forgive me for speaking so." "No, there's no fault," she said politely. Sticking to an understanding that the patient is a woman of lovers, Prophet Andrew appeared to stumble badly in misjudgment. "He should have been replaced," he said. "He's not the first. A lot of them have left you, if I can try to count them. But I don't want to go into that matter." "No," the patient firmly objected, proud of her marriage and protective of respect for her children and, indeed, for herself as a respectable woman. "For me he was the first, and the father of my children. We were legally married." Prophet Andrew then recovered his way, declaring, "I don't see you together." The patient cooperated and explained away the prophet's apparent error, "No, we are not together, because I told him that I am getting out of the holy marriage. I am no longer interested in it."

Off the hook, as it were, and given the mention of holy marriage, Prophet Andrew took the opportunity to pray piously—and he tends to have a sanctimonious manner, when reflecting on his next step, "Lord of Heaven,

Holy Spirit, Diligence in the Great Hands of the Holy Ones." Then he turned to the question of her dwelling place and its occult dangers, "Where do you live?" he asked. 'Block 5 (a city neighborhood), she responded. He asked further, "In your own house?" She nodded in agreement and he continued,

> If you listen well, in the belly of the night, there's a very loud knock on the door. You wake and sit up. When the event happens, you are shocked and open your eyes, looking straight at the door. Then you hear a very soft tapping on the window.

The patient asked, "Do you mean in the room, or what?" "I am saying there's a knock in the house where you sleep," Prophet Andrew said. "Do you mean in the bedroom or the whole house?" the patient persisted. The Prophet evaded her question; after all, there might be no window in the bedroom:

> A knock sounds, you could look for a person coming inside the house. There's a time it happens in the belly of the night. Do you understand? Between two and three. It's said I should "quote" that time. When you wake up and lift your head from the pillow, and you look straight into the door, then you hear a soft tap on the side of your window. Say no, if you never heard it.

Again, the prophet was off the mark and the patient did say, "I never heard it; I never noticed it."

Prophet Andrew finds his way, again, through prayer addressing God, "Elder who rules with the sword of Spirit." The prayer became a shifter from one plot line to another in the victim story. The prophet abandoned the trail of the pillow, door, and window, the moment of half-sleep in the night, and went for another fabricated object, her glasses. "You used to wear glasses?" he asked. "Or are you still using them?" "I am using them," she admitted.

With the hidden bit in mind, the eyes and the suffering behind the glasses, Prophet Andrew probed his way forward through interior dialogue about the patient's own pain,

> It was said first I should touch your eyes. It's said, Yes, don't you see that this person's eyes are already affected. It is said, I should explain it so. Even when you attend to your eyes, you feel that one eye is getting tired. It's aching.

Although still not right on the mark, the prophet got close enough for the patient to acknowledge the partial truth in his diagnosis of her physical symptoms. "It doesn't ache." She said. "But sometimes I see black, and some things are shaking. But it doesn't ache."

Prophet Andrew pursued more of the truth in his perception of her symptoms, "It's said, I should say you have been affected. Even the glasses you are using have been affected, because they don't correct your sight. Forgive me for speaking so." As he spoke, he stood up to model her suffering on his own hips, touching them in evident pain, "When I touch you on your hip, you have a pain that doesn't leave you alone. You could tell people that you should be massaged over your whole body, most of all on your hip." (Prophet Andrew is one of the prophets who cooperates with a physiotherapist in the treatment of patients.) "Yes, it troubles me," the patient confirmed.

Back to prayer, Prophet Andrew asked God for underlying reasons, recognized occult expertise, and asked the patient about another familiar object, her car. He thus opened another line of investigation, moving from one fabricated object to another, from her pillow, door, window, glasses to her car, still on the hunt for the means of hidden witchcraft.

Prophet Andrew reported and then asked, "I pray hard, and ask the King of the Voice of the Prophets, Why is it that there are some reasons for this? There's occult expertise applied there. Whose is the green car you are using?" The patient makes a minor correction, using "blue" in English, "There's a blue car." "Is it yours?" he asks. "Yes," she answers.

Accepting the patient's agreement to car ownership and ignoring the issue of the mistaken color, Prophet Andrew reported more of his interior dialogue. The moment had come for him to turn to the more shocking aspect of the victim's story:

> It's said I should myself look for it. What amazes me is I saw you going through the bush with this car. It is said your life could have been taken by this car. Do you hear what I say? Did you once have an accident with this car?

Rather than being shocked, the patient answered mildly about a minor accident, and not one involving her directly:

> It had an accident when I was at school. My children were using it. They'd gone to watch a movie. They say the wheel got loose, but they were driving slowly, leaving the filling station."

Recourse to prayer, but very briefly, again suited the prophet, who is not ready to abandon the car topic so easily. "The Mighty Judge," he prayed and then asked, "When you now go into this car, where is it?" "It is there," she answered. Prophet Andrew unpacked more of the car topic, rehearsing her experience of the car's oddity:

> When you enter this car, it makes you shake. It makes your heart full of dismay. You find that when you go with it, you feel like giving it to someone else to drive.

The patient agrees, "Yes, it is so." Prophet Andrew is himself a great lover of cars and proud of his chauffeur's skill in driving, but much to his regret he owns no car himself. Here he conveys his understanding of her feelings about the car she owns and apologizes for his apparent rudeness. "It doesn't make you yourself happy," he says, "and you will forgive me, our mother, for speaking in this way, but your troubling things are many. Where are your children?" "They are there [in her house]," she replies.

Prophet Andrew now raises the question of treatment. He is aware that Prophet Matthew has been coming and going impatiently, but so far not speaking in diagnosis, as if more than anything he wants to get on with a treatment, if it is paid for. Prophet Andrew asks, deferentially but conveying expected interest—he gave me the impression of a man about to close a financial deal—"We don't know whether you had only come for the diagnosis, or whether you also seek help." "Also help," she says.

In the expectation that this well-paid patient is going to pay and pay well, Prophet Matthew takes over. He suggests he has had to get a perspective on the patient from a distance—thus explaining his coming and going, and also his suspicion that the patient herself as well as her things can't be taken at face value. Perhaps she is hiding something, right inside her body. Another one of his patients calls him "a bruiser," tough enough to be hard to deal with in the roughest slum, even though he appears baby-faced. He was about to shock the patient and shake up her poised manner, and as he did so—conveying that even her preciously thin body could balloon round the belly and make her unfit for a nice, ready-made "size"—he used a great deal of strong body language, writhing in pain and gesturing around his own belly. Verbally, his reported threat—"your belly will swell"—became a relentless chant, battering her again and again and again, in the overpowering torrent of the prophet's words:

> To me, as this man was talking to you, it was said I should *lebelele*, inspect you, by first moving back a bit. I should look hard at you. I asked the Power of Heaven why it is said that I should look hard at you. It was said that in the past you swelled in your belly—it raised. I ask the Power of Heaven. It is said there is *seemo singwe*, another situation that is going on and is amazing here.

> Your belly raises. There is a pain that goes on staying inside your navel, and it is as if it would strike inside the pit of your stomach. I asked the Power of Heaven why this situation is going on as it is. It was said there is a situation of *sejeso*, oral poison. That was fed to you sometime ago. When you are resting, you feel scraped inside your belly. Sometimes you feel your belly twisting. When I follow it up, it is said your belly will swell, your belly will swell, your belly will swell, and you will never have a "size" (never be able to wear a ready-made dress cut to "size"). I go asking. It is said you have pains that arise in your belly. When they arise your joints start being tired. It is said you suffer from oral poison that eats you inside, and your liver, too, is getting spoiled. Something is completing its work. I go seeing your belly swelling and swelling, and it will always lack a "size".

Prophet Andrew reinforced Prophet Matthew's diagnosis and went on to ask about the patient's past treatment for a sexual disease:

> This concern, *kgang* (affair), he's been talking about has already affected you. Your very womb does not stay well. You yourself can see you have been affected by this concern. I don't know if I am oppressing you. Did you ever try to drink *monepenepe* (a species of acacia whose pods are used medicinally to treat venereal disease)?

The patient answers, "Yes." Prophet Andrew continued on her womb and oral poison, then he took her further on their home journey together by a river, and, eventually, he saw inside her for a revelation of her internal bleeding, its occult cause, and her mortal danger:

> When I ask, it is said that you arranged for your womb to be cleansed. It is said that I should tell you that you have oral poison, which is not letting you stay well. This is another concern, not just the womb. Yes, you can scrape the womb, and end up having your womb removed—and I don't know if it is the thing to be removed at the hospital. Listen to me, my mother, because it is not well.
>
> When I go and pray, and when it comes to me, I see you pass over there. When I call you, I see you return, ending up there. I go and see you being given to me, and it is said I should cross a river. I go following you, and I cross the river. When I go, it is said I should wait for you. I see you being rolled and rolled in the river. I ask the Mighty One why are you being rolled in the river. It is said I should *tshegetsa*, hold you fast.
>
> I see inside you. I don't know if you are troubled by nose bleeding or what—because when I go praying, it is said that it is inside you. You will find that inside the pillow you're using there's *melemo*, a medicinal substance working. It has been sent to work on you. Your head aches, when you sleep. I go and am told to *reetsa seemo*, listen to a

> situation that is so. There's a medicinal substance working inside the pillow you're using. The medicinal substance has been stored so that you can suffer nose bleeding and be choked by blood while sleeping. You would bleed through your nose and be found dead in your blankets. It is said I should go and attend to such a situation. Do you hear me, mother? I don't know whether you are *tshabelwa,* prone to suffering nose bleeding? There's a situation that is not going well.

The patient allowed for earlier nose bleeding, admitting, "When I was growing up, while I was young." Prophet Andrew stuck to his story line and turned to a further object of occult attack, her pillow, which gets him into another error he then has to explain away:

> But it is said this thing will come back again. It has been made so as to bother you again. The medicinal substance is working inside your pillow, the one you are now using. Do you hear me, our mother?

Once again, the patient dissented and contradicted the prophet—she doesn't use a pillow anymore:

> I don't use a pillow. That's ever since things were dug up from our yard at home, where we come from. And the things coming from the pillow frightened me. Now I use a blanket instead of a pillow. I just wrap a blanket up.

Prophet Matthew is an artful dodger, par excellence, however. Very quickly, without a moment's hesitation or reflection in prayer, Prophet Matthew confidently explained away his apparent mistake, by turning her blanket back into her pillow:

> But the thing comes. It is there inside the blanket you are using. It comes and enters the blanket. The blanket you are now using is the pillow, and it is inside the bed. You have to lie down with your head on this thing. Your dreams get *tlhakatlhakana,* jumbled and mixed up. You don't know what's happening. When you wake up in the morning, you feel dizzy, right inside yourself. It was said I should attend to such a situation.

Prophet Matthew warned the patient she was in mortal danger. Reaching a climax on the way to costly treatment of her yard, he directed her attention to the need she has in her situation to exorcise, to get rid of the demon (*thokolosi*):

> Your grave, well, you can die in your sleep. You can find that you bleed through your nose. There's a situation arising, going on where you stay. It is said that I should seek for something like a *thokolosi,* demon. It is going inside your yard, inside the house you are using. There is a

> situation that is going ahead in your yard, and it is a hairy thing. Do you hear me, our mother?

The patient agreed, "Yes." The patient's sister interjected, "Where in Block 5 (the patient's city home), or where?" Both prophets answered simultaneously, "Where she stays."

Prophet Matthew continued and gave his disclaimer that he diagnoses not of his own will, but under the guidance of the Holy Spirit. If he, in turn, shocks and amazes, then it is because he has been told to reveal shocking and amazing things:

> You yourself see something appearing to wake you up. During the day, your heart throbs in panic inside you, it throbs very fast. It is this thing throbbing along with your pulse and the flow of your blood. Do you hear what I'm saying, mother? Myself, well, I don't much like having to diagnose; it is that it was said I have to tell you about the situation that is so shocking and amazing.

Given that the patient actually was herself worried and amazed, Prophet Andrew immediately seized the moment to prove he was right even earlier on her situation, when it comes to men: "This concern [the demon at work] stops you from staying with any man." Responding silently, the patient nodded her head, seriously.

Again, with the use of touching body language, this time from the bottom to the top of his chest, Prophet Matthew alerted her to what he sees better than she does through the rest of his scan of her inside condition:

> You see in the present situation, it is said, *iteetse*, you should take care of yourself (attend to yourself). Sometimes when you wake up, you find that there is a foam in your chest. It is said the thing is stirring up forcefully in your belly. It fills up lots of foam in your chest. Your chest stays like a knocked-out car engine, at times. You can say that you walk with difficulty. You have lots of bile. This thing starts right from the bottom and spreads through your chest. It is said I must scan inside you. You are dressed with water in your lungs. Your lungs are dressed in such a condition of water you could just fall down. You suffer fits. When you pay attention to the condition of your body, you see that a joint of your body is not right and alive.

With a view to the future treatment, Prophet Andrew turned to her memory of an earlier exorcism, which led her to give up her pillow, when she was frightened by its revealed nasty contents. "The people who helped you," he asked. "where did they come from?" "They were from Eloyi church," she answered. "They came to my mother's place." "Did they come to help you or someone else?" he continued. She repeated, "They were from Eloyi church and came to my mother's place." "Which branch of Eloyi?" he asked. "Ramotswa [near the city]." "And they didn't help you?" he asked further. "I am not an Eloyi member," she answered. "My younger sister belongs to Eloyi."

Prophet Andrew went ahead, insisting upon the demon troubling her and needing to be exorcised:

> This concern he's talking about is such that even if you enter your house, you'll find it's as if a fuse is burnt. It smells acrid, *sisi,* not good. Don't you hear it happening that way? You can say sometimes it's as if something burning swept through the house.

In the same vein, Prophet Matthew added:

> It's that this thing I'm talking about takes your clothes and they disappear one by one. Even your cash disappears. It was said I should go and show you about this situation I'm talking about. I myself will stop there. I don't want to examine much.

Having reached a climax in diagnosis, the prophets drew the patient to the main aim at the end of their journey: exorcism. Hustling for their fees in paid treatment, I perceive, the prophets began to wind the patient up and reel her in—they conveyed that they might run out of patience, the way other people have with the patient. They cautioned her that they were about to stop; they intended to discharge her the way a patient is discharged in a hospital. But it was up to her to provide for the needed next journey by paying for treatment and exorcism.

Prophet Andrew said, "We are going to discharge you, our mother, and you can ask any difficult questions." "How do you help when the troubles are like this?" she asked. "We help when things are like that," he answered, "and it's up to you."

Worried that the consultation is to end before her worst fears and troubles were dealt with, the patient brought out, at last, the concern that had actually been uppermost in her mind. It was the concern that drove her to come to the prophets: "You didn't reach my workplace. I have troubles at work." "Mother, this thing can split you away from all people, including us," Prophet Matthew warned; he wanted her to attend to the demon and exorcism. "Even the person helping you can run out of patience." "Just as you are now running out of patience with me?" she worries. "No," Prophet Matthew assured her, "we are not running out of patience."

But Prophet Andrew had clearly had enough. He was determined to get the patient to make up her mind on the exorcism. He started taking off his robe to signal the end of the consultation, "You see me, I am disrobing. I have disrobed." "People can be very impatient with you. You can end up saying people hate you," Prophet Matthew cautions her. In very real distress, the patient cries out, "Oh such troubles, I just see no help I can get. But my sister said she is taking me to people who will help me, but if they fail, there's nothing we can do."

Prophet Andrew was determined to close with her in getting her agreement for payment. "You see the robes," he said, "I have taken them off; I have stopped work." She sighed, "When I saw you disrobing, I felt there's no help for me. I tried to get help from other people, but failed." Prophet Matthew again reassured her, "I can't fail you," and he was joined by Prophet Andrew, "I too can't fail you, even though you are older than I am." Hopefully, she called out, "Yes, help me now. But you have disrobed!" "I am putting on my shoes so we can go and help you now," says Prophet Andrew. "Where? At home?" she asked. "Yes," he answered. "Let's go," she urged.

Prophet Andrew was now hustling for the cash he needs as an unemployed prophet. He wanted to make the patient understand that money is the problem, not because prophets have to be paid, but because there are costs in getting the goods needed for their work in treatment. This is the way he finessed the prophets' fees:

> The trouble is the things we work with need to be bought, and cost money, so we have to postpone doing it until tomorrow. We have to find those things. If money were not a problem, we would come knocking at your house this evening. The things we were talking about, I'll take them out for you and give them to you.

"Are you tired?" the patient asked. "You know I am tired, but I haven't done anything at all," Matthew answered, and Prophet Andrew added, "No, we've finished." In something of a rush to get intercession with the Holy Spirit for her job and prospects for more higher education, the patient hurriedly pulled out some documents. One letter announced her likely transfer to a district capital in the west of Botswana; another delays or rejects her application for another course at the University of Botswana. She handed the documents to Prophet Andrew and said, "Don't you see how things differ? I want to reverse this letter for my transfer. And everything! As you see me I want to resign from work. The other letter, I want to make the UB (University of Botswana) people open their mouths I have long applied to them."

Prophet Andrew promised to pray on her behalf. This ends my record of the consultation, because at his request to take away my camera, I leave to allow them to deal with the payment in private. The prophets and the patient are alike in being sensitive over evidence of payment. It is, of course, against church rules, and it is an awkward aspect of prophets' hustling. They take great care to disguise or hide it, apart from hints and winks, or the occasional boastful moment, as in showing me the check from a physiotherapist.

Over the whole of the diagnosis in both cases of home consultation, there is one progression that needs to be made more explicit. I have in mind the leveraged subjection of the patient to domination by the prophets as holy hustlers. The collusion between patient and prophet, negotiating the way past fumbles and errors, is unmistakable. So too is the tug-of-war in the moments of the patient's resistance and contradiction of the prophets. Unmistakable, also, is the emotional impact, in the last case, from painful recall of bereavement to being moved by shock and amazement. But what needs to be made even more plain is the prophets' overwhelming or even battering of the patient by the end of such successful diagnosis.

The very expression of contradiction is itself a feature of the leveraged subjection in diagnosis. It is no paradox to say that. Eliciting contradiction as an open expression is standard dialogical work—business as usual, as it were, for a prophet. The elicitation is usually done with politeness in a formula, such as "Do you hear and understand?" or "I am not sure if you remember this" or "I don't know if you are aware of this situation" or "Tell me, if I am saying something that doesn't exist" or "Am I oppressing you by saying something false? Say if you agree, or disagree." After the elicitation, what is also standard dialogical work is glossing by the prophet. His glosses make sense of the contradictions between his prophecies and the patient's denials or uncertainties by bringing out what he knows better than the patient, the hidden truth.

THE CASE OF GREED AND THE NOT-SO-CLEVER ELDER

The following case illustrates subjection and the shocking approach in diagnosis by Prophet Johannes, when he was on a visit to the church's Gaborone branch. The patient was an elderly man, a stranger from the southern district capital of Kanye. He was short, and Prophet Johannes towers over him. I was filming from below upward, closer to the patient's eye level, and I was aware of how much Prophet Johannes' long arms flail threateningly about the patient's head—a windmill was whirling wildly, I felt, and the image of the robe waving conveyed that. In this case as in others involving elderly, relatively prosperous men as the main patients, Prophet Johannes focused on the occult attack against victims and objects of greed, such as wells at the posts where patients' keep their cattle. Prophet Johannes addressed his patient:

> It is said I should seek an owner of a white Toyota Hilux van [one of the most popular colors and makes]. I see people are massing together. I see that you will be struck by lightning at the early rains. It is said that I go and tell that. Do you understand me, sir?

The patient nodded, "Yes."

Prophet Johannes appealed in prayer, "God of the Israelites, The Diligence of the Jews, King Full of Peace and Glory, Jerusalem the Mighty, The Diligence of Heaven."

Then the prophet asked, "Whose child got lost?" "I don't know," the patient answered. Sticking to his topic, Prophet Johannes pushed ahead, "Yes, the child got lost and returned." The patient continued to profess ignorance, "I don't know." Domineering, Prophet Johannes stretched his long arm and reached with his hand close to the patient's face, "It's a child about this high. Who is it?' " The patient shrugged and again denied knowledge, "No, I can't say." Prophet Johannes pursued the story, "The child got lost, and went to some people who brought the child back." "No, I don't know who that is, I don't grasp who it is," the patient said with some bewilderment.

Prophet Johannes offered more circumstantial detail for the location of the person and the place, in the pasture area of cattle posts away from the village center:

> It is now said I should look for a certain patient. This place if you look at it closely, you see it's outside the village centre and is at the plowing area, by a river, with a big drift where the road crosses. The road dips down. Where do you go on it? Which place is it?

"It's the other side, after Kanye," the patient said, no longer at a loss and finding a familiar place to match landmarks in the prophet's journey. Prophet Johannes then asked, "Is this where your cattle post is?" The patient agreed, "Yes."

Prophet Johannes revealed:

> It's not going well there. The quarrel over the well is not favoring you. Your herd is straying and not prospering. There's nothing you grasp well. The King of Life said I should go and tell this. But I myself, it is said, I should say it is a quarrel over the well. Do you understand me,

> sir? [The patient nods silently.] If you don't stand up for yourself, the lightning of the early showers will strike you. Lord of Life said I should go and tell this. But the war is said to be over the well. One says it's my father's, the other says . . . King of Life says I should go and tell that. I myself don't grasp it well.
>
> Inside your body, sometimes you feel palpitations on your skin. Did you understand me? It's as if you are fearing something. You are pulled like this [he gestures roughly]. Sometimes you are so dressed in pain it is like a belt splitting your waist [he shows on his own waist].

The patient replied, standing stiffly, "I can't bend forward."

Prophet Johannes kept on the track, while exposing more of the patient's symptoms:

> Sir, sometimes you fail to support your position. Your knees, well I know you are an elderly person. Your knees are wobbly. But this wobbly condition changes, sometimes it gets better, sometimes mainly when you are at the cattle post, it gets very heavy, you feel intense pain. I don't know whether you know this?

"My feet swell full up," the patient admitted.

On the authority of his spiritual message, Prophet Johannes attributed that to witchcraft and went on telling its danger in death for others already: "To me, it was said, you are being eaten and bewitched for the well. And there are others who are already dead, under the earth. Do you know this situation?"

"I don't understand it," the patient admitted. Prophet Johannes pressed on, "You don't understand it. It was said, I should seek three people, already under the earth. One is not a grown-up, but already a man, older than me, but he died a sudden death."

This report elicited recognition by the patient: "It's my younger brother." "Sir?" Prophet Johannes interjected. The patient explained, "It's my younger brother who comes after me." Prophet Johannes took up the patient's tone and implied something about the nature of his loss, and amplified it later, "Don't you know that he was the one who stood head and shoulders, the most clever among you? You know that?" He agreed, "Yes."

Prophet Johannes drove home that the patient's expressed ignorance is part of his predicament, his inadequacy in the face of clever attack:

> He was cut off first. It was well known that you don't know much about lots of things. You only realize too late, after something happens to you. I myself was told to say this. You only realise too late. You are the useless ones. He knew the law, and was able to sue. So he was cut off first, to get rid of him. Do you understand me, sir?"

"Yes, sir," the patient agreed. Prophet Johannes then concluded the diagnosis, with a promise of future help to protect against the witchcraft, "Let me not go further. You will be helped."

While subjection dominates many of the moments in diagnosis, these cases also document the reaching beyond that in hope. There is always the promise of the body redressed to be at peace. It is a promise that is all the more appealing because it comes from one who, as a charismatic prophet, is not merely a figure of Power but also a submissive devotional subject within a community of suffering. In Christian faith healing, holy hustling is as much the undergoing of loss of bodily control by the devotional subject in compassionate service as it is the dominance of the artful dodger in diagnosis.

8. Prescribing Christian Cosmetics

Moving Bodies and Intercorporeality

A good number of Apostolic usages, beliefs, and practices support my argument that prophetic prescription aims at redress through Christian cosmetics. Most striking in such Apostolic counteraction is the colorful visibility of their cosmetics on and for the body, primarily the triad of green, white, and red, according to the desired good. Earlier, in Chapter 5, I spell out the color coding as a matter of consensus among the Apostolics even after their schism. Here my interest is in the analysis of cosmetic counterfabrication as a distinctively Christian preoccupation in prescription. Accordingly, I want to stress this immediate point on Apostolic visibility: the occult must be undone and seen to be undone in a significantly Christian way, to dress the Apostolic in the Holy Spirit. Later in this chapter, I relate my account of cosmetics to what I consider to be "intercorporeality" and discuss body language, the somatic, and empathy.

For illumination, visibly taking the person out of a spiritual condition of darkness, the Christian candle so familiar in the churches missionaries established is the appropriate alternative to the lamp of the diviner and witchfinder. Hence, too, the highly appropriate cosmetic material that commonly manifests the Holy Spirit is the refined, pure wool of the lamb, which is worn round the body, on the waist, arm, or leg. "The Lamb of Heaven, the Lamb of Heaven," Apostolics sing to God, and so too on earth do they adorn themselves cosmetically, seeking His goodness in life with the blessed wool of the lamb. The good fabric redresses the bad, as the Word of God undoes the evil witchcraft fabricates.

Besides manifestly heightened visibility, there is a further aspect in the effectiveness of Apostolic cosmetics: their very fabrication. We might say after Levi-Strauss that Apostolic cosmetics are cooked, never raw. These are used for the cosmetics:

wool, usually called "wool," by the English word

Sowatsho, holy ash

Tomololo, sacrificial blood in holy water

refined sea substances, such as salt or sand

the vapor from burning paraffin.

All these cosmetic means are processed. They are refined and made fit for their holy use by being transformed to a higher condition. One higher transformation, in the cosmetic, is the means of another, in the person: for example, as I pointed out earlier, ash is changed by the fire of sacrifice, and so too, Apostolics say, is the person changed by using it.

Given this argument about the effectiveness of fabrication in heightened visibility and higher transformation, it has to be appreciated, also, that the cosmetics are costly and commodified. Most are imported, in part or whole; nearly all are bought. They often come ready-labeled from a shop (the wool and candles, for example) or a pharmacy (the bottled sea sand and salt), and buying is true even for the products sacrifice transforms. The fact is that in the city and commonly in the countryside, too, the vast amounts of firewood and the sacrificial animals needed for a great sacrificial pyre are costly and usually have to be paid for.

In so far as the notion of an "occult economy" may be helpful for the discussion of Christian reformation, we could use it to highlight a change. We might say that Christian cosmetics have now become commercial goods in an occult economy, whereas in the past traditional Tswana cosmetics were not. Traditional Tswana cosmetics were made up of substances one could gather for oneself or get an expert to collect from things and beings at hand or in the wild. The fee for the expert's knowledge and work was in a sense not commercial but compensation in the generous gift of the grateful patient. Admittedly, the notion of the gift applies to the church's ideal for unpaid service by prophets. All the same, recreating cosmetics in Christian reformation, the Apostolics get their cosmetics through trade and commerce.

Somewhat despite themselves and in self-defence, the Apostolics engage as commercial consumers in what has now become, strikingly in Botswana's capital early in this twenty-first century, a pressing, if not overpowering, consumer society, apparently brimful of imported goods, mainly from South Africa, if originally from elsewhere, increasingly from China. The Apostolics consume cosmetics against being eating up by witchcraft, which they regard as usually being bought and probably imported. For example, as mentioned earlier, fabricated demons are said to be imported by mail; further, they are also said to bear a barcode, a warning of their shelf life, as in a shop. The import of fabricated evil is undone by the import of counterfabricated good; what redresses consumption, the negative, is the positive, counterconsumption: the black by the white. Commercial consumption rules overwhelmingly in Christian prescription.

Carrying forward my earlier remarks on power dressing by prophets, I would also extend my basic argument about counterfabrication and Christian cosmetics in order to highlight the pervasive concern for attractiveness and proximity to God. The argument applies to Apostolic vestments that, like Christian cosmetics, figure in prescription. The afflicted person has to be *diapolwe,* undressed and then dressed afresh, just as the cosmetics have to undo the contact, *moamolole,* with polluting or maliciously harmful and occult things. Lavishly fabricated, gloriously visible, and high in commercial cost, the robes, the copes, and the miters as vestments are the effective means of investing Apostolics with the spiritual capacity to combat evil and draw near to God's goodness. The vestments manifest also hierarchical authority, being made by a seamstress or tailor under the direction of the bishop or archbishop. Christian cosmetics and vestments make their bearer attractive to God, above all.

A further account of prescription in actual practice is needed to illustrate my argument and push it a stage further. First, a brief comment on the delivery of prescription is useful. Bishop Boitshepelo's innovation introduces a clinical, modern aspect to Apostolic prescription. In his branch of the church as in a clinic, prophets sit behind a desk, and in front of them, patients sit, waiting in line for prescriptions. For these, the bishop and the prophets not only use his standard hospital-like form but, like hospital doctors, dictate prescriptions to a secretary. Voluntary and unpaid, she writes them down, usually rather laboriously. When demand is high, the bishop takes a batch of forms, each filled-in with the patient's personal details, and he dictates every prescription in the patient's absence, sometimes looking at the patient's picture on a church registration form. Such innovation extends prescription from being fit for consumers in a consumer society to being fit also for the people processing and bureaucratic practice of a city.

For my evidence from actual cases, I give a brief example, first, from Prophet Matthew's practice. Then I return to a series of prescriptions by Prophet Joshua for Martha, my assistant Njebe's wife, starting with the one already listed in Chapter 1.

Prophet Matthew's prescription, which follows, came on a weekday morning, when the session is set aside for diagnosis and prescription. Unlike a Sunday service, such a session has no sermons or long prayers. The prophet sat on a desk, about a small step raised above the patients seated in rows in front of him. By his right hand was a church form, and next to that a Bible, on top of which lay his cell phone, ready for use, though closed, on standby throughout his diagnosis and prescription. The patients took their turns in a line the way they do in a clinic. Talking very quickly, as is his wont, Prophet Matthew dealt confidently and briskly with about five patients, all strangers; first, he offered each his diagnosis, and then to the voluntary secretary sitting next to him, he dictated the prescription for the person in turn, before he handed over to another prophet.

The following prescription is the one that Prophet Matthew gave for the patient he diagnosed in "The Case of the Renter and the Duped Child" (see Chapter 3). The prophet dictated this:

> The bath against tribulations *meleko* (ordeals and trials). Drinks. Green strings and red strings. Many colored candles. The burnt offering.
>
> The warm water to be drunk for three days, with three drops of salt and paraffin.
>
> The candles of many colors to be blown over with a green whisk, for two days, early in the morning.
>
> The white and green strings are to be worn for 29 days.
>
> The bath should be with 14 white candles, and the washing done outside, near a river. The body is to be rubbed with mud all over, then washed with milk and *sewatsho,* ash.
>
> With a goat, a burnt offering should be made near the place where you live. The *tomololo,* sacrificial blood in water, the *metse a metona,* great water, should be prayed over, while the trident is between 7 white candles.
>
> A drawing should be made on all the joints.

This is an exemplary prescription. In contents, it is a collection from what is standard in Prophet Matthew's and other prophets' prescriptions: candles and strings of different colors, various baths and rubs, of vapor, water, milk, sacrificial ash, and goat blood, and drinks, of salt, tea, paraffin. Also in the standard way, and after clinical or modern pharmaceutical practice, the prophet's prescription specifies the number of days and the times in the day for various applications. Still in the standard way, it concocts in stink, sharp taste, skin feeling, perhaps gut reaction, what is sensuously memorable and highly distinctive—indeed, it is even deliberately offputting, in the stink of *tomololo*, for some people who are not Apostles or even their enemies. Viewed as a whole, the prescription offers a blend of healing methods, from cleansing of the whole external body, to rubbing away dirt on the skin, to cleansing the inside of the body through drinking, to creating a surround of fresh air, spiritual wind, by spraying greenness and wholeheartedness, to casting off darkness by illumination, to the sustained protection of the patient with the wool of the lamb for a whole month, short of one day.

Normally, the prophet says almost nothing to explicate the prescription as to the choice and significance of the prescription contents, and patients do not ask or much concern themselves about such specifics, whether the choice of contents or the special schedule. The usual attitude of patients is ritualistic or, one might say, magical, their intent being to get an authorized formula and to follow it precisely. By contrast, prophets, pastors, and bishops read much conventional spiritual significance into prescriptions, according to an orthodox consensus on color, illumination, sacrifice, redressing with wool, drinking for cleansing the inside of the body, and bathing and washing for the outside.

Turning to a whole series of prescriptions by a single prophet, I begin with the first one that Prophet Joshua prescribed for Martha. It was almost at the start of her attendance at Eloyi and before she was baptized in the church. Martha herself came to Eloyi after a long quest for healing by traditional doctors and gynaecological treatment by Western hospitals. Martha's husband, Njebe, is a man-about-town. Njebe was once the security manager for a large, popular hotel, and he has very good close friends and a wide circle of acquaintances. Having had a long period of unemployment, he has had the time to keep up his contacts with that circle—a favorite meeting place, and for him a highly convivial one, being the casino of his old hotel. A nursery school teacher, Martha has been more of a loner than her husband, and when she felt isolated and shunned by other people, she came to accept that she suffered from *sefifi*, occult darkness and bad luck. It is a condition in which one feels lonely, because the *sefifi* (sometimes called, in Zulu, *senyama*, blackness) leaves one in the dark, usually ignored by others.[1] Her suspicion, opened out in diagnosis, was that with the aid of a demon, *tokoloshi*, a cousin had been secretly ruining her sex life by displacing her in bed with Njebe.

In the following, I repeat Prophet Joshua's early prescription for Martha to bring the text together with his exegesis:

1. She should bathe, while five red candles are lit around her. All her joints should be sealed with the image of a moon.
2. Her bed should be tied with a red cord and a cord of many colors, crossed.
3. She should be prayed over with long tapers and a red cord fastened around her body.
4. She should be bathed with boiled river water.
5. A bottle of the water should be kept for her pillow.
6. A many-colored cord should be tied around her loins, doubled.

Reviewing the text at my request and with the form in front of him, Prophet Joshua made me understand that Martha was doubly afflicted, in the flow of her blood and by *tokoloshi,* a demon. Prophet Joshua regarded Martha as having the relatively lower spiritual rank of a person with the gift of the moon (not that of the sun and the higher rank, which the archbishop revealed, several years later, when he overturned another of Prophet Joshua's prescriptions).

By the time of this exegesis, Prophet Joshua had come to know Martha well as his patient in repeated consultations. Like any regular patient, Martha has come to him for *itekodisa,* self-examination and reporting on one's state of health. I know of this practice from Martha and others, but I did not witness *itekodisa* or myself record it; it keeps prophets and pastors informed of regular patients' health, and it is meant to be one of the preparations, as a Christian practice, for *bolelo,* public confession before one makes a sacrifice.

Prophet Joshua's prescription was to deal with different things, he explained, troubles in Martha's yard and in Martha herself. Martha was not "bedding down" well; her pillow and mattress had to be dealt with, because they have been worked upon and fabricated with a demon. Martha needed to have *dithapo,* strings of wool, underneath and around her bed, so she could get better sleep, and for the same reason, she had to have a small bottle put in her pillow. There had to be a string round the bottle so that the blood in her veins (her strings) should flow well and be aroused, for they "become lazy," not able to do their work. The need is *tsosalosa ditshika,* to loosen the veins. She had been worked upon to mix things up, and that is why she had to have the mixed-up, many-colored string crossed with the unmixed red one, loosening her veins. Prophet Joshua prescribed the bath of the red candles, because "with the red we fight evil spirits. We light the candles right around, and pray for them." Martha's troubles were blood, he stressed, but also working upon her is "something like" a *tokoloshi,* demon. The red candles were to drive it away.

Martha's attitude to the prescription was that it must be carried out meticulously. Otherwise, it wouldn't work, she was convinced. It had to be correct to work. Her faith in Prophet Joshua was great. Martha took great care in the exorcism at her yard to make sure that the exorcists completed the prescription, after they crossed her yard's entry with salt, dug in the yard's four corners, where charms might be pegged, and in each corner buried a blessed bottle of holy water. Martha got the leading pastor to read out the prescription and check its fulfillment. Over a longer period, she continued to sleep with the wool strings and freshly blessed bottle of water under her pillow. She bathed regularly with holy water, and wearing her robe with the image of a moon, she regularly and faithfully attended church.

Despite Martha's own faith, meticulousness, and regularity, however, her troubles did not wholly go away. Eventually, she did feel her menstrual pain easing, and she found warm conviviality in the church that undid her sense of isolation and loneliness. But, in the meantime, she continued to worry about the evils bothering her. It was unsettling for her that the neighbors' dogs kept defecating in her yard, though she was reluctant to pay for the new gate her husband, Njebe, suggested as a practical solution for this attack of, possibly occult, dirt. What worried her was that the neighbors might be in cahoots with someone else, her village relative whom she had long suspected of witchcraft.

Martha maintained her good faith by readily explaining why the Apostolic redress was working at best only partially. Her explanation was that the Apostolics did fail to complete the prescription perfectly. She must—and did—keep trying to get it right and, as time passed, to get fresh prescriptions to meet further troubles.

Several years later, still a patient of Prophet Joshua's and now baptized in the church, Martha had a troubling dream. She told it first to her husband, Njebe, who interpreted it as calling for a burnt offering. In turn, Prophet Joshua confirmed this interpretation during diagnosis.

This is the dream in the version Martha gave me, in her own words in English, after the diagnosis:

> When I was sleeping, I was dreaming there was a big bath, looking as if someone was doing the washing. Inside the water there was some black stuff. That black stuff splashed on me. Then I started dusting that from me. And then I emptied the water from the bath. After I emptied

> all the bath, there were about three sheep inside, slaughtered. But the blood was coming out. But the sheep was just looking as if they were still alive. And then from there on the other side I went somewhere, and I saw the people holding the other sheep but that one was alive. And then from there, on the passage from the house where we were staying it was full of salt.

As I understand it, in her dream she saw a bath overfilling with dirty water after being used for washing. Reached by the overflow, she got splashed with dirt. The bath, fully drained, revealed about three sheep. Having been slaughtered, their blood was flowing. But the sheep were apparently not yet dead. Going somewhere, she found one alive, held by people. Going further, she saw the passage of her house full of salt, as it would be to drive away a demon.

In diagnosis, told of her dream, Prophet Joshua saw that her condition, having been worked upon with dirt, called for the counteraction through the burnt offering. The diagnosis, which he gave in a great torrent, along with his prescription, at the church service, was this:

> She should be served with a burnt offering of a nubile kid about so high. This kid must have not yet given birth. She should be bathed with its blood. A drop of blood must be put in water. And she should drink it.

Later, at my request, Prophet Joshua unpacked his diagnosis and prescription. Martha had troubles in her yard. When she should be pregnant, she suffered a miscarriage or something else. She needed to sacrifice a goat as a burnt offering, to cleanse herself, and even the offering is to counter *baloi,* the witches who are trying to shorten her days. The goat must be a young female kid, one not yet having given birth, in order to exchange her shortened life for the kid's longer life and for birth.

Sometime ago, in earlier diagnoses, Prophet Joshua told me, he warned her that she needed to make a burnt offering. Before carrying that out, she entered her period, so she couldn't complete the sacrifice—menstruating women are not allowed to use anything from church during their period. To put things right, she had to have the burnt offering made and then wash with its blood the very same day, and at least seven days after her period. She should have drunk drops of the kid's blood with milk, water, ash in *morito,* tea, without sugar and very salty to drive away the demon.

According to this interpretation, Prophet Joshua differed from his patient's explanation of the failure of prescription and treatment. Unlike Martha, he explained that the failure is because she was not in a fit state, due to menstruation, to carry out the guidance from the Word. Further, she was at fault herself for delaying the fulfillment when able to do it.

Great as Martha's faith continued to be in Prophet Joshua and his prescriptions, Martha was determined to have her burnt offering made by the person and in the place of her own choice, even if that meant in Prophet Joshua's absence. She wanted it made by the archbishop at his headquarters in Tsetsebjwe village, and not by the bishop in the city, where Prophet Joshua would also attend.

The bishop was confused, does not get things right, Martha told me—by his "confusion" she implied that he is himself bewitched or not in his right condition. Even more, he was not like his father, the archbishop, and his father's sister's son, the pastor-general. The bishop fails to pray through the night by the fire and tend it, until it goes out by itself. Instead, the bishop lets it go out in his absence. The archbishop and the pastor-general tend it prayerfully, and they have the singing and dancing go on until late in the night.

Earlier, in Chapter 6, I give the whole of the pastor-general's prayer for Martha at her burnt offering, and I analyze its significance at some length. I want to rehearse that more briefly here in order to draw out the application in accord with prescription. Such prayer at sacrifice, like virtually all Apostolic prayer, resonates with appeals by an intercessor for nearness to God. God is High in the Heavens. Below is the Apostolic who is the subject of the prayer. Distant from God and the healing angels, she is in a dire condition in which she has been dressed—other people have put it upon her and made turmoils agitate her soul—and she must be undressed. May what has been fabricated, making her in unfit contact, be undone by God, the intercessor prays For her sake, the intercessor calls upon God to receive her hand bearing the kid of sacrifice. She herself, the intercessor declares, raises it up, and her soul with it, in God's mighty name, which evokes compassion, salvation, healing and refuge from the suffering on earth.

Dressing redresses. The prayer speaks forcefully to understandings and experiences that inform prescriptions for Apostolics. I want to stress, again, their concern in prayer and in prescription to dress the subject afresh, casting off an old unwanted dressing, which is disempowering and which is commonly felt to be maliciously fabricated. I have already discussed, it will be recalled, in Chapter 2, power dressing by the prophets themselves.

For Apostolics, during diagnosis, the moving body of the prophet surpasses the mere body-in-motion. In spiritual transcendence, the prophet's body becomes the agency of moving others in harmony with the Holy Spirit. The intent is that by others' hearing his prayer, by their clapping and singing ever more loudly and joyously with him, led by other prophets, and by their seeing his body suffering under the control of the Holy Spirit, they too become with him bodily in tune with the Holy Spirit. Hence, a useful starting point for a discussion of the moving body in prophetic practice, of body language, the somatic and empathy, is not the body itself. Instead, it is the intersubjective relation of bodies in communication, which phenomenologists call intercorporeality, which needs to be foregrounded (Merleau-Ponty 2002).

That said, I must say something, nevertheless, about the background in popular ideas of the body. Like the diviner, the prophet draws on popular ideas of disease as a disturbance or blockage of the right flow of body fluids (Livingston 2005:104). In accord with that, for AIDS, for example, the prophet follows the archbishop's teaching on the bad flow in the body. Thus, Prophet Joshua explains to me that he knows what hospitals say about AIDS and blood cells but he accepts the archbishop's teaching on the disease and its symptoms. The disease comes, he tells me, according to the archbishop, from *setshwabu,* the pit of the stomach, the epigastrium, and goes to the navel, which gets soft and sore. You feel something hot, something like salty water comes out, with dirt. Your bowls get loose, your veins get tired, because in your head your fontanel gets soft like a small child's. Things then affect the spinal cord and the person starts complaining about headache. Such understandings of flow and blockage within the body are taken for granted by prophets and their patients as prophets visibly trace out the flowing course of an illness during diagnosis.

The prophetic diagnosis, I propose with regard to intercorporeality, is a divinatory séance turned Apostolic in vicarious experience. Even further, prophecy, if born of divination, grows with and beyond it, as bodily practice. This argument carries forward my earlier one that Apostolic prayer is an act which re-creates ancestral intercession as Christian intersubjective care.

It is useful to comment briefly on corporeal realities in wisdom divination in order to substantiate my argument. Wisdom divination is microdramatic, among other things, as I document in *Ritual Passage, Sacred Journey* (Werbner 1989), in my films *Séance Reflections with Richard Werbner* (Werbner 2005) and *Shade Seekers and the Mixer* (Werbner 2007), and elsewhere (Werbner 2001). Thrown down, the divinatory lots are seen to display a miniature tableau of significant others, friends and foes, around the subject. In place of their bodies are, as the lots, the bones or shells of other creatures, often including predators of the night, such as the leopard, and browsers of the day, such as the duiker (antelope). Perceived truths about the significant others, their inner attitudes, their dispositions toward the subject, are read from the lie of the lots. Similarly read is the subject's own condition, perhaps symptoms of suffering in the belly from the rising up of the round side of a divinatory bone.

Put in semiotic terms, such reading uses the lots as corporeal indexes and icons to make visible the truth of otherwise invisible conditions. The semiotic usage goes further, however, for some lots are also souvenirs and mnemonics. For example, for a diviner the bone of a leopard is a souvenir of a fortunate escape from the predator. As such souvenirs, the lots remind diviners of their own experiences and enable them to bring their own experiences to bear on those of their clients, to reach what are regarded as true insights. Elsewhere I argue that the lots are "a means for the embodiment of and thus the recall and reflection about, personal perceptions from the diviner's own life history" (Werbner 1989:32). On this basis, I suggest that "the discourse of divination resonates with experience, with echoes of the passions and suffering of a lifetime" (Werbner 1989:34). Empathy is at play in wisdom divination in this and in other ways. Moreover, the diviner uses body language and gestures, such as holding his hands with one pressing upon the other to indicate the oppression of the client. But what the diviner does not do is use or regard his own body as a vehicle of vicarious suffering.

Apostolic prophecy puts a Christian imprint on the exhibition of the moving body. The interior truth can still be read on the surface: that remains axiomatic in prophecy as in divination. But prophecy carries forward the corporeal visibility in wisdom divination and turns it into intercorporeal consciousness of the presence of the Holy Spirit. Reflected in the suffering body of the prophet is that of the patient, who is also brought into heightened self-awareness and communication with the Holy Spirit by the prophet, consciously knowing the Word in himself. As I describe earlier, the prophet follows the example of the archbishop in moving patients in harmony with the Holy Spirit. Only then can they experience relief from their suffering and be in harmony also with other people, for as the archbishop tells me with regard to the burden of *sefifi,* occult darkness, "When you are with other people, their bodies are not in harmony, *mmele ya bone ga e utlwane,* with yours."

The prophet begins by turning his own gaze inward. Sometimes, he writhes and sweats in discomfort, wracked by the suffering of the other that he shows he feels more fiercely than the other, and even in advance of the other. According to the understanding he conveys from the Holy Spirit, the prophet brings his hands along his own body, with evident pain. He touches one troubled part after another and is emotionally overcome, uttering a torrent of words, as he announces the course of the patient's pain and the nature of the illness. His moving body is meant to convey *kutlwelo botlhoko,* sympathy in suffering (literally mutual hearing of pain and bitterness) and *tlhomoga pelo,* being moved by pity (literally the removal of a thorn from the heart).

Such passionate intercorporeality is realized during a service in between musical moments of both great vibrance and intensely moving harmony. Both are very highly valued by Apostolics, who go to great lengths to create them as spiritual experiences. As I argue in Chapter 4, Apostolics seek to be at one with Spirit in the sound of their hands and their voices, in the very movement of their whole bodies.

THE EVIDENCE FOR CHRISTIAN INTENT

That said, an obvious question has to be asked. I am arguing not merely for the spiritual and existential importance of passionate intercorporeality in prophetic practice but even more for distinctive consciousness and intentionality. In other words, my argument is there is conscious, deliberately Christian intent in Apostolic intercorporeality. The question is: Where is the evidence, and how to arrive at it?

The difficulties in answering that lead some anthropologists, at least recently, to become the patients or apprentices, even copractitioners, of prophets, shamans, sorcerers, and various religious specialists. That is not my own approach, although somewhat jokingly prophets made me out, as a photographer, to be something of a "prophet," a cinematic seer, and although on an early visit the archbishop did attempt to volunteer a diagnosis for me.

The archbishop's attempt, alas, was not much of an experience of intercorporeality—perhaps, an Apostolic might say, because of my lack of faith in the Word. The archbishop began his tracing of the course of my apparent affliction by indicating my head and telling that my troubles start with severe headaches. What some might call a scholarly stoop in my usual posture might have given a misleading clue to the archbishop, I admitted later to my research assistant, Njebe. But the fact is the archbishop got it wrong; I do not suffer severe headaches, a fact that went well with Njebe's leaning toward skepticism about diagnosis in Eloyi. The archbishop then quickly and rightly read the truth, I guess from the doubting expression on my face, and he abandoned his efforts.

Although for evidence I rely primarily on conventional fieldwork and ethnographic methods in anthropology, I try to open out more of the answers through my film *Holy Hustlers,* which accompanies this text as a part of this book and about which I say more in the Conclusion. In advance of that, I want to draw attention to my use of film to elicit evidence of the conscious, deliberately Christian intent in Apostolic intercorporeality. I elicited this evidence from the archbishop, the bishop, and several prophets, Joshua, Andrew, and Johannes, by showing them my raw footage of prophecy. Many of their comments are already cited above, but given Prophet Joshua's prominence and his extensive, revealing commentary in *Holy Hustlers,* I want to provide another important part of the evidence by reporting more of Prophet Joshua's remarks on watching himself sing, dance, and diagnose.

Prophet Joshua noticed himself frozen still as a statue and remarked, "The song stopped, so did I, standing like a statue, waiting for it to start." He then drew my attention to the harmony in movement and in rest between himself, the singers, and the Spirit. "They sing with Spirit," he explained, "joining me as I am with Spirit, and we stop together." Together we viewed his eyes opening painfully, then looking around wildly, and his face, marked by grief, deeply troubled and pouring with sweat. In response, he volunteered his remarks on compassion, on his vicarious suffering for the sake of prayerful intercession with Spirit, from whom he wants healing for his Apostolics:

> The people prayed for are suffering from different kinds of illness. I have to feel their pain for them, and put myself in their position, feeling as if I am them, as if they are my mother's own children or even my parents. That's why you see my face looking full of sorrow and dismay. I want them to be healed.

Prophet Joshua took care, as we watched, to make me appreciate that his very movement in song and dance, when shared by the Apostolics, inspires faith which is healing:

> They can be healed by faith, seeing and hearing how I sing and dance. I dance with grief, I show compassion, so that they will stay with the hope that they will get healed and dance like me.

Seeing himself catching hold of a patient in hysterical distress, he pointed out to me that his rough handling, while very physical, is also spiritual: "I am holding that one, because I was shown by Spirit to take that one, the person with troubles."

Listening later, we could barely hear what he told his patient, and Prophet Joshua explained that at the time, under instruction from Spirit, he knew what to say, the reasons for her troubles. But now, having told her, he no longer had the vision, which he called "her film," and could not recall it. "Spirit is instructing me the reasons I tell her, but afterward I forget," he said, "I finish talking to her, and her film I've been seeing passes away." The whole experience was painful, he recalled, because he was at one with Spirit in grieving over the patient's turmoil and pain. "It was hard, very difficult." He explained, "Heaven was speaking about someone not well. Her condition was troubling us terribly, and Spirit was grieving painfully." Listening and watching reflexively with Prophet Joshua, I became convinced that one of his strongest motives for being a prophet is, indeed, healing. It is a passionate motive, which is grounded in his faith that in attending to the suffering of others he is at one with Spirit, doing the work of Spirit and revealing the hidden truth.

In this second part of the book, starting with Chapter 6, one of my main interests has been the linguistic force and importance of prayer, diagnosis, and prescription for Apostolics. On that basis, I turned from verbal communication to consciously shared experience, to empathy, the somatic, and intercorporeality, in Apostolic practice. To complete part two, I take up problems of Christian reformation from generation to generation and the ongoing debate about approaches to syncretism and antisyncretism.

9. Old and New in Christian Reformation

THE FOUNDATIONAL TEXT: SYNCRETISM/ANTISYNCRETISM

"New Wine in Old Wineskins" is a controversial chapter in Bengt Sundkler's *Bantu Prophets in South Africa,* the foundational text in the study of Zionist, Apostolic, and other Christian churches in southern Africa (first published in 1948 and revised in 1961). Named after a saying by Jesus, the chapter puts forward arguments at the heart of an enduring debate, including theological disputation, about the bringing together of the new and the old in religious change from generation to generation.

To keep Apostolic prophecy in view while considering its place in that debate, I want to comment first on a vision that Prophet Joshua told at a Sunday service during a diagnosis before an exorcism. His vision authorizes him to take on the guise of a *sangoma,* medium, and deal with a *tokoloshi,* demon—it is a cunning lad, fabricated in the form of a remarkably long, tricky snake by a *sangoma:*

> Hallelujah! The Voice of Spirit said I should run, sing songs like those of the *Magwasha* [i.e., *sangoma*] witchfinders, and wear a skirt like them. I asked Heaven, "Master, why do you show me that?" It was said, "There's a snake, so long, and it's alive. This snake was made by men wearing skirts, and made a long time ago, at its birth." The God of Heaven explains that. This snake is amazing, because it doesn't grow old. It's a lad, and so long. God of Heaven tells that. It is said that on the ground, we should spread out multicolored girdles at the entrance. I asked if it should be shut inside the yard. "This snake will amaze you. It can get out of the house, run away, and drive people away."

The new prophet in the old skin skirts—possibly the prophet knew the words of Jesus:

> People do not put new wine into old wineskins. Otherwise, the skins burst, the wine spills out, and the skins are ruined. Rather they pour new wine into fresh wineskins, and both are preserved. (Matthew 9:17)

These are words that echo down through the Christian era into our own literature in the anthropology of Christianity. The moral, and some might say the lesson for anthropology, too, is "Save the new." Arguing for that, the anthropologist Joel Robbins writes,

> The rhetoric that surrounds studies of syncretism is familiar: Christianity is just a thin veneer overlaying traditional culture; what looks like change is just a case of people pouring old wine in new skins as they seize on elements of Christianity that are similar to elements of their traditional culture; people feign conversion to get the material benefits the mission has to offer, but it is their traditional beliefs that are still most important to them. . . . (Robbins 2009:2; Robbins 2003)

"Old wine in new skins"—Robbins bends the saying of Jesus somewhat away from its significance in the spoilage of the new by the old, but there is no mistaking his criticism, and its force in current debate, to which I return later.[1]

For the young city-wise and street-smart Prophet Joshua, however, the revelation he himself receives speaks to an experience, an intimate feeling, of the past still working powerfully in people's lives in the present. The claimed authority in the prophet's revelation does come immediately from God in the present—it comes from divine inspiration; the young prophet is asserting against established church doctrine. In opposition to a founding generation of early Christians, he speaks for his own generation moving forward by going back to deal with the continued presence of the past. Those early Christians, primarily based in the countryside, were more concerned to emancipate themselves and their church from the spiritual claims of the ancestors and their veneration. For the early Christians, the priestly code of Leviticus offered them a way of purity. According to that code, priests became ritually clean, fit, and holy. Hence they could sacrifice not to the ancestors but directly to God. This was at once emancipating, because it set the old spirituality aside as polluting, but because there was no loss of the means of spiritual exchange in which a person detaches one part and reattaches another—the sacrifice that copes with problematic dividuality—it was also an accomplishment of resilience for the early Christians.

The young prophet's generation, living in the city and still belonging in both the city and the countryside, brings its own, opposed perception to bear on Christianizing. The city youth question whether they need to emancipate themselves the way the founding generation did. Less concerned with purity and pollution, they now take sacrifice for granted as an Apostolic practice. What the founding generation despised begins to be desirable: the stuff of insightful dreams inspired by the dead. There is a spiritually powerful connection that the new generation does not want to lose. The young prophet's generation primarily wages a more intense war against the materiality of witchcraft, against the malicious, harmful fabrication of occult things—it is distinctively a new war of their own in that it is against demons, and their imported, alien commodities.

As a visionary, the prophet recovers the dismissed yet still hidden things of old, while he wonders what God wants of him. Why wear the old skin skirt? Should he pour himself into it? Should he dress, dance and run with it? Is the message that by doing this, he will save by overpowering it? Or perhaps it is also a streetwise truth: to out-trick *moitseanape*, the bad old trickster-seer, using his own tricks? What is striking, however, is that as a visionary the prophet claims divine inspiration for the reprise and Christianizing of something beyond Christianity, something that a missionary might well call heathen.

This leads me back to Bengt Sundkler, the missionary for whom the question of syncretism as heathenism was a pressing concern. Something needs to be said about Sundkler himself, given the towering influence of his work on charismatics. My remarks are meant, among other things, to acknowledge something old in the anthropology of Christianity: the contribution and influence in ethnography of Christian scholars, not themselves anthropologists.

As a Swedish missionary, Sundkler was outstanding. Originating Zionist ethnography, he published, very sensitively, a wealth of dreams, hymns, prayers, and leaders' portraits along with his insights into the ecstatic practices and schisms of Zionists. In 1949, following publication of *Bantu Prophets*, he was appointed to the chair of Church History at Uppsala, and in 1961, he came to hold, also, the post of bishop in Tanzania.

Not surprisingly, however, in the late 1940s Sundkler applied Jesus's saying to what he judged to be syncretism, and he did so in the way one might expect from a devout and faithful Protestant missionary of his times. In the 1940s, and Sundkler recanted later by cutting this passage in the revised version of his book (1961), he did argue, "*The syncretistic sect becomes the bridge over which Africans are brought back to heathenism*" [italics in the original] (Sundkler 1948; also cited in Adam Ashforth 2005:189).[2]

Sundkler revised his reactionary contention—reactionary by his own lights —by the time of the second edition of *Bantu Prophets in South Africa* (1961). His later view is that the African religious change was more new than he had appreciated, and it was actually in a positive direction. After all, it was fundamentally away from "heathenism" toward Christianity.[3]

But in Sundkler's earliest view, syncretism was bad for the future of Christianity in Africa: an adulteration. He could not accept what members of the new churches claimed about prophecy. Seeing the purity of prophecy with an eye to the true spiritual value, they would insist that their prophets were not at all like diviners, given the fact that diviners are not inspired by the Holy Spirit. At best, Sundkler could have taken it as a claim in religious argument, in the demonizing of diviners. We might say its truth was oppositional, if weighted by the fundamental, overarching value of the Holy Spirit for prophets. In that fundamental respect, prophets and diviners have nothing in common, as Zionists could say: diviners are Other.

It is important to recognize that the syncretism against which Sundkler inveighs, if temporarily, comes at a certain phase in Christianizing. If not the first phase of Christianity—the phase about which Robbins writes for Papua New Guinea—it is, significantly, an early phase. In it what is still being contested is the very emergence of "religion" itself as a sphere distinctively set apart in spiritual purity. If primarily seen by embattled participants as a struggle about specifics, such as the regard for spirits and the dead, for example, it is nonetheless contestation that is more radical, even fundamental, and broad in its implications. This is the point I put forward in my own discussion of syncretism as it is politicized in relation to antisyncretism:

> . . . the management of identity and difference is actively reworked to fit the insistence upon setting apart a sphere of "religion" as the lasting, the pure, and the authentic. As such, it is shown to be a sphere which is quintessentially definitive of the self in contrast to the Other. (Werbner 1994:213)

Underlying Sundkler's view is a simple assumption about syncretism. It has recently been challenged, but it still runs through much debate about the bringing together of the old and the new or the opposition to that in religious change. It is the assumption that syncretism is one process, that what people talk about under such a rubric for religious change can be taken by itself. In my view, Rosalind Shaw and Charles Stewart make a convincing case against that assumption in their forceful introduction to *Syncretism/Anti-Syncretism* (Shaw and Stewart 1994). Following their lead, I argued:

> Subsumed at its broadest, the relation between the tendencies [of syncretism and antisyncretism] is what we might call coimplication; it is a mutual involvement, but according to context, the involvement is an *encompassment* of one tendency by the other, or their complementarity, or their significance as causes and effects, or the *tension* between them as conflicting tendencies. And, in specific cases over time, it may be all of these, or a combination of a number. (Werbner 1994:213–214, italics added)

Sundkler himself kept a certain stance toward issues of African religious change. Because these still resonate importantly in current debate, sometimes put in terms of syncretism, rehearsing at least part of Sundkler's approach is useful for our perspective on Christian reformation and, in particular, religious change through prophecy among Apostolics. I present my comments on two issues arising in Sundkler's foundational text, while I bring out certain implications for my own study.

The first issue reaches well-known truisms in anthropology about the cultural constraint on innovation. There is a need for the Zionist "to act in the categories and according to the patterns with which he was familiar, namely those of the Zulu diviner" (Sundkler 1961:260). Here we face what anthropologists now call the predicament of culture, a concept, as Clifford points out, that anthropologists find it hard to do without and yet, now, hard to do with (Clifford 1988). The catch, for the anthropologist no less than the missionary, is familiarity, which currently breeds contempt, because anthropologists have become uneasy about a possible disciplinary bias toward seeing the old in continuity, and too much ignoring breaks in newness.[4]

Holy hustlers as Apostolic prophets do form a vanguard for religious change. Where an older generation of diviners brought to bear the richness of a highly poetic, evocative, and ambiguous oral tradition, the wisdom of maturity and the personal understandings of a lifetime, the young prophets talk, in the new church of Conollius as in the old Eloyi, in the common language, sometimes argot, of the city. Recognized for their cleverness, they go on using their streetwise insights to advise about the cunning of others, and how to cope with that. In diagnosis, the concern of these prophets, known as street kids, continues to be not the individual conscience or social reform but the sordid world of malice—an important concern of diviners, also—and their mission is to expose its threat and, by interceding with the help of the Holy Spirit, to overcome it, at best temporarily, never absolutely.

The schism between Eloyi and Conollius gives prophets a fresh opportunity to make the most of their penchant for roaming the country, somewhat after the example of roving diviners, since they do not feel themselves bound exclusively to one congregation. Traveling across the country on church errands, the young Apostolic prophets recruit members. They mobilize them at services and exorcisms, and they themselves become a city team that is exemplary for church unity, trust, and loyalty to the new archbishop. To some extent, prophets take on more of a pastoral role, and even preach on occasion, in the making of the new church, during the early days of transition. There is unmistakably a heady sense of revitalized faith, of renewed community, much aroused and quickened by the prophets themselves.

The second issue in Sundkler's classic assessment of religious change among Apostolics and Zionists is that of the main modeling or priority in the mix of old and new. In Sundkler's judgment, "The basic pattern from which Zulu Zionism is copied is that of diviner and witchfinder activities rather than that of the Christian church" (1961:242). Against that, James Kiernan argues that Zulu Zionist prophets are radically new, in sociological terms, because unlike traditional diviners, the prophets serve, actively and deliberately, in the building of fresh community and in the moral reorientation toward the conscientized self. Yet, perhaps hedging his suggestion somewhat, Kiernan admits, "Nevertheless, it is undeniable that, in some respects and to some degree, Zionist prophets (some more than others) model their behaviour on that of diviners" (Kiernan 1992:237).[5]

NEW SUBJECTIVITIES: CHRISTIAN DISCIPLINE, SATAN, AND SALVATION

The practice of Zulu Zionists in Durban highlights the making of moral agency in ways that are familiar in classic accounts of Christian discipline among Protestants. Influenced by Calvinism through the Dutch Reformed Church, Durban's Zulu Zionist prophets hold members to a puritan code of conduct. The prophets actively expose members' lapses, publicly denounce their moral faults, and demand, with a spiritual mandate, that members give witness by confessing transgressions (Kiernan 1977:249). "In the process of divining," James Kiernan reports, "the way [a member] has comported himself as a Zionist, or as a potential Zionist, is subjected to a careful scrutiny at the end of which the prophet will interpret his behaviour either as blameworthy or worthy of reward" (Kiernan 1976a:359). Zulu Zionist prophecy evokes from the subject what some anthropologists might say is the voice of "modernity," or perhaps merely its Calvinist version: the voice of conscience in self-examination and self-policing. That "modern" Calvinist inner voice, like the Zionist subjectivity, is itself policed on behalf of the church by charismatic prophets.

Given our focus on Apostolic prophets who are labeled "street kids," at least by their enemies, it is significant that Zionists freely liken their charismatics to children, "in that their behaviour is irresponsible and unpredictable" (Kiernan 1976a:359). The Zionist moral policing is put in the care of those who are themselves not easily disciplined and who, speaking with the gift of the Holy Spirit, are answerable to nobody for what they say. The charismatics are the undisciplined, and the would-be disciplinarians are the pastors and the preachers; between them the balance is so precarious, in practice, that they often have to deal with friction and resentment.

While also regarded as irresponsible, unpredictable, and hard to discipline—as befits charismatics—Apostolic prophets are not arousers or keepers of others' conscience. Some, like the Zionists, do become resentful and involved in friction with preachers and bishops, and there are times, too, when the balance between prophets and pastors is more than uneasy. But if Christian discipline crops up in pastors' sermons, in gossip among ordinary Apostolics and in the attempts by church committees to regulate Apostolic morality, it is marginal for prophets, and especially in diagnosis.

Even more widely in the congregation, among the Apostolics there is little of the policing of sin or making Apostolic subjectivity more deeply intersubjective through confession.[6] Confession is called for when the subject has to be set aside, before God, in a fit state of purity to offer a sacrifice. The prophet's instruction, then, is "*boipolelo*, confess (report on yourself) before the Hand of Life, in front of the pastors." Confession is thus a matter for a very special occasion, made authoritative by being in the presence of pastors, who represent the hierarchy and church elders.

Chapter 5 documents a rare confession. A pastor-general makes it, as I report, at one Conollius service, immediately after Eloyi split in two and while the tension between the churches was high. This pastor-general had been grossly humiliated and driven from Eloyi. Obviously in great torment, he whispers into the Conollius archbishop's ear, while the music drowns out his voice from other Apostolics' hearing. The occasion was exceptional. I witnessed no other such confession during a service. Unlike the highly Calvinistic Zulu Zionists, the Apostolics have no great devotion to confession, no constant mutual surveillance of sin in the congregation, although dreams are often reported, especially by Mothers of the Church and other prominent Apostolics, to be interpreted primarily by the bishop or pastor-general.

In this respect, the Apostolics are more like the Gwembe Tonga Apostolics, among whom Thomas Kirsch observes a similar disregard for confession:

> . . . the confession of sins was almost nonexistent in the African indigenous churches I attended during my field research, the sole exception being the African Apostles of Johane Maranke, where the churchgoers had to confess their sins publicly before entering the area where services were being held. (Kirsch 2004:708, note 13; Colson 2006)

Self-revelation clearly varies in its importance from one Apostolic church to another. Hence it cannot be argued that there is a Christian model of self-making that the different Apostolic churches embrace uniformly or in common.

There is, however, a moral and theological attitude that Apostolic prophets do share with many other prophets in southern Africa, including Zulu Zionists (Kiernan 1997:249), but not in West Africa (Meyer 1999). It is the attitude to Satan. Where West Africans diabolize imaginatively, and make much of the Devil in everyday life, Apostolic prophets, like many other southern African prophets, do not; they say nothing of Satan in diagnosis. Preachers talk of Satan in sermons, but Satan, who does not loom in the popular imagination, hardly figures in everyday Apostolic concerns.

What might appear to be Apostolic exceptionalism needs to be recognized as practical religion, this-worldly and minimally salvationist, which is more widely observed among Christians elsewhere. Fenella Cannell points this out on the evidence from her own fieldwork among Catholic Filipinos:

> . . . the poor and rural people with whom I lived are relatively uninterested in the classic Christian "economy of salvation" (see also, Cannell 1999:137–62). People in Bicol rarely spontaneously mention the ideas of heaven or hell, and I have never once heard them mention the notion of Purgatory. Although they have a keen sense of moral behaviour, they are also unlikely to refer to the possibility of damnation when talking about wrongdoers. (Cannell 2006:144–145)

My own evidence for Apostolics and that of Klaits for Baitshepi Apostolics (Klaits 2010:27–30) is strikingly comparable, and like Catholic Filipinos, Apostolics are not "deeply invested in a morality within the economy of salvation, which is centered on sin, repentance, and justice in the next life" (Cannell 2006:145). Among Apostolics, the salvation of the individual is a concern at baptism and in sacrifice that requires confession and then promises an exchange for individual salvation or at least well-being, as I show in Chapter 6.

FROM GENERATION TO GENERATION: CHARISMATIC DIRECTIONS

The continuing response to Sundkler's foundational text represents a seemingly endless debate—by missiologists or theologians, by church members themselves, by various opponents of the churches, and not only anthropologists—about the syncretism and antisyncretism of Apostolic, Zionist, and Pentecostal churches in southern Africa (see also Daneel 1974). It is a debate dominated by the Christian missionaries and theologians and largely dismissed by the anthropologists until recently.[7]

The most important exception—and now a classic in its own right—is *Body of Power, Spirit of Resistance* by Jean Comaroff (Comaroff 1985). She uses "subversive bricolage" to conceptualize implicit cultural resistance through the reworking of contested signs of authority. Elsewhere and at some length in a contemporary review article, I gave one of the earliest appreciations of Jean Comaroff's study as pathbreaking in its time, and thus worthy of strong criticism (Werbner 1986). There is no need to spell that out here, although I consider that the balance in debate, even well beyond African anthropology and in the wider debate on agency, has turned against resistance theses of the 1980s, such as that of Jean Comaroff.[8]

For present purposes, my summary of the ongoing debate on the new and the old from generation to generation in Apostolic and Zionist churches must be brief. Of recent scholarly and historical accounts, the most insightful are, in my view, by David Maxwell (2006, 2007), David Chidester (1992:112–145), Matthew Engelke (2004, 2007), and Adam Ashforth (2005:184–193). Put simply, and without regard to contradictions or blind spots, the accounts illuminate the change in Sundkler's attitude toward syncretism and conversion and, following his rethinking, changes in the attitudes of white and black Christian leaders of so-called mainline churches in South Africa. Some Christian leaders now see what are called

African Initiated Churches—in itself an awkward label (see Maxwell 2007—as having "a genuine Christian mission in Africa" (Ashforth 2005:190.); others equate the churches with American Pentecostals in a global fellowship and minimize the importance of their African distinctiveness or even differentiation as Apostolics and Zionists (Anderson 1999, 2001). Still others fault them for their quiescence, their failure to speak truth to power, to openly oppose the apartheid state.

The underlying question is a simple one. Is there a dominant direction to change in African charismatic churches? If so, how can this be understood, without falling back on gross oppositions, such as heathen versus Christian, or traditional versus modern? The answers vary, but what is striking is the burden of the old legacy of the linear as history. There is evident difficulty in refashioning the question to take into account reprise and the redirecting of change from generation to generation under conditions of religious pluralism. There is also difficulty in keeping in the same perspective several things—the persistence over the *longue durée*, the generational turns and returns, and the possibly dominant direction of change, at present.

An outstanding exception, overcoming these difficulties in important ways, is David Maxwell's landmark social history of the Zimbabwe Assemblies of God, Africa (known as ZAOGA), *African Gifts of the Spirit* (Maxwell 2006). As it is about transnational Pentecostalism, and thus beyond my present focus, I must treat it here all too briefly, and perhaps too hurriedly.

What is immediately relevant for my purposes is that Maxwell presents his study of charismatics, in my view, from a basic sympathy with a young generation critical of their elders for losing sight of the original way of the Apostles.[9] Maxwell's illuminating book analyses ZAOGA as a movement from generation to generation in which there is a dialectic between its egalitarian ideals, after the Apostles and early Christianity, and its increasing insistence upon hierarchy and authoritarianism. Maxwell's account traces a dramatic expansion from the establishment of the church, on a small scale, in leveling and intimate fellowship by labor migrants to its transnational eminence as a vast, centralized, and bureaucratic organization. We get to appreciate the extent to which the preoccupation with Biblical Christianity, with images of rupture and the fiercely adversarial intolerance of services for the ancestors, is another manifestation of what amounts to an enduring cycle in ecstatic, societal cleansing. Rupture turns into social rapture of a different kind, with regard to the *longue durée* in African history.

Maxwell's analysis shows continuities with early personal security cults—these are the many, ephemeral cults that offer personal protection against witchcraft, cleanse even the accused witches, and renew moral community.[10] In the same perspective, Maxwell addresses the new along with the old: the reworking of the cults in the popular embrace of Pentecostalism, its rituals, and its key tenets of personal salvation and repentance, sanctification, divine healing, and faith in Christ's imminent return.

THE *LONGUE DURÉE:* AN EARLY CULTURALIST ARGUMENT

African Gifts of the Spirit opens the way for a long-term perspective on Apostolics and Zionists, and perhaps other southern African religious movements also. In his view of both continuity and transformation in personal security cults, Maxwell deploys selectively for southern Africa some of the arguments Craemer, Vansina, and Fox raise in their seminal article on religious movements in Central Africa (1976). At first sight, the arguments by Craemer et al. seem to have a striking resemblance to Sundkler's in that they look to culture, above all. In enduring culture, they find deep-seated orientations that persist or change very slowly through transformations from precolonial to colonial to postcolonial times. But unlike Craemer et al, Sundkler has in view *the* culture of *the* Zulu. After all, he writes in agreement with many southern African anthropologists of his time, perhaps fewer now than in the past, who write of *the* culture of this or that people or ethnic group.[11]

Craemer et al. subvert that familiar cultural agreement. Against it, they make up culture from their analysis of what is common among people across a whole region of Central Africa. It is regional culture, not ethnic culture, about which they theorize in their approach to religious innovation and the transformation of religious movements. In defense of their reconceptualizing of culture, they contend:

> Culture in Central Africa is less homogeneous and less particularistic than has generally been supposed. One culture does not exist for each ethnic group, for each shares part of its ethnic make-up, especially the fundamental aspects of its religion, with many others. (Craemer et al. 1975:475)

Given regional culture as their object of analysis, Craemer et al. go on to argue for certain basic parameters—indeed, a hierarchy of encompassing value—that frame the direction of change over the centuries and, they suggest, perhaps even millennia. Arriving at these basic parameters entails a high-order abstraction, by which the analysts discern "the most encompassing value orientation in the common culture—namely the fortune–misfortune complex (Craemer et al. 1975:468). Within that, going from the encompassing paramount value to the more specific values, are distinct constellations; these focus on goals, in specific terms, such as impunity and invulnerability, and security and protection. There are simple assumptions, lasting and shared across Central Africa, that inform the pursuit of these specific goals, for example, the assumption that "disclaims personal responsibility for mishaps and calamities by attributing them to the intervention of significant others" (Craemer et al. 1975:473). Dedicated to such specific goals and informed by unchallenged assumptions, security cults wax and wane, nevertheless; they appear to change in one form after another, often with a dialectical impact making one a significant counterversion of another or a series of others.

That is not the profound truth for the Central Africans, however. Somehow, to the engaged people themselves, each cult looks brand new, as if having nothing in common with the others. Although a curiously unproblematic fact for the analysts, it is one that matches the similar truth Sundkler found among Zionists devoted to the new and in denial of anything in common with divination. Like Sundkler, Craemer et al. see beyond that "truth," given the determining priority that paramount cultural value has in their analysis. It is not a matter of arguing for syncretism in some pejorative sense. Craemer et al. are of course not with the early Sundkler, troubled by the bridge in modern Zululand back to "heathenism," as it were. But they are arguing, comparably in a culturalist approach, about enduring encompassment. That is not the encompassment by what is introduced or received, say, Christianity, as the missionary wants but, at first, finds astray. Instead, that which endures is on the receiving side—it is the encompassment by what is already there, culturally, that enables the reception.

More specifically on Apostolics, here is the gauntlet they throw down:

> The specific quality of Central African religious movements is not that prophets can don snow-white garments and take up shepherd's crooks and attire themselves with different signs of rank and hierarchy, as they do among the Bapostolo. All of that was already there in germ before the movement began, when the Scriptures were first read and were beginning to be understood and brought into line with older basic forms of symbols and rituals. (Craemer et al. 1975:472)

The argument is that even at the initial reception, the frame for encompassment and apparent innovation was already culturally established.

Pushing their culturalist argument to a deliberately even more provocative conclusion, Craemer et al. thunder against much of the conventional wisdom—indeed a basic assumption—among anthropologists and other scholars of so-called new religious movements. Ironically, perhaps, they attack situational novelty as an assumption in their own scholarly culture in order to defend in Central African culture the contrary, the persistence through changing situations, even "enormous changes", of the old, or at least "core elements" of the old:

> Contrary to the allegations of some writers these movements were not purely or even primarily reactions to the stresses of the colonial experience or modernization, they were an integral part of the precolonial Central African tradition, and they were primarily religious in nature. (Craemer et al. 1975:465)

The movements are, indeed, movements, full of innovation—brand new in the eyes of participants—but the analysts as outsiders see move after move, the very changing of movements, to be "an integral part of the precolonial Central African tradition," very much alive in religion across the centuries.

It is obvious that for Africanists, whether anthropologists, social historians, or missiologists, what is controversial—much too hard for many to take—is the minimizing of reaction and with that, transcultural agency. In this culturalist argument, the situational is not only outside the problematic, it is explicitly dismissed as irrelevant. Hence there is no priority for present circumstances or current context, for "radical forms of cultural resistance" or protest, for the "invention of tradition," for modernization and, by implication, globalization and millennial capitalism. The culturalist argument is wholly apolitical, without "argumentative imagination," in my terms for religious change involving image and counterimage, debate and counterdebate (Werbner 1994:212).

It is as if to say, going against the grain of common sense, that the great debates in the study of Christian and other movements are, in a word, misguided. Or worse, fluff. And yet, for all that, what is largely agreed—or at least to my knowledge never questioned by Africanists—is the basic common sense in this early version of the culturalist argument that we might call reception by encompassment.

THE NEW CULTURALIST ARGUMENT: AFTER DUMONT

Because the very notions of hierarchy and encompassment are matters of basic common sense, Craemer et al, who are otherwise given to conceptual explicitness and prescriptive definition, make no effort to spell out what they mean by their basic ideas. The debate, they imply, lies beyond that common ground. It is remarkable, however, that the challenge in a fresh turn in the anthropology of Christianity comes precisely from rejecting the familiar common sense, reconceptualising it, and advancing an alternative.

Arising outside Africa, in concepts and theories originally generated by Louis Dumont in wider theoretical comparison with Hinduism in India (Dumont 1977, 1980) and developed by Joel Robbins with evidence from Pentecostal and charismatic Christianity in Papua New Guinea (Robbins 2009), this fresh turn stands on its head the culturalist argument for reception by encompassment. In the new version, the reception by encompassment makes for radical change, because the encompassment is not at all the old swallowing up the new.

Like Craemer et al., Robbins accepts that values organize culture. Although a group of 390 people, known as Urapmin, provide his case study for culture in the Sepik area of Papua New Guinea, Robbins sees change among Urapmin against a wider background, against variation in charismatic revivals that swept across Papua New Guinea. Robbins does not regard the Urapmin case as typical, but as extreme, in some respects. Fundamentally, his approach, like that of Craemer et al. for Central Africans, is built upon the recognition that there is a paramount cultural value (Robbins 1994, 2004). For Melanesians, this is relationalism:

> In cultures in which relationalism is the paramount value, it is social relations that are valued most highly and other elements (including both persons and things) are evaluated on the basis of their ability to help create and maintain such relations. This does not mean that one never finds holist or individualist representations in Melanesian cultures, only that these are not the most highly valued ones and hence not the most fully elaborated. [Robbins cites Dumont 1980:420, fn.118d, and p.237.] (Robbins 2009:12)

Beyond a measure of overlap with the culturalist argument, and following Dumont, Robbins puts forward a model using alternative ideas of hierarchy and encompassment.

His Dumontian model could be thought of, for our purposes, by analogy between elements of a culture and Russian dolls. They are of a specially inclusive kind—they fit not merely one inside the other but are included both according to size and importance in value and also *relatively* according to contraries in pairs. To follow the analogy in terms of a gender pair, the bigger doll is the man to the smaller one and is the woman, in turn, to an even bigger doll, and so on. Each element can thus stand for a thing and its opposite; that is relative. As Robbins puts it, citing Dumont (1977, 1980), cultural elements (beliefs, ideas, things, etc.) are arranged in hierarchies such that

> the more valued term of a pair encompasses its contrary: that is, in some contexts the more valued term can stand both for itself and for its contrary, as in English the lexeme "man" can stand for both "man" and "woman," or "goods" can stand for both "goods" and "services." (Robbins 2009:1–2)

No doubt an Africanist more familiar with segmentary models could translate that into a hierarchical version of fission and fusion, in which fission at a lower level turns into fusion at a higher one, always with an increase in value (i.e., power). But that would leave the model merely a matter of alternation, or in a more loaded word, static.

Robbins takes his model beyond such overly familiar translation by addressing more of the changeable organization of value in culture. In addition to encompassment, he weights the elaboration of cultural elements, that is, their rationalization such that the greater values dominate, or rather, in a risky step toward a conflict-free view of holistic culture, such that the greater values are not contradicted by the lesser:

> . . . more valued elements tend to be more elaborately worked out, more rationalized as one might put it in Weberian terms, and to control the rationalization of less valued ideas such that they can only be worked out to the extent that they do not contradict more valued ones. Finally, it is only in less valued context that less valued ideas are able to approach full expression. (Robbins 2009: 2)

Unlike Craemer et al., when Robbins puts a culturalist argument of his own, he finds a place in his theoretical model for context and situation, and thus for change being many different things at once. His model foregrounds selectivity but denies disparity—cultural elements are never merely disparate, they always have to be rationalized, as it were, taken on board according to their value, and thus drawn into cultural integration. Hence, according to this model, there can be radical change in which specific things from the past, old ideas and practices such as to do with ancestors, surface still, but they are marginalized in value or importance; they are residual, and they are brought into line with the new paramount value. People keep them restricted to certain limited situations only, and they pursue change by working hard to subordinate the value of the old to that of the new. The point is straightforward. Recognizing radical change for what it is, and not focusing on the marginal residue, is the whole thrust of the model. There is an old bias in anthropology, Robbins contends: the overemphasis on continuity.

In disagreeing with Robbins, and perhaps in the considerable but not exclusive attention I give throughout this book to resilience, to reprise, and to the recovery by one generation of what an earlier generation discards, I might appear to suffer from that old bias. One part of my predicament is that I do not claim to know and, worse still, doubt I can know what the paramount value is in any regional culture among southern Africans.

There is another part, and this limits for me the value of the Craemer et al. version of culturalism, also. It is that I continue to write in the intellectual tradition of the Manchester School (Werbner 1990b), even as my work encompasses, in a Dumontian sense, work in other traditions. Foregrounded still, in my analysis, is the importance of the situation as it is actually contested.

That means at least two things. With regard to value, it means an appreciation of multiple valorizations that are disparate, some overt, others covert, and possibly contradictory, according to intent and who does the valorizing. With regard to the integration of culture as a whole, it means a good measure of skepticism about totalizing.

Included in that skepticism is the question of totalizing Christianity itself, of course. What is problematic is perhaps least marked during first-phase Christianity in certain parts of the world, such as among Urapmin. It is, however, striking where Christianity has a history of evolving over centuries, or where, in the presence of religious pluralism, each church is but one site of contestation among many.[12]

Fenella Cannell spells out this problematic:

> . . . however unyieldingly orthodox the form of Christianity that may be visited on another culture, it can never contain only a single message with single possibilities of interpretation, because Christian doctrine is in itself paradoxical. (2006:43)

This paradoxical nature is such that, she suggests, "even orthodox Christianity contained within it the shadows of its own alternative ways of thinking" (Cannell 2006:43). The challenge this raises for the new anthropology of Christianity is important. If in the past anthropologists have recognized in theory the complex character of Christianity, they now need to grasp this complexity in practice in order to reach more sophisticated models that take account of Christianity being "in tension within itself" (Cannell 2006:43).

In agreement with that, I continue to argue, as in *Syncretism/Anti-Syncretism* :

> As historically situated agents [people] are able to compartmentalize one sphere of social interaction from another, participants disagree among themselves not merely about the desirability of syncretic change, but also about its actuality. (Werbner 1994:212)

New wine in old wine skins, old wine in new skins, young prophet in old skin skirts—all seen to be politicized, highly contentious, embattled in the seeking for power. Writ large as truth, for some it is Power and perhaps for others it is heathen or heresy or cult practice, unbecoming a Christian church. The moral high ground is contested.

"THE SACRED SELF," THE INTRAPSYCHIC AND THE INDIVIDUAL

In the broad literature on the individual, the self, or the permeable dividual, the question is often put as Spiro does in the title of his article on the subject: "Is the Western Conception of the Self 'Peculiar' within the Context of the World Cultures?" (Spiro 2003). I want to turn the question around, away from the peculiar, and toward issues of comparison in Christianity.

At one extreme of Western individualism and the discrete self, the studies by Thomas Csordas of the Charismatic Catholic Renewal movement in New England illuminate the unfolding predicaments of a self recreated for ritual healing with the presuppositions of American folk psychology and psychotherapy (Csordas 1990, 1993, 1994, 1997).[13] The movement is remarkable, and considering it here opens out a broader perspective on religious change in relation to alternatives, the relational and the discrete self. The comparison also brings into relief, by way of introduction, important features of Apostolic prophecy and charismatics that I discuss throughout much of this book.

This American movement, Catholic Charismatic Renewal, is a telling example of the remaking of the modern revivalist legacy that Apostolics also recreate. While the American movement illuminates an extreme contrast, it too shares certain features and rites with Apostolic charismatics, for it is a distinctive development, as a Catholic movement, within the worldwide efflorescence of movements originating in late-nineteenth- and early-twentieth-century Protestant or Pentecostal revivalism. For my understanding of the development of Catholic Charismatic Renewal, I rely on Thomas Csordas's landmark and highly influential ethnography (1990, 1993, 1994, 1997). In this development, individualism is intensified within the community of the faithful, and the overwhelmingly increased preoccupation in religion is with the discrete and, above all, the emotionally injured self, its autobiography, its levels of consciousness, its emotional life and psychotherapy.

What is most distinctive about the Catholic movement is that it brings charismatic healing together with certain disparate influences—the Catholic and the Pentecostal with the professionally psychotherapeutic and the "North American," (that is, more specifically, the cultural themes and dispositions of the New Englanders in Csordas' classic ethnography). Of great spiritual concern to these New Englanders is the healing of memories. It is a concern that is grounded in an American folk psychology, which turns healing into a biographical process preoccupied with the self. But rather than any self, among New Englanders and perhaps more broadly in North America, it is "the true self" as it is popularly conceived to be both conscious and unconscious and also engaged with an internalized other. For the New Englanders in Csordas' study, even spiritual healing becomes "premised on the folk psychodynamic model of bringing unconscious contents into awareness, and including overall concern with the 'true self' or identity" (Csordas 1994:54).

Csordas finds this basis in the presuppositions of a psychology he considers to be widely shared in North America:

> . . . both repressed and conscious memories are regarded as significant constituents of the "self" in North American ethnopsychology. First of all, memory is a powerful *symbol* of the self, such that access to memory is access to a privileged zone of communion with that "other who becomes myself." (1994:110)

Many of the charismatic New Englanders come to regard themselves as the subjects of abuse as children (by a parent, not a Catholic priest in the cases Csordas reports[14]), and they seek religious liberation from the burden they find within themselves, the burden of the internalized other (commonly, a disabling parental figure). Reconciliation is important, though not so much with significant others who are living but primarily "reconciliation with the alterity of the self" (Csordas 1994:132). Above all, the charismatic New Englanders are seekers of an intimate Other who is sacred, the God they can experience embodied and incarnate within themselves. "The spiritual career of any Charismatic," according to Csordas, "is likely to include many . . . instances of healing such that the sacred self can be understood as a pastiche of ritually transformed memories of varying degrees of autobiographical significance" (1994:11). Ritual thus comes to the rescue of the discrete self through autobiographical revelation and sacred treatment in healing that is analogous to psychotherapy.

The Catholic healer uses techniques which are similar in form, though not in content, to "techniques used in image-oriented psychotherapies" (Csordas 1994:75). A simple image, such as that of an afflicted body part, is expected to come spontaneously to the Catholic healer, who gets the patient to elaborate the image by locating it in a known life situation and thus turning a "word of knowledge" or guided image into therapeutic imagery. Both Catholic and Apostolic healers involve the patient in the situating in his or her life world of the revelatory imagery given by the healer. But Csordas distinguishes such revelatory imagery from imagery that is therapeutic, and he finds, "Therapeutic imagery occurs not to the healer but to the patient and constitutes the experiential resolution of a problem" (1994:75). For the Apostolic charismatic as healing prophet and the patient, virtually the opposite holds true, and there is a striking contrast to the imaginative process in divinatory and healing dialogue. What Csordas describes as Catholic "imaginal performance" privileges the patient's imagery over that of the healer, rather than the opposite among Apostolics, that is, the privileging of the prophetic imagery.

The contrast extends to the passage in revelation through dreams or visions. For Apostolics, these access communication with others, living and dead, outside the person, and reveal hidden truths about his or her situation. Earlier I show that the Apostolic prophet as intercessor carries out a visionary walk for reconnaissance of the hidden in the world around the patient. By contrast, the spiritual voyage is, for the Catholics, the patient's own, and it is into the interior of the self in its discreteness. Attention in such Catholic charismatic healing focuses above all on the individual rather than the current relationship with others, and it is dominated by "an ethnopsychological preference for finding an intrapsychic locus of problems" (Csordas 1994:121). Apostolic prophets have little or nothing to say about forgiveness, but forgiveness is essential, and it must be reached by the patient for Catholic imaginal performance to be successful in making the self sacred and thus healed.

There are three pivotal ethnographic features in the Catholic charismatic healing of memories, Csordas suggests:

> 1) that the mergence of autobiographically significant memories is attributed to revelation; 2) that such memories are construed as in some way traumatic; and that healing requires forgiveness of the trauma's perpetrator; and 3) that a privileged mode of healing is an imaginal performance of the traumatic event, or an enactment of a problematic scenario with Jesus in the role of healer. (1994:143)

Here the difference between the Catholic and the Apostolic movements is particularly striking. Earlier I show for the Apostolics the overwhelming weighting—with empathy, vicarious experience, intercession, and spiritual mediation—upon the charismatic healer in his relationship with his patient and the Holy Spirit. By contrast, although aided or even explicitly guided with imagery by the Catholic healer and also subject to prayer and the laying on of hands,[15] sometimes by a whole group, the Catholic patient is spiritually more on his or her own, and hopefully, with the deity , of course.

It is the Catholic patient who bears or even writhes with the moral passion, who has to unveil and reveal his or her own memories, who reenacts trauma spiritually, and who becomes personally creative of a "sacred self." In the most desirable moments of transcendence through "imaginal performance," the one who cultivates the reception of eidetic imagery is the patient and not the healer (not the prophet, as among the Apostolics). The patient is the medium for unmediated communication and for direct communion with God, in felt tactile contact, as it were, in the imaginary embrace of Jesus or the Virgin Mary.

Csordas asserts:

> The embrace from Jesus, observable as his characteristic action in countless episodes of Charismatic healing of memories, is as phenomenologically real qua embrace as are the words he speaks in the recesses of the imagination. There is no more convincing a way that the deity can be both incarnately present and readily accessible. (1994:163)

The swoon is perhaps the most dramatic instance of a fundamental difference in the recreating of religious experience from the legacies of a shared Protestant tradition. It is, I suggest very briefly by way of introduction, that for the Catholic charismatics the swoon becomes the religious experience of communion in bliss, but for the Apostolics it is an experience of shock in disgust, in obnoxious contact with the demonic—the prophet becomes the implacable "sniffer dog" grimly clenched on his prey, his swoon is the very hounding down of hidden witchcraft.

Csordas traces the Catholic term for the sacred swoon, "resting in the spirit," back to the Protestant, "slaying in the Spirit," where Spirit refers to the Trinitarian Holy Spirit, and he explains:

> A person slain in the Spirit is forcibly rendered "as if dead" by the power of God, and hence falls in the sacred swoon. Uncomfortable with this term, leaders of the Catholic movement promulgated "resting in the Spirit" as an alternative. Their intent was to eliminate the connotations of violence on the part of a deity conceived as intimately loving and gentle. (1994:231)

For the Catholic charismatics, their practice is letting go, which they describe as "surrender" and "submission" and which they understand "as giving oneself over to the divine will not just for the moment, but in a moment that symbolizes commitment. Resistance is thus thematized as resistance to the power of God" (Csordas 1994:236). Charismatics say they undergo a calm and relaxed state in which their thoughts are slowed and they become most open to divine healing. Sometimes, they have a sense of peace that changes their lives; sometimes, they experience the "voluptuous gratification of succumbing" in which "there is both release through resignation to one's lot, and the sharing of a slice of heaven as the reward for devotion" (Csordas 1994:251).

When Apostolic prophets swoon, they, like the Catholic charismatics, are usually caught by others, falling backward into waiting arms. There is a display of trust and support and of a subsequent feeling of being energized (often with arms raised and shouts of "hallelujah" or "glory my Lord"), comparable to that among the Catholics. By contrast, however, Apostolic prophets swoon by falling down, limp yet rigidly clenching, by hand or mouth, bits that are evil things, the demonic, fabricated material that they sniff out, in evidently overwhelming disgust. Their swooning keeps more to the Protestant tradition of "slaying" in that it dramatically manifests violence, but not in the "spirit," not in submission to the all powerful God—it is in demonic attack, which the prophets publicly confront, expose, and resist. Apostolic practice thus turns the Protestant legacy dramatizing overwhelming submission into a compulsive impulse for public service, suffering on behalf of the afflicted others. Moreover, rather than a practice of individuality, it is one of dividuality—it is participating in dangerous, permeable contact with the nasty bits of others, the very opposite of the Catholic charismatic preoccupation with the sacred self.[16] If the Catholic charismatic swoon is assuaging, the Apostolic has a tactile shock effect, reverberating beyond the prophet himself, for it heightens the attention of everyone around him to the threat that participation has in their lives. With the Apostolic swoon comes one of those moments in ritual physically and very immediately intensifying the collective perception people have of something fundamental in their being in the world—their very dividuality in its frail vulnerability. I am tempted to suggest also that the Apostolic charismatics' practice in the service of others is kenosis, self-emptying and self-humiliation, recreated in exorcism, not as a divine act of Christ but as a human ordeal of dividuality.[17] If the Catholic healing concentrates on psychologizing, on the personality of the afflicted to change the person's stance toward the world, the Apostolic healing is more sociocentric—it includes personal counseling that is intended to shock and have a powerful impact on the situation in which the person finds herself or himself.

It might well be asked whether the Catholic healer is like the Apostolic prophet in taking on the pain of the patient, in feeling empathy and having vicarious experience. Is there a similarity in mimesis? One answer is given by a woman who is herself a Catholic healer:

> Sometimes when I'm praying, I will be with a person and begin to cry. Not cry as if they were my own tears, but as if the suffering of the other person or the joy—it can be either—were moving though me. Cleansing me maybe, or as if I were representing Jesus and at that point taking on the pain. So I'll just be with them and I'll find tears moving down my eyes. I just know it's different than when I cry. But it's as if I'm the vessel for that. That's very powerful in me. (Csordas 1994:92)

In commenting on this passage, Csordas stresses "the insistent 'as if' used by the healer" that points to "the image's relation to the healer's self, combining the essential indifference and detachment of imagination with the existential commitment to the suffering patient" (ibid.). Csordas adds:

> Another healer explicitly stated that "I cry a lot. But it's not from sadness." Neither, in her view, is it from empathy, but from "being moved" by "the intensity of God's presence." (ibid)

On the whole, Catholic healers do not understand themselves as sharing a patient's emotional state or feeling empathy; nor do they serve as surrogates in mimesis to heighten awareness by mirroring back an interior or hidden condition. The contrast with the Apostolics is striking, and I discuss it at length later.

Because the self as culturally constituted in much of everyday life for the New Englanders is the discrete self, rather than the relational self of the Apostolic charismatics, the practices of the New Englanders and the Apostolics embody fundamentally different ways of being in the world. Yet they draw on a common legacy from Pentecostalism or revivalism and appear somewhat similar, at least at first sight. Accordingly, sacred forms and rites, which the Catholic and the Apostolic charismatic movements apparently share, take on unlike significance; they evoke very different perceptions of the human condition, very differently felt experiential qualities that radically mark one movement apart from the other. "The sacred self" is a ritual accomplishment in personality transformation by Catholic charismatics that has no parallel among Apostolics. What my analysis shows is how the different modes of charismatic healing advance the variation in self processes. Each mode carries that forward, I argue, according to the constituting of either the discrete self, as popularly conceived among American Catholic charismatics, or the relational self, as among Apostolic charismatics of Botswana.

CHARISMATICS AND ALTERNATING PERSONHOOD

The analysis of personhood by Africanists is rich in insight, much of which is yet to be given adequate weight in Christian research. Many Africanists recognize the importance of the relational self,[18] which is "imbued with the presence of others" (Piot 1999:19). Specifically for one Tswana-speaking group, Jean Comaroff finds the relational self labeled *seriti* (Comaroff 1981:644). In the Introduction, I have spelled out this term and its usage more fully (see also Werbner 2007; P. Werbner 2009). More briefly, rehearsed here, *seriti* has come to be translated in English as "dignity" by many people in Gaborone; for some, *seriti* no longer has any metaphysical or substantial meaning, but for Apostolics, and most influentially Eloyi's archbishop, *seriti* as the essential shade or aura of a person, which is substantial, does have a metaphysical significance.

Comaroff herself offers this acute insight, which resonates widely for the relational self in southern Africa:

> Tshidi depict the self as enmeshed in a web of influences, a field of relations with other people, spirits and natural phenomena, none of which are set apart from the self as static, and objectifiable states of being and all of which are linked to the self in terms of continuous strands of influence. (Comaroff 1981:644)

But how far does this insight inform her classic work on Zionists? One might argue that it is more by neglect than anything else, because it is not explicitly theorized any further.[19] The question at issue is: How and what can our understanding of the relational self add to the study of Christian reformation?

Part of the answer lies in bringing together the concept of the relational self and that of the dividual. I suggest that the relational self is an aspect of the dividual, and that much that has been discussed under the rubric of relationality is better conceptualized as dividuality. This step in argument makes it possible to reconsider even further the conventional wisdom about the making of the individual and the overriding force, in religious change, of a Christian postulate of individual salvation.

My argument calls for a shift in analysis within the study of charismatics and, more broadly, within the anthropology and social history of Christianity. Too little in the broader literature has been analyzed apart from the stress on the individual, and there is a major gap in interpretation at the opposite extreme, where the charismatic self is outstandingly relational.[20] The study of charismatics in Africa has yet to contribute to the wider debate and to address the problematic relations between charismatics' individuality, their selves, and their dividuality: How is each defined and changed in relation to the others?

Part of the reason for the neglect of this question comes from conventional wisdom about the individual as a construct in Christian history. Christianity brings the rise of the individual, as much scholarship suggests for many parts of the world. Christianity itself, so the argument runs, places the individual and the salvation of the individual at the very center of the religion's theology. It is, some would also argue for the most recent missionary spread of Christianity, a fact or, perhaps, an artifact of modernity, or even print capitalism and globalization (Comaroff and Comaroff 1991:60–68). Against that, however, my argument looks to the *longue durée* from a pre-Christian past. I find that among charismatics, and more broadly across southern Africa, over generations what endures is alternating personhood. That is, over the *longue durée*, the person continues to be variable. One might say there are two persons in one: an individual and, alternatively, a dividual, someone who is composite or partible and permeated by significant others' emotions[21] and shared substances, including life blood, body dirt, or sexual and other fluids. In other words, something of the person is in significant others, and reciprocally; each partakes of the life of the other. Of course, it might be argued, against a meaningful concept of dividuality, that everyone is in a certain respect a dividual, because sharing substance is a universal condition. To be useful in ethnographic analysis, a concept of the person must have cultural and experientially felt limits for the subjects themselves. Perhaps most important is that being a dividual, subject to the substantive influence of others, is a matter of some concern for the person, who has to deal with the risks and dangers of shared substance, of being composite, permeable, or partible.

The implications of the unstable yet long-term twinning of individuality with dividuality, I argue in this study, are many. They are problematic for the people themselves no less than for the anthropologist. Some of these implications are important for studies of what has been called the modernity of witchcraft (Geschiere 1997; Moore and Sanders 2001); others, for theories of change in religious practice, such as the Christianizing of animal sacrifice and demon exorcism (Barrington-Ward and Bourdillon 1980, Werbner 1997); still others, for problems of self and other and intersubjective management in ritual (Bateson 1958; Kapferer 1983; Werbner 2002). But these studies fail to explore the dialectic between dividuality and individuality that is at the center of the present study. My account brings the conceptual framework of alternating personhood to bear on the study of witchcraft, demonic exorcism, sacrifice, aspersion, and charisma among southern African Christians from generation to generation.

THEOLOGICAL LEARNING: DIVIDUALITY IN THE ANTHROPOLOGY OF CHRISTIANITY

A confession is in order, perhaps true to the present field of study. It might appear that an old anthropology of Christianity was light on theological learning. In that regard, however, the new anthropology has its heavyweights who seem to know more of Christian theology as it has been evolving over the millennia from the early church—they demand that the rest of us, too, know more and, consequently, say more about central dilemmas recurrent in Christianity itself (Webb Keane 1997a, 1997b; Fenella Cannell 2006:12–14).

The obvious difficulty is twofold. First, one needs to know which theologians or historians of Christianity matter—those with a focus on unequivocal law and moral discipline, or on existential paradoxes, ecstasy, and mysticism? How and why do they matter for the study of holy hustlers who are charismatics?

The second difficulty is itself paradoxical, or at least about Christian paradox. The more the learning, the more the theological disputation: where one anthropologist insists that *the* paramount value in Christianity is the salvation of the individual (Robbins 2009), another is equally sure that, as Fenella Cannell asserts:

> The idea that Christianity constructs, through the Incarnation, an absolutely new relation between man and the world might be said to be the central proposition of the religion. (Cannell 2006:14)

My confession is that, with admitted naivety, I have had to suspend judgment. Below I address a legacy, from the fifteenth century, of "coincidental theology." Otherwise, I have largely backgrounded Christian theology, so far, in order the better to open out interests in ethnography that my study of Apostolic holy hustling shares with other innovative research in the anthropology of Christianity.

On that basis, however, I must now make a more direct response to Cannell's call to be theologically informed and attentive to the "tension in Christianity." But my response has to be the naïve one—largely ignorant of theological learning and yet with a felt sense of Christianity's paradoxical nature.

"Learned ignorance," the theological legacy of the fifthteen-century Cusanus, I find illuminating, as it is now being recovered in a series of historical and theological debates.[22] As a mystic and as an exemplary Renaissance man, Cusanus brought together in himself much that now appears paradoxical—he was at once German humanist, philosopher, scientist, mathematician, diplomat, and Roman Catholic cardinal. His approach to dialectics made him a forerunner of Hegel and Marx, and, perhaps, even Dumont. His influence has been forcefully brought to bear in modern studies of the history of religion perhaps most prominently through the work of Mercea Eliade.[23]

Most to the point of the present challenge in the anthropology of Christianity, the arguments of Cusanus located at the very heart of Christian theology the tension between contraries or opposites. In what is now called "coincidental theology," he fathered the notion of *coincidentia oppositorum*. Literally, it means the coincidence of opposites. The coincidence is in interactive opposition, and not the co-instantiation that is little more than copresence. Cusanus's arguments about the implied tension at the heart of Christian theology open out the interaction between the contraries, such that there is a mystery, that is, the transcendence of the opposites. The lifelong challenge for Cusanus as a mystic was the comprehension of the incomprehensible—the mystery of the Incarnation of Christ, God, and man.

Apostolic prophets might well find themselves more in tune with the Catholic Cusanus than with the Calvinists or certain other Protestant theologians in that like the Apostolic prophets he hardly attended to sin or the agony, torment, and death of Christ on the cross. His theology was a move away from the late-medieval devotions to the passion of Christ. Like the prophets, also, while practically aware of good and evil in this world, he had a transcendental vision of a cosmos that is fundamentally harmonious and beautiful. The Apostolic religious aesthetic—that beauty beckons God and the faithful to each other—would appear to meet the one in the Catholic tradition of Cusanus in the Renaissance.

Theological polemic surrounds the vision of Cusanus in a way that Apostolic prophets too might be criticized. Because Cusanus had so little to say about the agony of Christ, the Catholic theologian Walter Andreas Euler has had to defend Cusanus against Protestant critics. They object that Cusanus overlooks the fact of human sin, ignores the need for salvation, and "abandons the cross of Christ in his theology" (Euler 2000:405). Against that, Euler has to turn from the magnum opus and other monumental works of Cusanus to find the needed theological proof. Euler hunts selectively—I found myself being reminded willy-nilly of the prophet as sniffer—to rediscover the truth in the details of occasional sermons by Cusanus.

Euler answers yes to his own question, "Does Nicholas Cusanus have a theology of the Cross?" (Euler 2000). But the affirmative answer is not easily come by; it requires skilful glossing, reasoning about arcane things, and it is in itself an object lesson in the paradoxical nature of Christian theology.[24] It is, as it were, a cautionary example for anthropologists who would found the anthropology of Christianity on encompassment, according to the idea of a simple hierarchy of value in Christianity. Vast religious polemic awaits them: not new tribal cosmologies, but old worlds within worlds of polemical Christian scholarship, often profoundly dividing Catholic and Protestant theologians.

That said, I am tempted nevertheless to bend the reasoning of Cusanus to our interests. According to Cusanus, "Christ is in every person who is directed to him in a complete, living faith" (Cusanus, *De Docta Ignorantia,* cited in Euler 2000:415)—that is, the dividuality of the faithful. Apostolics realise the same dividuality in their devotion to the dew of Jesus, which unites the faithful with Christ. With living faith, however, comes the true individuality, Cusanus argues, "The individuality of each person remains untouched." (ibid.) and each person differs as an individual in the level of unity with Christ. Cusanus arrived at what we can consider to be a Christian model of dividuality and individuality not as simple or exclusive alternatives but as radically constituting each other. They are mutually constitutive in and through Christ.

To pursue this model of dividuality and individuality as mutually constitutive, I want to say more about a problematic in approaches to personhood. If Christianity promises the individual salvation, what does it offer or do for the dividual and the relational self and how does that bear on the study of charismatics and holy hustling?

Dividuality, like the relational self, has, until now, got rather short shrift in the recent anthropology of Christianity. There are two exceptions which point a more productive way forward.[25] The first is Simon Coleman's study of the charismatic gift in the Swedish Faith movement (Coleman 2000, 2004, 2007). Coleman's account runs against the grain in much research on Protestantism in Europe, which has been heavily influenced by Calvinist conceptions of subjectivity, the autonomous individual, and individualism. Coming under an alternative influence, the Swedish Faith movement owes much to nineteenth-century American revivals. These revivals, according to Coleman,

> were founded on explicitly rational principles of efficiency; partly through their influence there was a generalized shift among American Protestants from Calvinist notions of predestination to Arminian forms of Christian self-conception. (Coleman 2004)

Mark Mosko's recent papers on syncretism and on partible personhood and sacrifice in Melanesia are the second exception (Mosko 2001, 2008, 2010). Mosko makes his contribution from the region where, of course, the relational self and dividuality are now felt to be mother's milk—Robbins would speak of paramount value.[26] It would take me too far from my present focus to rehearse at any length the complementary arguments Coleman and Mosko advance. Instead, a simple conclusion must be drawn.

What both the European case and the Melanesian one make plain is that Christianity is more than compatible with dividuality. As the European case shows, in the presence of a stress on the individual, Christian practice can create dividuality afresh, in surprisingly substantial ways.

In the presence of a prior stress on dividuality, exemplified by the Melanesian case, newly introduced Christian practices can exaggerate and accentuate dividuality. Dividuality triumphs, but the practices do not cease to be recognizably Christian, at least in the eyes of the people themselves and perhaps the missionaries also.

The Swedish Faith Movement promises believers a desirable break from the Swedish religious and cultural mainstream. Its practices are deliberately intended to transfer spiritual substance between persons by means of words; it fosters the mutual interpenetration of believing persons. Even more, dividuality is brought to bear alongside and in tension with individuality, especially in Faith ideology:

> The individual person "owns" linguistic properties of the self and "gains" from strategic deployment of spirit-filled resources. Yet in another sense the believer is "dividualized" (cf. Busby 1997: 275; Strathern 1988:348) through the constant need to externalize and exchange the spirit part of personhood. (Coleman 2004)

The person who is an individual, in one sense and yet, in another, dividualized—if this, like holy hustling itself, is a paradox, then it needs not to be dismissed, reduced, or marginalized but comprehended more comparatively. For Apostolics in common, their dividuality is substantive; it is a predicament of being permeated by others' substances that they manage and recreate in part through sacrifice and in part through cosmetics, including the dew of Jesus. For holy hustlers in particular, the dividual emerges, most strikingly, in the passion to be other during vicarious suffering—a compulsion to take on the pain of the other that is imposed from without. In tandem with that comes the assertion of the prophet's own autonomous even willful individuality.

My approach throughout this book has been comparative in order to illuminate both the differences among Apostolic and Zionist churches and also the significantly diverse perspectives on the direction of religious change. I have brought into relief what holy hustling in Eloyi and Conollius fosters by comparison to religious practice in certain other churches. I have addressed transformations that Christianity has effected in moral agency, sociality, and discipline, in ethos, in aesthetics, and in subjectivity. My intent has been to locate prophecy and holy hustling in a context of ongoing debate and discourse—and a historiography of certain writing on religion—in which anthropologists have to make their own contributions alongside, and not always in opposition to, missionaries and other committed Christians, theologians, and social historians. In this debate, I have taken up arguments about syncretism and antisyncretism and theoretical reasoning on the nature of value and the cogency of totalizing in cultural models. My focus has been on major transformations that prevail as Christianity is reformed in southern African Apostolic churches. Given the tension between dividual and individual and the bringing together of contraries in holy hustling, this study of Apostolics opens the way to a new and wider comprehension of prophecy and reformation in the anthropology of Christianity.

Conclusion From Film to Book—*Dianoia* and *Noesis*

THROUGH TEXT AND BEYOND TEXT

Much of this book engages with the counterbearing of the invisible on the visible, and the inaudible or ineffable on the audible. Many paradoxes of the presence that is somehow an absence prevail in prayer, diagnosis, prescription, and exorcism. Prophecy realizes that counterbearing through very different moments. Some come in the mastery of the materiality of witchcraft, others in the patients' subjection and submission, and still others in revelation and the embodiment of the Word in the devotional subject. Perhaps most paradoxical and yet most highly valued by the Apostolics themselves are the moments that represent the redress of the afflicted body in the calming dew, the peace of Jesus, the very Incarnation that is, for Christians, the Presence of Absence.

The engagement with these moments of dynamic counterbearing is pervasive in my film *Holy Hustlers* (2009). Perhaps that is so in any film where what you see is not what you get, because it is conditioned by what you are led to apprehend is beyond sight, and what you hear resounds with the unheard yet understood. The moving image surpasses in the imagination its own corporeal and material presence. Its accompanying sound or even silence resonates with hardly heard truth. Being cinematic, it is moving and, in a word, evocative. If touching, it brings memories close, even of taste and smell, well beyond the audiovisual's sight and sound.

To say this leads to very broad issues of the presence of absence in communication, knowledge, and felt experience. In anthropology and more broadly, there is a growing topic of interest, commonly labeled "Beyond Text."[1] This turn in research reaches beyond the written word to study how communication works through performance, sounds, images and the use of objects.[2] In this Conclusion I take up this turn but reverse it in order to bring more into relief the dynamic interaction—where the image and the written word or the readable text work with and upon each other in ethnography. On this basis, I compare church aesthetics; I analyze the sensual experience in ritual in order to complete my exploration of how charismatic practice makes subjectivities among Apostolics.

By presenting *Holy Hustlers* in the context of this ethnography, my intent is to open out the question of the integration of text with film. Of course, each might be taken as an object in itself, open to critical analysis. The question could become comparative: In an ethnography, what is better done by text or film, and how?[3] And are they complementary or in tension? [4] Or do image-based techniques of research "reinscribe the body and the senses into ethnographic practice" and thus better suit "phenomenologically inflected perspectives" (Grimshaw and Ravetz 2005:7)?

The visual anthropologist Anna Grimshaw addresses the challenge of integrated ethnography by asking one part of the question in this way, "What kind of contemporary synthesis is achieved between two areas of practice, film-making and the ethnographic?" (Grimshaw 2005:17). In answering that she seeks to disclose how such a synthesis might open out kinds of ethnographic knowledge that are different from the kinds that are "articulated through the framework of a discursive anthropology" (Grimshaw 2005:18). Her approach separates one kind of ethnographic knowledge from another. It might bring visual anthropology closer to certain fields in the creative arts, but at the risk of further divorcing visual anthropology from the rest of anthropology—a consequence subversive of her clear intent.[5] By contrast, my own approach seeks greater integration through the ethnography that works a substantial film into a book-length text.

Given the fact that the film *Holy Hustlers* is the father of the book, my focus is processual. In what ways, does the film, and its reception, influence the later text or give it a boost? More broadly, how do my film and text belong in one process and form parts of a single ethnography? There is another challenge: to shed light on the filmmaking itself, from the shooting to the editing to the feedback through early screenings. In this book, I do not take up that ethnography of film production, because, in my view, it is a challenge that calls for a metafilm, a film about the filmmaking, and beyond that an accompanying text, perhaps a metatext: in brief, a metaproject for the future.[6]

TEXT WITH FILM, PROPHECY WITH ETHNOGRAPHY

Within my present focus, I want to address certain contributions that text and film make in this ethnography, while responding also to a basic challenge. This is to be more reflexive about creativity with words and imagery, mine in ethnography and that of prophets in prophecy: How does one bear upon or even become a version of the other?

To begin with, I want to tell the story of being myself the object of an accusation, not quite of witchcraft but perhaps in a common family of resemblances—of being perceived to betray significant others. Shortly before starting to write this book, I met one of our students at the University of Manchester's Granada Centre for Visual Anthropology (GCVA).[7] A man who had risked life and limb for his remarkable documentary on mountain climbers, the student was one of the GCVA filmmakers whose collective criticism of my work in progress has made my whole series of films more accessible. My method has been to screen rough cuts of my films to the GCVA and other audiences in the same way that one offers a paper in progress to an academic seminar. The GCVA audience was the one that put the imprimatur on the director's cut: intelligible, at last. My interlocutor was thus aware of my intent to make my series of films full of arguments, in anthropology, across disciplines, and, hopefully, reaching beyond the academic community.

"What are you going to do next?", asked the student. In unmistakeable dismay, perhaps even disgust, he heard me saying that I was going to Japan to write a book at the Graduate University for Advanced Studies, Minpaku, in Osaka. "So you are going to turn back to writing" was his critical response to my apparent betrayal of the true way in visual anthropology. He had no time for my answer that I had never given up writing, and he found an excuse to walk away quickly, if politely.

On reflection, thinking about the view that in filmmaking I had crossed over into visual anthropology and then was crossing back to social anthropology by writing a book, it occurs to me that there is a misconception. Perhaps it is a matter of dogma or even faith among true believers, like devout Apostolics, who feel beleaguered and thus perhaps defensive. What is being misconceived is the place of writing *in* film. It is as if the less text in an ethnographic film, the better, with the best being the textless film, free of narration and even of subtitles and translation, simply pure—no author speaking in the "voice of God," no intervention in word or image from outside the primal happening, that moment of blissful cine-trance in the actual location of the filming. A story has to be told, but not in text, and certainly not scripted. Instead, the ethnographer has to be dumbed down, or even mute and speechless, never daring to make a judgment or offer an opinion—let the observed action itself tell the story and let the practice speak for the ethnography and, in a word, emerge.[8] Even the subjects have to be somewhat silenced, or at least beyond direct conversation with the filmmaker: interviews are out.[9]

That is, in my view, not ethnography, though it may be a cinematic marvel, and even profoundly moving as observational cinema. Even further, I would argue that the film about charismatics calls for the ethnographer to dare to speak with the "voice of God," because the ethnographer is the one who listens with a watchful eye to the implicit and a whole context of tacit understandings, not otherwise transparent or cross-culturally accessible. If the charismatics are consciously cinematic seers, aware of making out bits and glimpsing reality beyond them, so, too, must the ethnographer as filmmaker deliberately go beyond the surface of things. Or, to push the analogy further, the ethnographer becomes *malgre lui*, a prophet making the unsaid and the unseen known.

"I have had the lecture," said Paul Henley, the founding director of the GCVA, when he shuffled in his chair, with characteristic body language, long slouched now upright, after watching an unsatisfactory beginning for a rough cut of my film *Shade Seekers and the Mixer* (2007). "When," he continued frankly, "does the film start?" Admittedly, there are limits of tolerance in narration, and currently the going rate is at most several lines of spoken text at a time. But, as my colleague agrees and himself advocates constantly, what has to be found afresh in each ethnographic film is the right balance between commentary and observed action. The filmmaker has to face a dilemma of getting one thing right at the expense of the other, either discursive explication or immediate representation. To resolve that in practice is to take up a pressingly open challenge. If there is an academic movement now emerging under the rubric, "Beyond Text," there needs to be a countervailing one, "Through Text and Beyond Text."

This leads me to the archive that I find inviting in *Holy Hustlers* and my other films. In this book, I draw continually from that archive, because my aim is to explicate cultural assumptions and the implicit, to contextualize tacit knowledge even to the extent of a longer lecture than film watchers otherwise tolerate. I recover the archive's subtitles for Apostolic texts, conversations, and interviews, and for commentary, the narration in the archive. I cite and elaborate all of those words and texts at the needed greater length. In some instances, I take the bits out of their context in the filmic story and bring them together afresh, again in a story, of course, but in the ethnographic narrative I write for purposes of analysis. Often, that restores more of the words of an original whole, perhaps a dialogue that had to be cut for the sake of the flow or pace of the filmic story, or even due to the limits of the images. In other instances, I present words listed more fully to locate them in distinct semantic fields, apart from speech. Given the fresh perceptions and new knowledge I myself gain from the moving images I recorded and watch again and again, I bring more of the verbal, from my notes and related literature, to bear in the ethnography. In other words, I deconstruct and reconstruct in moving from filmic text to book text.

There is an obvious parallel with the practice of the prophets: what they find fabricated they fragment, and what they receive in fragments they counterfabricate. Not for them, the natural attitude: theirs is the attitude which defamiliarizes the familiar. The ethnographer, too shares something of the feeling prophets have of being driven to fragment and counterfabricate by an overwhelming compulsion, and not by the desire of an autonomous individual. Ethnographic knowledge is collective knowledge, with the author(s) thrown in.

The filmic archive goes well beyond texts, of course. It registers costumes, deeds, moods, flashes of experience, the look of an eye, the warmth of a face, the pace of feet, the sway of bodies, the wreckage of the holy place, the bleaching heat of the conference tent, and very much more that is sensuous, material and sensual beyond my powers of recording otherwise. It yields immediate knowledge of mimesis and empathy, knowledge that makes contact with powerful religious experience. It has the quality that, in writing on intercultural cinema, the film critic Laura Marks would call "tactile" (2005:xi–xii). Hence it is the kind of archive that does not merely document details but, in refreshing my memory, animates my ethnography toward the vivid in felt experience. In my response to my own film, I feel driven to write ethnography that is more evocative and hopefully more memorable than any I might otherwise have written.

CINEMATIC AND CHARISMATIC AESTHETICS

Even further, my early screenings of *Holy Hustlers*, especially in Kyoto, Tokyo, Beppo, and Osaka in Japan, as well as in Europe, in Manchester, Leeds, Oslo, Liege, Ghent, and Tervuren, drive home to me that there is an aesthetic problem in the very evocativeness of cinematic experience. Sensuous or material as that experience is, it is after all audiovisual. But is that true to what the prophets themselves experience as cinematic seers? And does that fit their own aesthetics? Or is there a need for a text on the senses that goes beyond what film can present or recall? Perhaps even in communication, the cinematic seers intend to go beyond not merely words or texts but beyond images also?

Here comparative ethnography is illuminating. At the beginning of this book, I stress dazzling brilliance and resonant vibrance when I give my first impressions of the young prophets dancing fervently during Apostolic services. The brilliance is, on reflection, all the more overwhelming because of a striking contrast. I have in mind the contrast to certain Apostolics in other churches in Botswana and Zimbabwe whose appearance is relatively plain (Werbner 1985). In his important study of Friday Apostolics in Zimbabwe, Matthew Engelke brings out the contrast in a way that points to the major difference in aesthetics in the force and appeal of things, among Apostolics (2007:233–37).

Having described the Friday Apostolics' plain white robes, Engelke argues that their significance is in "their simplicity—their levelling effect" (2007:233). "The robes are another statement," he concludes, "about why things should not matter in the religious life." They are supposed to be "insignificant in their materiality" (2007:233). This simple, leveling aesthetic has its egalitarian force where a discourse of equality prevails and where a faith that is live and direct is the deep intent in Christian practice. In accord with that, the church rejects and devalues things, including the Bible, it puts overriding value on words, as charismatic gifts of the Holy Spirit. The leveling church practice entails a hierarchy of the senses, and it overwhelms the faithful with loud sound, fully, perhaps equally, shared sound, at the expense of the other senses being minimized as the means of access to the divine presence.

If Friday Apostolics seek to escape materiality by blanking out the richness in material things, Apostolics in Eloyi make their own spiritual escape—to be close and at one with the Holy Spirit—by saturating, indeed, super-saturating prophets in their inner holy circle with gloriously moving color. It is a supersaturation that is moving not merely for people but, above all, for the angels, for pleasing and attracting them from heaven. God's Kingdom in Heaven is glorious, Apostolics say, and so too on earth must they make themselves and their holy space glorious and pleasing to the Lord. The visibility-in-motion of prophets, whirling with splendor, reveals the invisible, God's presence, by making that closer to people on earth.

Even further, on the moving bodies of the whole Eloyi congregation, what is revealed in their imagery of celestial bodies—star, moon, sun, the unequal sources of holy light—and in the many colors they use is not equality or leveling but the blessing in an economy of charisma—an order of distinction and excellence. It is, at once, both a living and moving embodiment of unequal suffering and also a faithful practice for healing that. Memorialized in the varied imagery are the understood ways, as the prophet says, *malwetse a a farologaneng,* sufferings have differed. There is a significant resemblance to the revelatory imagery of Zulu Zionists in their township near Durban. Commenting on the Zionist insignia and emblems as mnemonics and indices of personal suffering, James Kiernan remarks perceptively, ". . . [they] stand out as mute testimony to the fact of outside malevolence and . . . [with them] members are placed along a scale of excellence, some being clearly more battle-scarred and proficient than others" (Kiernan 1979:20).

In Eloyi, the Apostolic aesthetic is movingly sensuous. Superlative beauty beckons to each other God and the faithful, according to the Apostolics' aesthetic. Unlike the Friday Apostolics' aesthetic, but like that of the Zulu Zionists, the Apostolics' aesthetic is multisensual, without a simple hierarchy of the senses. Accordingly, this aesthetic is realized visually, tactilely, and materially—indeed embodied—in laying on hands and manhandling, in rich dress, substances, and cosmetics, including one that tastes very bitter, enough to be an emetic, another that stinks to high heaven. Sight, sound, taste, touch, and smell, all the senses are drenched to excess. It is a supersaturation exceeding the experience and the sensory memories of *Holy Hustlers'* spectators who are not themselves Apostolics. The senses are heightened, according to the Apostolic aesthetic, for the sake of nearness to the divine presence of the Holy Spirit and the angels from the heavens above.

Prophecy among Apostolics, if ridden with suspicion and obsessed with the hidden "underside of things," does not have the closure of a "hermeneutic of suspicion" (Ferme 2001:7). Prophecy, like divination, has a revelatory hermeneutic: it allows for bodily mimesis to reveal the interior, and for the inner truth to be seen on the surface. Clarity and clarification are no less important in prophecy than are ambiguity and suspicion. Accordingly, with that revelatory hermeneutic goes not an aesthetic of ambiguity but an aesthetic of the unmistakable, of, above all, the clear and splendid redress of the body sensuously for the glory of God.

Lest I be accused of making a fetish of continuity in prophecy, I need to stress a radical departure by churches. If religious change proceeds through innovations in space, particularly among Apostolics and Zionists, as I argue elsewhere (Werbner 1985), what is especially forceful in Christian reformation as a process is innovation in aesthetics. It is through innovations in aesthetics that Christians set the sensual appeals of their churches apart from each other and, even more, seek to raise themselves, in body and spirit at once, above others who lack their faith. They introduce a new tone in their lives. They are moved to create very distinctive aesthetics of well-being. At one extreme, for example, among the Friday Apostolics, the sensibility is plain, somewhat puritan, and tormented by the damning lure of material things. At another extreme, among Eloyi prophets, there is a richly multisensual aesthetic and their ritual experience is drenched in memorably excessive pleasure by things and by words. Reaching most intimately, it is through innovations in aesthetics that Christians reconstitute their felt religious experience.

The innovations in aesthetics and religious experience are biased, of course, and not value-free. I want to address the gender bias, in particular, given the masculine dominance of Apostolic prophecy in Eloyi. Again, the comparison to the Friday Apostolics is illuminating. Matthew Engelke's substantial analysis of hymn singing shows that Friday Apostolics turn to vocal music to bring them to the very heights of oneness with the Holy Spirit:

> It is through interventions [in singing] that the gendered dynamics of religious authority receive their most public airings. . . . Most of these interventions were made to disrupt lessons and testimonials in which women or images of womanhood came under fire. (Engelke 2007:221)

Among Friday Apostolics, as in certain other Apostolic churches, call-and-response singing provides a highly valued opportunity for the congregation to intervene in ways that control the significance of the singing.[10] In particular, among Friday Apostolics, the thrust tends to be toward leveling and, above all, against male chauvinism, so to speak.

More broadly, in this Zimbabwean church and others elsewhere in the region, there is a show or a withdrawal of support with the rise and fall of the singing or the selection of the hymn. The interactive singing in call-and-response conveys what a congregation judges about prophets and moves the service in its tone, its feeling, and in the very evocation of God's presence. As a consequence, the congregation's exercise of their own control frames prophecy among such churches.

By contrast, in Eloyi and Conollius, Apostolic prophets take the musical lead in their show of inspiration, just as they serve as the primary devotional subjects during the climax of ritual in trance. Support has to be elicited from the congregation, from the prominent women who are the

Mothers of the Church, above all but it is support strongly framed by youthful masculine control and by the foregrounding of youthful masculinity, and it is accordingly biased. What is celebrated and ritualized in the aesthetic and in the structure of feeling is youthful masculinity as heroic yet pitiable, as caring yet domineering, even bullying, and, perhaps most persuasively moving, as electrifyingly energetic—in the Tswana word, *matlakase*. In such transfiguration, there is a paradoxical fusion of contraries that empowers holy hustling and which brings about a radical departure in religious experience from one generation to another.

It follows that our getting the aesthetics right, at least for Apostolics, does demand ethnographic text, narration in words, beyond the images and sounds in filmed performance in order to reach the taste, touch, and smell that escape the recording media. My point is not to deny that my film and intercultural cinema in general is, in Laura Marks's terms, tactile and multi-sensory (2005, *passim*). I would agree with Marks that "the audiovisual image necessarily evokes other sense memories" (Marks 2005:148). But which memories and which senses are evoked? For *Holy Hustlers,* the reduction to the audiovisual so inflects the performance of prophets that audiences often enter into a moving experience of their own that is sensual, but it is not as memorably multisensual as it is for Apostolics. Instead, it is ever incomplete, perhaps ethnocentric, and often remarkably unlike the prophets' own memory-enriched experience.

That is why this part of my reflexivity turns to comparative argument and a rehearsal of relevant literature. My intent is to make the reader of this text a different watcher and listener of the film, one for whom the awareness of incompleteness enhances the cinematic experience itself.[11] Paradoxical as that may seem, it is nevertheless another instance of that consciousness of the presence of absence which takes us beyond the naïve apprehension of cultural difference in religious practice.

THE PRISM OF *DIANOIA* AND *NOESIS*

Another part of the question of the integration of film and text in ethnography brings out even more explicitly the bond between my creativity in ethnography and the prophets' creativity in prophecy. For this, I find it useful to reflect through a classical prism of ideas, which is suitably double-sided. The ideas are originally Plato's: *dianoia,* or reasoning, which is discursive, and *noesis,* or nous (literally, spirit) and intuition, which is immediately apprehended. On one side, the prism is distant from me and closer to prophets—coming from another era when for most people the say of seers could be the *logos,* the true word. It is, however, the reverse on the other side, in distance and closeness, in that I know my own creativity to be more fundamentally qualified, perhaps bothered, by the reprise of these ideas across the centuries in a tradition that is part of my own intellectual heritage.

Before I bend the prism somewhat for my own purposes of reflection, I need to let that tradition be spoken for, and clarified, with the philosophical authority, which I lack. The philosopher Clyde Lee Miller traces the historic tension between *dianoia* and *noesis* in the light of an unpublished lecture by Richard Rorty, given at Yale University in 1998:

> Richard Rorty has suggested that we may understand philosophy in the West as poised between *noesis* and *dianoia.* A good part of what philosophers have always done and still do is to become masters of discursive reasoning. They use understanding in reason to arrange the familiar and relative things of our own experience in comprehensive and elegant patterns. Indeed, scholars in every field of the humanities and social sciences present arguments, or at least informed and sophisticated discussions, that attempt to describe and redescribe, to order and think through the items of human experience and their contexts. But in principle at the level of *dianoia* everything is contextualised. Everything is open to redescription and recontextualizations. (Miller 2003:2)

To bend this to my reflexive interest is to see a moment of *dianoia* in Apostolic prophecy and in my ethnography. Highlighted for prophecy is the moment of what I describe as the rhetorical strategy of defamiliarization in the direct dialogue of diagnosis. The prophets, also, deliberately "use understanding in reason" (*tlhaloganyo*) to rearrange "the familiar and relative things" of patients' own experience. They talk in a way that Miller, too, would regard as businesslike (see Miller below, on the tone in *dianoia*).

For my own moment of *dianoia,* I redescribe and recontextualize the prophets' argumentation relative to that of divination. Even more, to document and then analyze the remarkable continuity in rhetorical art, I find that I have to recover a wealth of words. The pace of the film demanded short bursts, no circuitous argumentation, no rambling, no extended dialogue. There had to be cuts in talk, compression within subtitle limits, plainer speech without stylistic repetitions or ambiguous innuendo. The film simply would not tolerate the torrent of words in interior dialogue: the use of indicators of reported speech, of brackets and citation idioms, the glossing of flashes of thought and fleeting images. There was no space for the shifters from the interior to the direct dialogue, the tortuous ex post facto reasoning, the fumbling and tacking back and forth, with more or less collusion between patient and prophet to recover a line of interpretation.

Edited out was all that and much more that I have unpacked in the course of this ethnography. Very little of the defamiliarization in diagnosis remains in the film, which largely omits the prophets' narration of their visionary walk from the enigma of arrival to the exposure of the hidden fabrication undoing the patients' lives. Nor does the defamiliarization emerge as reconnaissance; hence, exorcism appears disconnected from diagnosis, rather than grounded in the foreknowledge that the art of prophecy constitutes.

That is not to say that watchers in the early screenings were aware of missing that, or that it is still such a presence of absence that it somehow disturbs or subverts the sympathy of those without firsthand experience of prophecy. Admittedly, a film critic at a festival screening did raise the question of whether an ethnographer can adequately film prophet-patient interaction without a second camera. But, in my view of ethnographic filmmaking, the problem of the number of the cameras pales before the current constraints on the number, the density, and the wealth of words. Where the ethnography of religious language demands parsing that wealth, the ethnographic film has had to get it right in pace and be appealing in audience sympathy at great cost in significant utterance.

"Your film would be better as a radio play," the famous British documentary director Paul Watson commented frankly at a screening of my early film *Shade Seekers and the Mixer* (2007). *Holy Hustlers* is perhaps a more cinematic film, because I could not help but take his criticism seriously. But my experience of taking the film beyond itself within this book is that only by bringing the interpretation together—the cinematic and the textual—can ethnography seize our digital opportunities without disabling cost in description, analysis, and cross-cultural communication.

There is, of course, much more that needs to be said about defamiliarization in prophecy and ethnography, but saying that best comes in response to further points Miller makes on the "tension in the dividing line between *dianoia* and *noesis*":

> We cannot limit our philosophical efforts merely to discursive reason without betraying a part of our own heritage. However much philosophers love to describe and characterize, to categorize and analyze, to reason logically and present the most perspicuous case they can muster there is another philosophical attitude that Aristotle captured in his

> well-known remark (following Thales) that philosophy begins in wonder. Another constant effort of thinkers in the West has been to get in contact with the unfamiliar and the ineffable, to point beyond to what resists categorization, even if they cannot easily talk about this or argue back and forth about it. (Miller 2003:3)

Where the divide between *dianoia* and *noesis* gets blurred for philosophers and after them, ethnographers, it is a transcendental moment for prophets, too. It is the moment when in their diagnostic interior monologues prophets talk of wonder, of being in contact with the unfamiliar and the ineffable, of losing their grip on themselves in a compulsion to become the other. As in prophecy, so too in ethnographic filmmaking; the tension is problematic, perhaps irresolvable, between *dianoia* as discursive commentary and *noesis* as imagery that resists categorization: one may threaten to overwhelm the other, and the right balance between them has to be discovered, often in a dialectic rich in uncertainties or even unknowables.

Miller enables us to pursue that further. He develops his line of reasoning in a way that makes the prism of *dianoia* and *noesis* even more illuminating for our interest in defamiliarization as prophetic and ethnographic practice:

> *Dianoia*, discursive thinking, dialogue and philosophical conversation deal with rather familiar things of ordinary experience, even when they reconstruct or deconstruct their ordinary construals. . . .
>
> But *noesis* thinks beyond such things and attempts to contact the unfamiliar – what transcends normal experience. . . . If the tone of discursive reason is businesslike and efficient, the tone of thinking beyond such discourse is one of being awestruck—of being a captive to wonder . . . we must not forget this second moment, even in philosophy, where one loses one's grip, because one is gripped by something else, something rather different than any or all of the things "dreamed of in our philosophy." (Miller 2003:3)

It follows that defamiliarization is far more than merely a practice of the stranger as fieldworker who undoes the natural attitude of local people—defamiliarization is virtually a staple of ethnography, mine included.[12] Or rather, that is so at least insofar as my approach to the anthropology of Christianity is in the tradition for which an original exemplar in anthropology is Ruth Benedict—this is what Clifford Geertz captures with his razor-edge wit:

> In her work as in [the English satirist Jonathan] Swift's (and that of others who have worked in this tradition—Montesquieu, Veblen,

> Erving Goffman, and a fair number of novelists), the culturally at hand is made odd and arbitrary, the culturally distant, logical and straightforward. Our own forms of life become strange customs of a strange people; those in some far-off land, real or imagined, become expectable behaviour given the circumstances. (Geertz 1988:106)

There is something, however, that Geertz's razor cuts away: the very raw nerve of *noesis*. Guarding against that slash, and thus recovering the *nous* in ethnography also, the philosopher Miller reminds us that:

> . . . we must not forget this second moment, even in philosophy, where one loses one's grip, because one is gripped by something else, something rather different than any or all of the things "dreamed of in our philosophy." (Miller 2003:3)

For prophets, their moment of *noesis* comes in vicarious suffering: they are overcome by the compulsion to be the other, to know and to feel as their own and inside themselves the patient's pain. In trance and when making contact with witchcraft substances, prophets lose their grip, being gripped by something else—the release becomes a moment of sheer exaltation, when they raise their arms and cry out to heaven, "Glory, my Lord."

If western philosophy as a whole is poised between *noesis* and *dianoia*, so too are ethnographic filmmaking and Apostolic prophecy. This ethnography reflects a recursive process, perhaps a dialectic of *noesis* and *dianoia*: the film, once made and seen with responsive audiences, has invited a fresh encounter by the ethnographer with the very depth and complexity of experience the film recalls but inevitably fails to reveal fully; and so too in the writing of the text, critical responses have driven the ethnographer back to the film, again and again, to watch and to listen for more immediate understanding, even for faith in the reality of remembered things and feelings. My conclusion is that the promising way forward in ethnography for the anthropology of Christianity is to reveal that poise—*noesis* and *dianoia* in tension—ever more dynamically through the arguments of words along with the arguments of images: it is a tension that has lain at the heart of this attempt to combine both texts and images in the representation of the Apostolics' experiences with holy hustlers of their faith and their quest for well-being.

Notes

INTRODUCTION

1. For a discussion of the changing usages of "charismatic" for Christian movements linked to late-nineteenth and early-twentieth-century American revivalism, see Coleman 2000:20–27; my own usage follows that of Engelke 2007 and Kirsch 2008, although the term "charismatic" itself is not used by English speakers in the main churches I studied.

2. In Africa, Thomas Kirsch has addressed these issues in a very sensitive ethnography of Zambian Christians, rich in insights into the volatility and situational uncertainties of a dispersed type of charisma among Tonga villagers (Kirsch 2008).

3. My usage follows McKim Marriot's seminal formulation on the person as dividual or divisible in India: "To exist, dividual persons absorb heterogeneous material influences. They must also give out from themselves particles of their own coded substances—essences, residues, or other active influences—that may then reproduce in others something of the nature of the persons in whom they have originated" (1976:111).

4. On the gendered community of suffering in a Ghanaian church, see Ishii 2008.

5. On the deliberate generating of spiritual energy or spiritual electricity in churches, see Niehaus 2001:35.

6. I say more about vulnerability in the time of AIDS in Chapter 5.

7. For the considerable proliferation of new Apostolic and Zionist churches in Botswana, the main site of the present study, James Amanze traces what he regards as the grafting of Christianity in distinctively local forms, and he argues that the success of the new churches has been due not to some break with the past but to their ability to incorporate into Christianity "some of the most cherished and dearest Tswana [ethnic and local] customs dealing with matters of belief in (*Modimo*) God, the ancestors, initiation ceremonies, worship, agricultural practices and more particularly healing . . ." (Amanze 1998:xvi).

8. On Zion City and American workers, see also Jean Comaroff 1985.

9. Baptism is controlled by the church hierarchy, and the charismatics who are my main subjects as faith healers are sidelined in that, as I explain more fully in Chapter 1.

10. James Amanze reports the testimony of the founders of other churches who suffered banishment, arrest, and imprisonment in the late 1950s. He sees this general trend: ". . . the 1950s was also a difficult time for the African Independent Churches in Botswana. Although the mission churches had lost power in controlling the formation of new churches, the traditional chiefs were still unwilling to give them freedom of worship because of the divisive nature of the new religious movements. The new churches continued to face open opposition" (Amanze 1998:83).

11. In an important study of the moral imagination in Botswana, Julie Livingston writes of "interconnectedness" for what is "dividuality," in my terms, and she relates that to the flow of substances between people. Livingston reminds us, ". . . there is a perpetual tension in Tswana thought between the individuality of each person, which is a defining feature of his or her humanity, and the interconnectedness of people and their hearts as reflected in procreation, language, law, and morality . . . In *bongaka* [Tswana healing practice], tensions between the social person and the inner/individual self are reflected in physiology and medical diagnosis: the heart is the center of individuality, the *madi* (blood, semen) is the substance of relationships and social life, and the *mowa* (breath or soul) constantly moves between the person and the environment" (Livingston 2005:166–67; see also Livingston 2009).

12. Problems of alternating personhood have arisen in early comparative debate about the dividual and individual in South Asia (Marriot 1976; Mines 1988; McHugh 1989). In her contributions Katherine Ewing writes of "multiple selves" and "shifting selves" that are context dependent, and she opens out debate "on how multiple self-representations are organized, contextualized, and negotiated in dialogue" (1990:274).

13. For a discussion of *kgaba* in another Apostolic church, see Klaits 2010:5, 194–96, 270–71, 309 n13.

14. See P. Werbner 2009. The notion of *seriti,* as involving regard in the eyes of others, is closely documented in my film *Shade Seekers and the Mixer* (2007), and in commenting on that, and in particular on *seriti* as a relational phenomenon that bears on respect and blessing, Klaits opens out the comparison to moral reflection among Apostolics (2010:172–174).

15. For a contrast in Ghanaian Pentecostal discourse, see Meyer 1998.

1. HOLY HUSTLING

1. Michael Taussig illuminates Walter Benjamin's insight into mimesis as a compulsion of persons to "become and behave like something else," and he argues that Benjamin's discovery of the importance of mimesis in modernity fits "a sudden rejuxtaposition of the very old with the very new" (Taussig

1993:20; see also Buck-Morss 1991:263–70). I return to the problematic of such a rejuxtaposition, and the importance of reprise for Christian reformation, in chapter 9.

2. It is worth noting the contrast to medieval devotional practice, mimesis, and empathy, all of which engaged the devout with holy others as alter egos. Laura Jacobus makes that plain in her account of Giotto's achievement in the frescoes of the Arena Chapel of Padua (2009a, 2009b). Giotto enhanced the viewer's devotional experience by imaging the interior of the chapel itself within his holy scenes. The viewers were encouraged to start with mental preparation before the image of the Crucifixion and then to reflect on a version of themselves as the others in the Passion. "Medieval devotional practices stressed such mental preparations, encouraging the worshipper to pray in a spirit of penitence, or to meditate on the sufferings of Christ and the Virgin Mary in order to truly understand the meaning of Christ's sacrifice for their sins. It was common to suggest that a devout frame of mind could be induced if the worshipper imaginatively engaged with holy personages such as the Virgin Mary or Mary Magdalene, empathising with their emotions or envisaging themselves taking part in the events of Christ's life" (Jacobus 2009:54). Later I say more about the prophets as devotional subjects, and in chapter nine I consider the comparison to a Renaissance sensibility toward the Passion of Christ.

3. Anthony Simpson points out how problematic self-knowledge is in Catholic formation for Zambian postulants. They are told by missionaries that "they must look inward to find out whether God's call was true," but their own understandings of personhood start from the proverbial wisdom that "you cannot look inside a person" (Simpson 2003:392).

4. For the example of urban slang among Dioula in Ivoire, see Newell 2007.

5. For the argument that this extra-hierarchical prominence gives women influence counter to the formal authority of men, who dominate the church hierarchy, see West 1975:50–51; for the alternative, among urban Zionists near Durban, where many women are prophets but all the outstanding, dominant ones are men, see Kiernan 1976a:357.

6. On the heightened sense of vulnerability in the time of AIDS, see Chapter 5.

7. On the comparison between wisdom divination and Apostolic prophecy in terms of the importance of empathy, see Chapter 8.

8. In the past, *sangoma* were distinct from diviners, who were not mediums or dream interpreters but who cast lots in one form or another of wisdom divination. Now there is less distinction in that *sangoma* also cast lots. On *sangoma* see Janzen 1992, 1994; on wisdom divination, see Werbner 1989, 2002.

9. For an account of similar change among Tonga in Zambia, see Colson 2006:235–265.

10. On this logocentric perception in another Apostolic church in Gaborone and the church's opposition to the logocentric expression in divination,

see Klaits 2010:156–159; and for the church's trust in the Christian voice and the word, see also Chapter 4; Klaits 2010:163–212.

11. On the power of the word among Zionist prophets in a township outside Durban, see Kiernan 1978:30.

12. On the agony of Christ, Iberian Christianity, and the reception in Africa, during different historical periods of the passages in the Christian drama, see Werbner 1997; on the wider comparison to Medieval and Renaissance practice, see also Chapter 9.

13. On the unorthodox use of incision by Prophet Matthew, see Chapter 7.

14. On fabrication and the invisible realm in Mozambique, see West 2005.

15. In the Conclusion I return to the sensual aesthetics among Apostolics and the contrast to Friday Apostolics in Zimbabwe, who do privilege the aural at the expense of the visual; see Engelke 2007.

16. On the unease with and even denial of empathy in the Catholic Charismatic Renewal movement, see Chapter 9.

17. An absence of the drum and dance is noted by Janzen (1994:165).

18. In the practice of Zionist prophets, James Kiernan finds similar negotiation and tolerance of error: "In divining, the prophet proceeds by a method of trial and error, so that the central place of error in prophetic utterance is readily conceded and it does not always operate as a discrediting factor" (Kiernan 1976:364).

19. On the problem of Christ's presence and distance, see Engleke 2007.

2. BETWEEN THE PROPHETIC AND THE PASTORAL

1. Apostolic churches in Botswana are differentiated by their practice of sacrifice as a burnt offering to God, as an offering also to the ancestors, who receive blood or the smell in accord with traditional practice, or as involving a traditional meal for a congregation (see Amanze 1998:190–92).

2. Kiernan 1991:36, footnote 6, citing H.-J. Becken in correspondence; on Apostolics, see also West 1975:177.

3. Njebe and Martha feature prominently in my film project *The Well-Being Quest in Botswana*—now a series of four films available from the Royal Anthropological Institute.

4. On Rouch and cine trance, see Henley 2009.

4. ESCALATING CRISIS: FAITH AND TRUST "UNDER DESTRUCTION"

1. *Tlotlo* is a notion of respect that extends to the idea of being worthy of regard by others, and it relates to what, in a wide-ranging study, *Honour in African History*, John Iliffe calls "householder honour" by contrast to "heroic male honour" (2005:155 and *passim*). Included in householder honor were assumptions about respectability. A legacy of the colonial era, in Iliffe's view, was the relative taming of heroic male honor by an accentuation of the

respectability in householder honor. "Respectability was the chief means" Illife suggests, "by which Europeans tried to domesticate African notions of [heroic male] honour, replacing their emphasis on rank and prowess with stress on virtue and duty. Africans, equally, adopted respectability to liberate themselves from ideas of honour no longer in tune with reality" (2005:246).

2. An example is the critical letter by attorney Mothoothata M. Lesole written on 29 January 2003 on behalf of The Eloyi Christian Church (apparently at the request of the bishop and archbishop) to the Registrar of Societies:

> In one of your letters to your office it is complained that there is no confidentiality in the Church file, as some people [i.e., the Bishop] seem to know everything. Why should a complaint be made in a corner when it concerns a public institution? One is puzzled when one has regard to section 37 of the Societies Act CAP 18:01 which provides for inspection of documents. . . . The Church submits and requests that you must confirm to the Complainants that your office does not have power to give the requested intervention and that they must use the General Body as provided in the Church Constitution. If they are unhappy with the decision of the General Body, the Courts, and not your office may hear their grievance. (Registry of Societies 2003a, H28/26/721 (62))

The Registrar of Societies accepted the lawyer's advice and passed it on, in a letter of 18 February 2003 to the complainant from a dismissed executive committee:

> Like I mentioned, the societies section does not deal with disputes of societies. Any problem that comes up within your society can be best dealt with through your constitution following the prescribed committees including the general membership. If all efforts fail to normalise the situation, especially where the constitution is being violated, the aggrieved party can use the Court of Law as an intervention. (Registry of Societies 2003b, H28/26/721 (63))

5. SCHISM, INNOVATION, AND CONTINUITY

1. On the widespread use of wool in Apostolic and Zionist churches, see West 1975:117.

2. On purity and the wide use of white robes, see West 1975:177

3. For my account of that, see Werbner 2004; for an account based on fieldwork in Mogoditshane, the urban base of the Eloyi church, and an argument about generational perspectives on death in Botswana's time of AIDS, see also Ritsema 2008. Ritemsa provides evidence of a difference between generations

in expectations. I did not find in Eloyi similar evidence of the younger generation resorting to rationality and a discourse of numbers in interpreting AIDS deaths.

4. In Chapter 9, I consider the avoidance or unease about empathy among Catholic Charismatics in New England, who accentuate individualism and the discrete self and who rely upon presuppositions from North American folk psychology and psychotherapy (Csordas 1994).

5. Wholeheartedness is valued among Apostolics, as it is more generally among Tswana who are not church members. But such empathy differs from the one that prophets compulsively undergo.

6. For evidence from Botswana's capital on the acceptance of death and suffering as a condition of modernity and development in Botswana's time of AIDS, see Ritsema 2008. For an insightful account of perceived vulnerability among Batswana in this time of AIDS, see Livingston 2009.

7. The best account for Botswana (primarily south-eastern Botswana) of the recomposing of the self and personhood in relation to changing medical ideas is Livingston 2005.

6. PERSONAL NEARNESS AND SINCERITY IN PRAYER

1. The prophet's logocentric assertion is a Christian orthodoxy widely shared by Apostolics and Zionists, which Kiernan reports in words almost the same as the prophet's: "The usage of water therefore testifies to the power of the word which is spoken over it and which transforms it from ordinary water into powerful water. The power of air, breath, voice, word is mysteriously transmitted to the water which is then suffused with the power of spirit" (Kiernan 1978:30). In the same vein, Engelke comments on substance and the power of blessing, in particular for holy honey, "Regardless of the ingredients or their preparation, however, I was told that what mattered was the blessing conferred on it by the Holy Spirit. Indeed, holy honey, like all apostolic medicines, is understood to be powerful because of its spiritual properties. As a substance it does not matter" (Engelke 2007:226). On the transformative power of the voice among other Apostolics in Gaborone, see also Klaits 2010:163–212.

2. *Tumelo,* which I translate as faith, is also commonly translated by Tswana as "belief." As Klaits reports, "In Tswana, 'belief' and 'faith' are rendered by the same term, *tumelo,* which derives from the verb *go dumela,* to agree" (2010:23). Klaits prefers to leave the term untranslated by one word, and he highlights "divergences between *tumelo,* and certain connotations of faith and belief common in contemporary Euro-American usage" (ibid.). My understanding of *tumelo* is close to Kirsch's view of belief among Gwembe Tonga: "Belief was quintessential to their religious practices just because it had a certain performative power directed at 'the world outside,' namely the power to invoke spirits [for Apostolics, the Holy Spirit] and, therefore to invest rituals with effectiveness" (Kirsch 208:702).

7. DIAGNOSIS, RECONNAISSANCE, AND FABRICATION

1. For an analysis of the use of citation idioms to detach responsibility from diviners in West Africa, see Graw 2009.

2. On the story of Martha and her husband's quest for well-being and the issues of impotence, infertility, and gynaecological illness, see my films Werbner 2005, 2007, 2008.

8. PRESCRIBING CHRISTIAN COSMETICS: MOVING BODIES AND INTERCORPOREALITY

1. Three of my films (2005, 2007, 2008) closely regard Martha's life and her subjectivity as a patient, and they disclose the personal meanings of *sefifi* for Martha and her husband, Njebe. The films also provide much documentation and ethnographic illumination complementary to this book's account of patients' subjectivities. My most recent film (2009) is similarly complementary, with regard to intersubjectivity, but focuses more on the charismatic prophets.

9. OLD AND NEW IN CHRISTIAN REFORMATION

1. For a response that brings the rejuxtaposition of the old and the new together, see Engelke 2004.

2. For a sympathetic appreciation of Sundkler's major books, and his last book, coauthored, flawed, and posthumously published, see Maxwell 2002c; see also Engelke 2003. In a review of a Sundkler "biography/autobiography/epistolary collection," Terence Ranger gives a remarkable, personally informed insight into Sundkler's sensibility and his sympathy with African religious experiences (Ranger 2003). David Maxwell reminds us, "In [Sundkler's] sequel to *Bantu Prophets—Zulu Zion and Some Swazi Zionists* —he reconsidered his judgements about the dangers in South African Independency and helped nudge it into a closer fellowship with the global Christian communion. Ecumenism was always a present theme in his scholarship" (Maxwell 2002c:434). It is worth saying that Sundkler and the leading anthropologist in Zulu research, Max Gluckman, became lifelong friends, who visited and exchanged ideas with each other over many decades, as I witnessed. Gluckman encouraged Sundkler in an early period, admired his work, and supported the publication of the revised version of Sundkler's classic monograph.

3. For personal communication with Sundkler on that, see West 1975:177.

4. Robbins finds this bias and proposes an alternative Robbins 2009; for his discussion of images and rituals of rupture among Pentecostals, see Robbins 2004:127–130.

5. See also his early accounts of syncretism, which he obviously admires as an innovative cultural creation, and the symbols for which he unpacks in

fine, subtle detail (Kiernan 1976, 1978). Kiernan's contribution on diviners and prophets is part of his very substantial and perhaps much-too-neglected body of linked work on Zionist religious creativity (Kiernan 1976a, 1976b, 1977, 1978, 1979, 1982, 1990, 1991, 1994, 1995).

6. The Apostolic tendency away from institutionalized confession is even stronger in Baitshepi, which lacks confession but encourages moral reflection through hymn singing (Klaits 2010:172).

7. See Kiernan 1994; for an appreciation of religious pluralism with multiple religious affiliations and seemingly contradictory religious orientations, see Kirsch 2004; for my own views on syncretism/antisyncretism, see Werbner 1994, 1997.

8. For further rethinking among South Africanists of the resistance thesis in Comaroff's argument, see Chidester 1992:134; and on the condemnation of the Zion Christian Church (ZCC) by the Truth and Reconciliation Commission, see Ashforth 2005:191. For the current need to move beyond the resistance thesis, or "the imposition of modernity," and to advance a different kind of anthropology of Christianity, see Cannell 2007:11–13 and Engelke 2007. For the wider critique of resistance, see Sahlins 2002:52-57; Asad 2003:71; Ortner 2006:42–62; and the feminist critique, Mahmood 2005:5–10).

9. Maxwell delivers his insights at the frontiers between social history and ethnography. His work, *African Gifts of the Spirit,* is strong in documentation—he rescues a vast correspondence by making the archive for the church correspondence from its founding—and the book has much strength from participant-observation. For a sympathetic approach to young Pentecostals in Malawi, see Van Dijk 1992.

10. For my earlier discussion of the dynamics of personal security cults from precolonial to postcolonial times, see Werbner 1989, Chapter 5.

11. This notion of culture remains common among the Melanesian anthropologists, more common than among the southern African.

12. For an insightful analysis of multiple valorizations seen against the problematic of belief under conditions of religious pluralism, see Kirsch 2004.

13. I note that Csordas' study precedes the twenty-first-century digital revolution whose impact on individualism and the discrete self may well be re-creating dividualism and the relational self in a new age. What the significance of that is for religious experience and charismatic practice is an open question.

14. Although*The Manual,* the critical report by Ray Mouton and Tom Doyle on child abuse, was widely circulated among American Catholic bishops in 1985, the scandal fully became public after Csordas' research in the 1990s. It is worth noting that the secrecy was such that it kept the painful problematic for both the priests and the patients themselves from Csordas' knowledge, despite his care for the record of cases in psychodynamic and therapeutic depth. *The Manual* (Mouton and Doyle 1985) is online at http://tiny.cc/yhsdw, and for an account of the church secrecy around child abuse, see O'Neill 2010.

15. About the laying on of hands, Catholic charismatics are remarkably and explicitly ambivalent in ways that Apostolics are not. The Catholics share with New Age healing an intent to evoke divine power as "energy," through the hands as "a kind of energy interface where divine love enters and negative energy exits the person" (Csordas 1994:54). Such energy is comparable to the spiritual electricity evoked by Apostolics. But Catholic supplicants can be uneasy in that they fear the intimacy, the intrusion into the self, and sometimes have a sense of "intimidation at being touched at all" (ibid.), perhaps in recoil against the repressed history of child abuse. For my account of intercorporeality among Apostolics, see Chapter 8 and also my discussion of handling by Bishop Boitshepelo in Chapter 3.

16. The demonology of Catholic charismatics is a major subject of a part of Csordas' analysis that I cannot address fully here. He argues for domains in their ritual language. That of demonology has a "representation of the redundant heaviness weighing upon the afflicted self in isolation," and an alternative, more positive domain of the emotions has "a semantic representation of the mutual implication or interinvolvement of sacred selves in the charismatic community" (Csordas 1994:188).

17. On the Christian theology of kenosis and its importance for defamiliarization and shock, see Bogdanov 2005:50; see also Emerson 2005.

18. See Riesman 1986; Jackson 1982:22–23; Werbner 1990a, 1996; Jackson and Karp 1990.

19. Jean Comaroff addresses theories of selfhood, but of the bourgeois self, when she and John Comaroff write on missionary conceptions of the person in the nineteenth century (1991:60–68). They remind us of the modern imagining of the radically individuated self, and they relate that to the Nonconformist missionaries' efforts to spread literacy. In Europe, according to historians of literacy, "its social impact was closely tied to the ascendance of the reflective inner-directed self: a self, long enshrined in Protestant personhood, now secularized and generalized as bourgeois ideology" (Comaroff and Comaroff 1991: 63). It is the further imagining of the radically individuated self that advances the development of the American movement of Catholic charismatics, as Csordas has shown (1994).

20. Frederick Klaits' account of Apostolic charismatics makes a landmark contribution in addressing this gap (2010).

21. On the relational self and the sentiments that Tswana speakers express, see Klaits 2010:2–6.

22. For the current relevance of his life and theology, see Casarella 2006; Blystone 1972.

23. See Wasserstrom 1999, Chapter 4, for a helpful guide to the modern impact of Cusanus and his idea of the *coincidentia oppositorum* for, among others, Gershon Scholem, Jung, and Dadaists; on Eliade and the *coincidentia oppositorum* , see also Valk 1992.

24. Although Euler answers "yes," he in fact also answers "no," in a feat of theology, "Does Cusanus Have a Theology of the Cross?" (Euler 2000). If you

understand theology of the cross in the sense of Luther's *theologia crucis*, then the answer must surely be no. If you understand theology of the cross more generally, as the attempt to ascribe to the cross of Christ a substantial meaning by means of theological arguments so that we gain insight into both divine revelation and the event of salvation (without reducing divine revelation to the event of salvation or vice versa), then the question, in my opinion, can be answered in the affirmative.

25. See also my discussion of composite personhood in Bwiti (Werbner 1990a), and on dividualism in birthing ritual (Werbner 1996). Thomas Kirsch objects to the view that the reformation of subjectivities through African churches should be seen as a move toward "reflective, inner-directed selves." He stresses the importance of the "spiritual permeability of the body" in new African churches and concludes that it has consequences in religious literacy, among other things, that run counter to early Protestant missionaries' ideas of' "reflective, inner-directed selves" (Kirsch 2008:11).

26. See Strathern 1988, the work that is, of course, the acknowledged starting point for both Coleman and Mosko, and to which I am indebted also.

CONCLUSION: FROM FILM TO BOOK—*DIANOIA AND NOESIS*

1. Beyond Text is the title of a major international conference convened at the University of Manchester in 2007 by Rupert Cox, Andrew Irvine and Chris Wright in combination with the film festival of the Royal Anthropological Institute. The conference shares its theme and title with a five-year project from 2007 on communication, which is funded in millions of pounds by the Arts and Humanities Research Council in Britain. On "the growing interest in areas of ethnographic interest that lie beyond discursive reach," see also Grimshaw and Ravetz 2005:6.

2. There is a related turn in the study of mass mediation among charismatics. These studies examine how charismatics use audiovisual media, in films and DVDs, or photographs to command a sector in the public sphere (Hackett 1998; Hughes and Meyer 2005; Meyer 2004, 2005; Meyer and Moors 2006; de Witte 2004, 2010). Apostolic charismatics have hardly begun to engage with such filmic mediation in Botswana. Hence mediation is tangential to my study, although I take into account sensational coverage, on Botswana TV, of Apostolic exorcism.

3. These questions are much considered in recent literature on ethnographic film; see Banks 2001; Grimshaw 2001; Grimshaw and Ravetz 2005, 2009, Heider 1990; Macdougall 1998, 2006; Postma and Crawford 2006; Russell 1999.

4. In a review article appreciating the seminal contribution of David Macdougall, Ivor Strecker comments on the price of MacDougall's influential "exaggeration of the difference between images (film, photography) and writing." Strecker suggests, rightly in my view, that the price is too high: As I was reading the agonizing text of "Visual Anthropology and the Ways of Know-

ing" [a chapter in Macdougall 1998] I felt like shouting: "Don't you know that you do with film, what you do with words, and with words what you do with film. Both are evocative and both need our interpretative attention. Either you start with the text and then conjure the images, or you start with the images and then conjure the text" (Strecker 2001:2008).

5. In stressing the dominance of discursive anthropology, Grimshaw acknowledges but somewhat underplays the major influence for more than a decade, especially in the anthropology of religion and ritual, of work on embodiment and the senses by anthropologists such as, among others, Csordas (1990), Taussig (1993), Stoller (1997), and Jackson (1998).

6. I have begun this project by recording in various countries the reception of the four films in my *Quest for Well-Being in Botswana* series. My intent is to make a film about that, tentatively titled, *Counterpoint.* For an ethnography of the production and reception of documentary film, see van Dienderen 2008.

7. For a participant's account of the Granada Centre for Visual Anthropology, see Grimshaw 2005:18–24. More of the issues in this present conclusion are raised in a wide-ranging interview with the GCVA's founding director, Paul Henley; see Flores 2009.

8. For the argument, dismissing "the conventional" and for a renewed defense of observational cinema "as a distinctive form of anthropology in its own right," see Grimshaw and Ravetz 2009.

9. For a perceptive view of wordy "intercultural cinema" and the shift away from verbal language, see Marks 2005:xv.

10. For Masowe Apostles in Zambia, see Jules-Rosette 1975, 1979; for Gwembe Tonga Apostolics, see Thomas Kirsch 2004, 2008; for Friday Apostolics in Zimbabwe, see Engelke 2007:210–222; for Zionists, see Kiernan 1990.

11. The ethnographic text is intended to enable the viewer to move from being a passive spectator to being an active participant experiencing the world of the film with an informed consciousness.

12. From a somewhat different perspective on discursive knowledge, Anna Grimshaw reaches a similar conclusion, "Observational cinema profoundly subverts traditional models of academic learning based upon discursive knowledge. Specifically, it works to defamiliarize, to render the familiar strange; and, as such, it mirrors the 'surrealist' experience enshrined at the heart of ethnographic fieldwork" (2005:23).

References

Amanze, James

1998. *African Christianity in Botswana: The Case of African Independent Churches.* Gweru: Mambo Press.

Anderson, Allan

1999. "The Lekganyanes and Prophecy in the Zion Christian Church." *Journal of Religion in Africa* 29 (2):285–312.

2001. *African Reformation: African Initiated Christianity in the 20th Century.* Trenton: Africa World Press.

Asad, Talal

2003. *Formations of the Secular.* Stanford, California: Stanford University Press.

Ashforth, Adam

2005. *Witchcraft, Violence, and Democracy in South Africa.* Chicago: University of Chicago Press.

Bakhtin, Mikhail

1984. *Problems of Dostoevsky's Poetics.* Edited and translated by Caryl Emerson. Minneapolis: University of Minnesota Press.

Banks, Marcus

2001. *Visual Methods in Social Research.* London: Sage.

Barrington-Ward, S., and Michael Bourdillon

1980. "Postscript: A Place for Sacrifice in Modern Christianity." In *Sacrifice,* edited by Michael Bourdillon and Meyer Fortes. London: Academic Press for the Royal Anthropological Institute.

Bateson, Gregory

1958. Naven: A Survey of the Problem Suggested by a *Composite Picture of the Culture of a New Guinea Tribe drawn from Three Points of View.* Stanford: Stanford University Press.

Beidelman, Thomas

1966. "Swazi Royal Ritual." *Africa* 36 (4):373–405.

1971. "Nuer Priests and Prophets: Charisma, Authority and Power among the Nuer." In *The Translation of Culture,* edited by Thomas Beidelman, 375–416. London: Tavistock.

Blystone, Jasper

1972. "Is Cusanus the Father of Structuralism?" *Philosophy Today* 164 (Winter):296–305.

Bogdanov, Alexei

2005. "*Ostranenie,* Kenosis and Dialogue: The Metaphysics of Formalism according to Shklovsky." *Slavic, East European Journal* 45 (17):48–62.

Buck-Morss, Susan

1991. The Dialectics of Seeing: Walter Benjamin and the *Arcades Project.* Cambridge: The MIT Press.

Buhrmann, M.V.

1977. "Xhosa Diviners as Psychotherapists." *Psychotherapeia* 26:17–20, 297–312; 27:41–57, 163–173.

Buhrmann, M.V. and J. Nqaba Gqomfa

1980. "Xhosa Healers." *Journal of Analytic Psychology* 26:297–312, 187–201.

1981. Xhosa Healers." *Journal of Analytic Psychology* 27:41–57, 163–173.

Cannell, Fenella

1999. *Power and Intimacy in the Christian Philippines.* Cambridge: Cambridge University Press.

2006. *The Anthropology of Christianity.* Durham and London: Duke University Press.

Chidester, David

1991. *Religions of South Africa.* London and New York: Routledge.

Casarella, Peter

2006. "Introduction." In *Cusanus: The Legacy of Learned Ignorance,* edited by Peter Casarella, i–xxix. Washington, D.C.: University of America Press.

Clifford, James

1988. *The Predicament of Culture.* Cambridge: Harvard University Press.

Coleman, Simon

2000. *The Globalisation of Charismatic Christianity: Spreading the Gospel of Prosperity.* Cambridge: Cambridge University Press.

2004. "The Charismatic Gift." *Journal of the Royal Anthropological Institute* 10 (3):421–442.

Colson, Elizabeth

2006. *Tonga Religious Life in the Twentieth Century.* Lusaka: Bookworld Publishers.

Comaroff, Jean

1981. "Healing and the Cultural Order: The Case of the Barolong Boo-Ratshidi of Southern Africa." *American Ethnologist:* 7 (4):637–657.

1985. *Body of Power, Spirit of Resistance: The Culture and History of a South African People.* Chicago: University of Chicago Press.

Comaroff, Jean, and John Comaroff

1991. Of Revelation and Revolution: Christianity, *Colonialism, and Consciousness in South Africa.* Chicago: University of Chicago Press.

1993. Modernity and its Malcontents: Ritual and Power in *Postcolonial Africa.* Chicago: University of Chicago Press.

Craemer, Willy de, Jan Vansina, and Renee Fox

1976. "Religious Movements in Central Africa."*Comparative Studies in Society and History* 18 (4):458–475.

Csordas, Thomas

1990. "Embodiment as a Paradigm for Anthropology."*Ethos* 18 (1):5–47.

1993. "Somatic Modes of Attention." *Cultural Anthropology* 8 (2):135–156.

1994. *The Sacred Self: A Cultural Phenomenology of Charismatic Healing.* Berkeley: University of California Press.

1997. "Prophecy and the Performance of Metaphor." *American Anthropologist* 99 (2):321–332.

Daneel, Marthinus

1971. *Old and New in Southern Shona Independent Churches.* Volume 1. *Background and Rise of the Major Movements.* The Hague and Paris: Mouton.

1974. Old and New in Southern Shona Independent *Churches.* Volume 2. *Causative Factors and Recruitment Techniques.* The Hague and Paris: Mouton.

Dumont, Louis

1977. *From Mandeville to Marx: The Genesis and Triumph of Economic Ideology.* Chicago: University of Chicago Press.

1980. *Essays on Individualism: Modern Ideology in Anthropological Perspective.* Chicago: University of Chicago Press.

Eisenstadt, Shmuel

1968. *Max Weber and Institution Building: Selected Papers.* Chicago: University of Chicago Press.

Emerson, Caryl

2005. "Shklovsky's *Ostranenie,* Bakhtin's *Vnenakhodimost* (How distance serves an aesthetics of arousal differently from an aesthetics based on pain)." *Poetics Today* 26 (4):637–664.

Engelke, Matthew
2003. "The Book, the Church, and the Incomprehensible Paradox': Christianity in African History." *Journal of Southern African Studies* 29 (1):297–306.
2004. "Discontinuity and the Discourse of Conversion." *Journal of Religion in Africa* 34 (1–2):82–109
2007. A Problem of Presence: Beyond Scripture in an *African Church*. Berkeley, Los Angeles: University of California Press.
2009. "Reading and Time: Two Approaches to the Materiality of Scripture." *Ethnos* 74 (2):151–176.

Euler, Walter
2000. "Does Nicholas Cusanus Have a Theology of the Cross?" *The Journal of Religion* 80 (3):405–420.

Fabian, Johannes
1979. "The Anthropology of Religious Movements: From Explanation to Interpretation." *Social Research* 46:4–35.
2008. Ethnography as Commentary. Durham and London: Duke University Press.

Ferme, Marian
2001. *The Underneath of Things: Violence, History and the Everyday in Sierra Leone*. Berkeley, Los Angeles, London: University of California Press.

Fernandez, James
1985. *Bwiti: An Ethnography of the Religious Imagination in Africa*. Princeton: Princeton University Press.

Flores, Carlos Y
2009. "Reflections of an Ethnographic Filmmaker-Maker: An Interview with Paul Henley, Director of GCVA, University of Manchester." *American Anthropologist* 111 (1):93–99.

Geertz, Clifford
1988. *Works and Lives*. Stanford, California: Stanford University Press.

Geschiere, Peter
1997. *The Modernity of Witchcraft*. Charlottesville: University of Virginia Press.

Graw, Knut
2009. "Beyond Expertise: Reflections on Specialist Agency and the Autonomy of the Divinatory Ritual Process." *Africa* 79 (1):92–109.

Grimshaw, Anna
2001. *The Ethnographer's Eye*. Cambridge: Cambridge University Press.
2004. "Eying the Field: New Horizons for Visual Anthropology." In *Visualising Anthropology*, edited by Anna Grimshaw and Amanda Ravetz. Intellect Books: Bristol and Portland, Oregon.

Grimshaw, Anna, and Amanda Ravetz
2005. Introduction." In *Visualising Anthropology*, edited by Anna Grimshaw and Amanda Ravetz. Intellect Books: Bristol and Portland, Oregon.
2009. "Rethinking Observational Cinema." *Journal of the Royal Anthropological Institute*. 15 (3):538–556.
Hackett, Rosalind
2006. "Mediated Religion in South Africa." In *Religion, Media and the Public Sphere*, edited by Birgit Moors. Bloomington: Indiana University Press.
Heider, Karl
1978 [1990]. *Ethnographic Film*. Austin: University of Texas Press.
Henley, Paul
2009. *The Adventure of the Real: Jean Rouch and the Craft of Ethnographic Cinema*. Chicago: University of Chicago Press.
Hughes, Stephen, and Birgit Meyer
2005. "Guest Editors' Preface." *Postscripts* 1.2/1.3:149–153.
Iliffe, John
2005. *Honour in African History*. Cambridge: Cambridge University Press.
Ishii, Miho
2008. "From Passion to Compassion: Healing Rituals and Gender in an Independent Church in Southern Ghana." *Japanese Review of Cultural Anthropology* 9:3–28.
Jacobus, Laura
2009a. "The Art of Experience. *Art Quarterly*" (Spring): 52–57.
2009b. Giotto and the Arena Chapel: Art, Architecture, and Experience. Turnhout, Belgium: Harvey Miller.
Jackson, Michael
1982. *Allegories of the Wilderness*. Bloomington: Indiana University Press.
1998. *Minima Ethnographica: Intersubjectivity and the Anthropological Project*. Chicago: University of Chicago Press.
Jackson, Michael, and Ivan Karp (eds.)
1990. *Personhood and Agency: The Experience of Self and Other in African Cultures*. Washington, D.C.: Smithsonian Institution Press.
Janzen, John
1992. *Ngoma: Discourses of Healing in Central and Southern Africa*. Berkeley and Los Angeles: University of California Press.
1994. "Drums of Affliction: Real Phenomenon or Scholarly Chimera." In *Religion in Africa: Experience andExpression*, edited by Thomas Blakely and Walter van Beek, Dennis Thomson with the assistance of Linda Adams. Oxford: James Currey.

Jules-Rosette, Bennetta
1975. "Song and Spirit." *Africa* 45 (21):150–166.
1979. "Women as Ceremonial Leaders in an African Church." In *The New Religions of Africa,* edited by Bennetta Jules-Rosette. Norwood: Aflex Publishing.

Kapferer, Bruce
1983. *A Celebration of Demons.* Bloomington: Indiana University Press.

Katz, Richard
1982. *Boiling Energy: Community Healing among the Kalahari Kung.* Cambridge: Harvard University Press.

Keane, Webb
1997a. "From Fetishism to Sincerity: On Agency, The Speaking Subject, and their Historicity in the Context of Religious Conversion." *Comparative Studies in Society and History* 39:674–693.
1997b. *Signs of Recognition: Powers and Hazards of Representation in an Indonesian Society.* Berkeley: University of California Press.

Kiernan, James
1974. "Where Zionists Draw the Line: A Study of Religious Exclusiveness in an African Township." *African Studies* 33 (2):79–90.
1975. "Old Wine in New Wineskins." *African Studies* 34 (3):193–201.
1976a. "Prophet and Preacher: An Essential Partnership in the Work of Zion." *Man.* n.s. 11:356–366.
1976b. "The Work of Zion: An Analysis of an African Zionist Ritual." *Africa* 46:340–356.
1997. "Poor and Puritan: An Attempt to View Zionism as a Collective Response to Urban Poverty." *African Studies* 36 (1):31–41.
1978. "Saltwater and Ashes: Instruments of Curing among Some Zulu Zionists." *Journal of Religion in Africa* 9 (1):27–32.
1979. "The Weapons of Zion." *Journal of Religion in Africa*10 (1):11–21.
1980. "The Problem of 'Evil' in the Context of Ancestral Intervention in the Affairs of the Living in Africa. *Man.* n.s. 17:287–301.
1990. *The Production and Management of Therapeutic Power in Zionist Churches within a Zulu City.* Lewiston: Edwin Mellen.
1991. "Wear 'n' Tear and Repair: The Colour Coding of Mystical Mending in a Zulu-Zionist Church." *Africa* 61 (1):21–39.
1992. "The Herder and the Rustler: Deciphering the Affinity between Zulu Diviner and Zionist Prophet." *African Studies* 51:231–242.
1994. "Variations in a Christian Theme: The Healing Synthesis in Zulu Zionism." In *Syncretism/Anti-Syncretism,* edited by Charles Stewart and Rosalind Shaw, 212–215. London: Routledge.

1997. "Images of Rejection in the Construction of Morality: Satan and Sorcerer as Moral Signposts in the Social Landscape of Urban Zionists." *Social Anthropology* 5:243–254.

2006 (ed.). *The Power of the Occult in Modern Africa: Continuity and Innovation in the Renewal of African Cosmologies.* Berlin: Lit Verlag.

Kirsch, Thomas

2004. "Restaging the Will to Believe: Religious Pluralism, Anti-Syncretism and the Problem of Belief. "*American Anthropologist* 106 (4):899–709.

2008. *Spirits and Letters: Reading, Writing and Charisma In African Christianity.* New York, Oxford: Berghahn Books.

Klaits, Frederick

2010. *Death in a Church of Life.* Berkeley: University of California Press.

Lambek, Michael, and Jacqueline Solway

2001. "Just Anger: Scenarios of Indignation in Botswana and Madagascar." *Ethnos* 66:49–72.

Lindholm, Charles

1990. *Charisma.* Oxford: Basil Blackwell.

Livingston, Julie

2005. *Debility and the Moral Imagination in Botswana.* Bloomington: Indiana University Press.

2009. "Suicide, Risk and Investment in the Heart of the African Miracle." *Cultural Anthropology* 24(4):652–680.

MacDougall, David

1998. *Transcultural Cinema* (edited and with an introduction by Lucien Taylor). Princeton: Princeton University Press.

2006. *The Corporeal Image.* Princeton: Princeton University Press.

Mahmood, Saba

2005. *The Politics of Piety: The Islamic Revival and the Feminist Subject.* Princeton: Princeton University Press.

Marks, Laura

2000. *The Skin of the Film.* Durham and London: Duke University Press.

Marriott, McKim

1976. "Hindu Transactions: Diversity without Dualism." In *Transaction and Meaning,* edited by Bruce Kapferer. Philadelphia: ISHI Publications (ASA Essays in Anthropology 1).

Matumo, Z. I.

1993. *Setswana-English Dictionary.* Macmillan: Gaborone.

Maxwell, David

2002a. "Introduction: Christianity and the African Imagination." In *Christianity and the African Imagination: Essays in Honour*

of Adrian Hastings, edited by David Maxwell and Ingrid Lawrie, 1–24. Leiden: E.J. Brill.
2002b. "Christianity without frontiers: Shona Missionaries and Transnational Pentecostalism in Africa." In *Christianity and the African Imagination: Essays in Honour of Adrian Hastings,* edited by David Maxwell and Ingrid Lawrie, 295–332. Leiden: E.J. Brill.
2002c. Bengt Sundkler and African Christian Studies. *African Affairs* 101:433–438.
2006. *African Gifts of the Spirit: Pentecostalism and the Rise of a Zimbabwean Transnational Religious Movement.* Oxford: James Currey.
2007. "Christianity: African Instituted Churches." In *New Encyclopaedia of Africa,* edited by John Middleton, 391–398. New York: Scribners.

McHugh, Ernestine
1989. "Concepts of the Person among the Gurungs of Nepal." *American Ethnologist* 16:75–86.

Merleau-Ponty, Marcel
2002. *Phenomenology of Perception.* London: Routledge.

Meyer, Birgit
1998. " 'Make a Complete Break with the Past': Memory and Postcolonial Modernity in Ghanaian Pentecostal Discourse." In *Memory and the Postcolony: African Anthropology and the Critique of Power,* edited by Richard Werbner, 182–208. London: Zed Books.
1999. Translating the Devil: Religion and Modernity among the Ewe in Ghana. Trenton: Africa World Press.
2004. " 'Praise the Lord . . .' : Popular Cinema and Pentecostalite Style in Ghana's New Public Sphere." *American Ethnologist* 31:92–110.
2005. "Religious Remediation: Pentecostal Views in Ghanaian Video-Movies." *Postscripts* 1.2/1.3:155–181.

Meyer,Birgit and Annelies Moors (eds.).
2006. *Religion, Media, and the Public Sphere.* Bloomington: Indiana University Press.

Miller, Clyde Lee
2003. Reading Cusanus: Metaphor and Dialectics in a *Conjectural Universe.* Washington, D.C.: Catholic University of America Press.

Mines, Mattison
1988. "Conceptualising the Person: Hierarchical Society and Individual Autonomy in India." *American Anthropologist* 90:568–579.

Moore, Henrietta, and Todd Sanders
2001. "Introduction." In Magical Interpretations and *Material Realities: Modernity, Witchcraft and theOccult in Postcolonial Africa.* London and New York: Routledge.

Mosko, Mark
2001. "Syncretic Persons: Sociality, Agency and Personhood in Recent Charismatic Ritual Practices Among North Mekeo." *Australian Journal of Anthropology* 12 (3):259–274.
2008. *The Sacredness of the Gift: Partible Personhood and Sacrifice in Melanesian Christianity.* Paper presented at the Annual Meetings of the Association of Social Anthropologists of the Commonwealth, the Australian Anthropological Society, and the Anthropological Association of Aotearao, Auckland 7–12 December 2008.
2010. "Partible Penitents: Dividual Personhood and Christian Practice in Melanesia and the West." Journal of the Royal Anthropological Institute. 16 (2):215–240.

Mouton, Ray, and Tom Doyle
1985 *The Manual.* Online at http:/tiny.cc/yhsdw.

Newell, Sasha
2007. "Pentecostal Witchcraft: Neo-Liberal Possession and Demonic Discourse in Ivoirian Pentecostal Churches." *Journal of Religion in Africa* 37:461–490.

Niehaus, Isak
2001. *Witchcraft, Power and Politics: Exploring the Occult in the South African Lowveld.* London, Sterling Virginia: Pluto Press.

O'Neill, Eamonn
2010. "What the Bishop Knew." *The Guardian* 3 April: 27.

Ortner, Sherry
2006. *Anthropology and Social Theory.* Durham: Duke University.

Piot, Charles
1999. *Remotely Global: Village Modernity in West Africa.* Chicago: University of Chicago Press.

Postma, Metje and Peter Crawford *(eds.)*
2006. *Reflecting Visual Ethnography.* Leiden and Hojberjeg: CNWS Publication, Intervention Press.

Ranger, Terence
2003. "Review: Marja Liisa Swantz, 'Beyond the Forestline: The Life and Letters of Bengt Sundkler'." *Journal of Religion in Africa* 33 (4):437–438.
2005. "Scotland Yard in the Bush: Medicine Murders, Child Witches and the Construction of the Occult: a Literature Review." *Africa* 7 (2):272–283.

Registry of Societies
1994. *Constitution of the Eloyi Christian Church.* 1994:12–20, H28/26.
2003a. Letter from Mothoothata M. Lesola to The *Registrar, 29th January 2003.* H28/26/721 (62).

2003b. Letter from The Registrar to Molefhe *Medupe, 18th February 2003*. H28/26/721 (63).

2003c. Letter from Molefhe Medupe to The Registrar, 8th *November 2003*.

Riesman, Paul

1986. "The Person and the Life Cycle in African Social Life and 'Thought'." *African Studies Review* 29 (2):71–138.

Ritsema, Mieke

2008. "Gaborone is Growing like a Baby: Life Expectancies and Death Expectancies in Urban Botswana." *Africa Development* 33 (3):81–108.

Robbins, Joel

1994. "Equality as a Value: Ideology in Dumont, Melanesia and the West." *Social Analysis* 36:21–70.

2003. "On the Paradoxes of Global Pentecostalism and the Perils of Continuity Thinking." *Religion* 33:221–231.

2004. *Becoming Sinners*. Berkeley: University of California Press.

2009. "Conversion, Hierarchy, and Cultural Change: Value and Syncretism in the Globalization of Pentecostal and Charismatic Christianity." In *Hierarchy: Persistence and Transformation in Social Formations*, edited by K. Rio and O.H. Smedal, 65–88. New York: Berghahn Books.

Russell, Catherine

1999. *Experimental Ethnography: The Work of Film in the Age of Video*. Durham: Duke University Press.

Sahlins, Marshall

2002. *Waiting for Foucault*. Chicago: Prickly Paradigm Press.

Schapera, Isaac

1934. "Oral Sorcery among the Natives of Bechuanaland." In *Essays Presented to C. G. Seligman*, edited by E.E. Evans-Pritchard et al. London: Routledge.

1955. "Witchcraft Beyond Reasonable Doubt." *Man* 55:72.

1969. "The Crime of Sorcery." *Proceedings of the Royal Anthropological Institute*: 15–23.

Schutz, Alfred

1944. "The Stranger: An Essay in Social Psychology." *The American Journal of Psychology* 49 (6):499–507.

Simpson, Anthony

2003. "Personhood and Self in Catholic Formation in Zambia." *Journal of Religion in Africa* 33 (4):377–400.

2009. *Boys to Men in the Shadow of AIDS: Masculinities and HIV Risk in Zambia*. New York: Palgrave.

Spiro, Melford

2003. "Is the Western Conception of the Self "Peculiar" within the Context of the World Cultures?" *Ethos* 21 (2):107–153.

Stoller, Paul
1997. *Sensuous Scholarship*. Philadelphia: University of Pennsylvania Press.

Stewart, Charles, and Rosalind Shaw
1994. "Introduction." In *Syncretism/Anti-Syncretism*, edited by Charles Stewart and Rosalind Shaw, 1–26. London: Routledge.

Strathern, Marilyn
1988. The Gender of the Gift: Problems with Women and *Problems with Society in Melanesia*. Berkeley and Los Angeles: University of California Press.

Strecker, Ivo
2001. "Creativity in Ethnographic Film." *Visual Anthropology* 14 (2):203–209.

Sundkler, Bengt
1948. (2nd edition, 1961). *Bantu Prophets in South Africa*. London: Lutterworth Press.
1997. *Zulu Zion and Some Swazi Zionists*. Oxford: Oxford University Press.

Sundkler, Bengt, and Christopher Steed
2000. *A History of the Church in Africa*. Cambridge: Cambridge University Press.

Taussig, Michael
1993. *Mimesis and Alterity: A Particular History of the Senses*. New York and London: Routledge.

Valk, John
1992. "The Concept of the Coincidentia Oppositorum in the Thought of Mircea Eliade." *Religious Studies* 28(1):31–41.

van Binsbergen, Wim
1993. "Independent Churches and the State in Botswana." In *Power and Prayer:* Essays in *Religion and Politics*, edited by M. Bax and A. de Koster. Amsterdm: VU Press.

van Dienderen, An
2008. *Film Process as a Site of Critique: Ethnographic Research into the Mediated Interactions during (Documentary) Film Productions*. Saarbrucken: VDM Verlag Dr. Muller.

Van Dijk, Rijk
1992. "Young Puritan Preachers in Post-Independence Malawi." *Africa* 62 (2):159–181.
1998. "Pentecostalism, Cultural Memory and the State:Contested Representations of Time in Postcolonial Malawi." In *Memory and the Postcolony: African Anthropology and the Critique of Power*, edited by Richard Werbner, 155–181. London: Zed Books.

Wasserstrom, Steven
1999. *Religion after Religion*. Princeton: Princeton University Press.

Weber, Max

1948. *From Max Weber: Essays in Sociology*. London: Routledge and Kegan Paul.

Werbner, Pnina

2003. *Pilgrims of Love: The Anthropology of a Global Sufi Cult*. London: Hurst and Company.

2008. "The Hidden Lion: Tswapong Girls' Puberty Rituals and the Problem of History." *American Ethnologist* 36:441–458.

Werbner, Richard

1973. "The Superabundance of Understanding: Kalanga Rhetoric and Domestic Divination." *American Anthropologist* 75:414–440.

1985. "The Argument of Images: From Zion to the Wilderness in African Churches." In *Theoretical Explorations in African Religion*, edited by Wim van Binsbergen and Matthew Schoffeleers, 253–286. London: KPI.

1986. "The Political Economy of Bricolage." *Journal of Southern African Studies* 13 (1):151–156.

1989. *Ritual Passage, Sacred Journey*. Washington, D.C.: Smithsonian Institution Press.

1990a. "Bwiti in Reflection: On the Fugue of Gender." *Journal of Religion in Africa* 20:2–25.

1990b. "South-Central Africa: The Manchester School and After." In *Localizing Strategies: Regional Traditions of Writing*, edited by Richard Fardon. Edinburgh: Scottish Academic Press; Washington: Smithsonian Institution Press.

1993. "Afterword." In *Syncretism/Anti-Syncretism*, edited by Charles Stewart and Rosalind Shaw, 212–215. London: Routledge.

1996. "Creative Dividualism: Reflections on *Mwana Ndi Mai*." *SMT Svensk Missionstidskrift* 84 (3):86–93.

1997. "The Suffering Body: Passion and Ritual Allegory in Christian Encounters." *Journal of Southern African Studies* 23 (2):311–324.

2001. "Truth-on-Balance: Knowing the Opaque Other in Tswapong Wisdom Divination." In *Witchcraft Dialogues: Anthropological and Philosophical Exchanges*, edited by George Bond and Dianne Ciekawy, 190–211. Athens: Ohio University Center for International Studies.

2002 "Postcolonial Subjectivities: The Personal, The Political and the Moral." In *Postcolonial Subjectivities in Africa*, edited by Richard Werbner, 1–22. London: Zed Books.

2004. *Reasonable Radicals and Citizenship in Botswana*. Bloomington: Indiana University Press.

2005. *Séance Reflections with Richard Werbner*. Manchester: International Centre for Contemporary Cultural Research; London: Royal Anthropological Institute.

2007. *Shade Seekers and the Mixer.* Manchester: International Centre for Contemporary Cultural Research; London: Royal Anthropological Institute.

2008. *Encountering Eloyi.* Manchester: International Centre for Contemporary Cultural Research; London: Royal Anthropological Institute.

2009. *Holy Hustlers.* Manchester: International Centre for Contemporary Cultural Research; London: Royal Anthropological Institute.

West, Martin

1975. *Bishops and Prophets in an African City: African Independent Churches in Soweto.* Johannesburg: David Philip.

West, Harry

2005. *Kupilikula: Dominance and the Invisible Realm in Mozambique.* Chicago: University of Chicago Press.

Wiegele, Katharine

2004. *Investing in Miracles: El Shaddai and the Transformation of Popular Catholicism in the Philippines.* Honolulu: University of Hawaii Press.

Witte, Marleen de

2004. "Altar Media's Living Word; Televised Christianity in Ghana." *Journal of Religion in Africa* 33:172–202.

Yoshida, Kenji and Brian Durrans

2008. *Self and Other: Portraits from Asia and Europe.* Osaka: The Asian Shimbun.

Index

Text: 10/13 Aldus
Display: Aldus
Compositor: Westchester Book Group
Printer and binder: Maple-Vail Manufacturing Group